...ed in the United Kingdom by MPG Books, Bodmin

...ished by Sanctuary Publishing Limited, Sanctuary House, 45–53 Sinclair Road,
...don W14 0NS, United Kingdom

...w.sanctuarypublishing.com

ISBN: 1-86074-367-6

Star
Nake

The Autol
Of Graha

Print

Publ
Lon

ww

Co

Ph

A
el
w
q

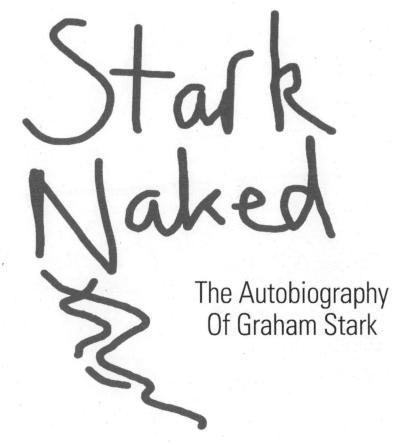

Stark Naked

The Autobiography
Of Graham Stark

Sanctuary

To Audrey, Christopher, Julia, Timothy and all the grandchildren,
who keep arriving at an alarming rate.

Acknowledgement

Without the efforts of John Kaufman this book would never have been published. Being an admirer of my photography and a magical audience of my stories and anecdotes, his suggestion of combining the two set me at the file of my negatives and the keyboard of my word processor. I remain eternally grateful.

About The Author

Graham Stark was born in Wallasey, Merseyside, in 1922 and made his first stage appearance at the age of ten at Wallasey Grammar School. His first professional engagement was in pantomime at the Lyceum Theatre, London, in 1935 when he was just 13 years old. Then, in 1939, he enrolled at RADA and made his first movie appearance in *The Spy In Black*, starring Conrad Veidt.

During the war years, after volunteering for the RAF, Graham joined Ralph Reader's RAF "Gang Show" and thereafter entertained the troops in all theatres of war around the world, along with fellow airmen Peter Sellers, Tony Hancock and Dick Emery. Graham's close friendship with Peter Sellers lasted until Peter's untimely death in 1980.

Graham has appeared in 99 films and has also directed two: *Simon Simon* (the British entry at the San Sebastian Film Festival in 1970) and *The Magnificent Seven Deadly Sins*. He was also awarded the Bucket and Spade Oscar in Cromer for best comic in the summer season of 1954!

Graham has been married to Audrey Nicholson since 1959 and they have three children: Christopher, Julia and Timothy. He still enjoys working in showbusiness and is busier than ever. He loves swimming, keeping his ever-expanding video library fully up to date and of course photographing his fellow actors in his studio. He lives in north London.

Contents

1 Not An Ounce Of Rhythm In His Body

Towering over the floating landing stage, on the banks of the River Mersey, is a monument to the great days of the British Empire when it really did rule the seas – the Liver Building. The shipyards of Britain built a fleet of ocean-going liners that spread the British way of life worldwide and, although the Kaiser may have tried to outshine us, Clydeside, the great shipyards of the Northeast, and Cammel Lairds on Merseyside set a rate of shipbuilding that was impossible to match. The huge links of giant chains slowed the launches as hull after hull slid down into the water. Britain had a worldwide network of great ships and one of the major fleets was the Canadian Pacific Steamship Company, allied to the Canadian Pacific Railway, which snaked its way coast to coast across Canada. Although the Liver Building was built for a famous insurance company, it became the Liverpool headquarters of Canadian Pacific, who felt the need to impress. And the Liver Building did impress. With clock faces 25 feet in diameter (the largest in Great Britain), the clocks were started at the precise moment that King George V was crowned on 22 June 1911. The twin towers that housed them were crowned with the famous Liver birds, and these levers or sea cormorants, made of copper, 18 feet high, fashioned with their wings spread in arrogance, gaze across the Mersey, masters of all they survey. The Scousers (the slang expression for all born in Liverpool) adopted the birds as their own, and to talk of the Liver birds in a familiar way was to be a member of the magical and extraordinary mixture of northerners and Irish that made up the population of the city. It was the birthplace of what seemed to be every other comedian in the British Isles and later, of course, the birthplace of a singing group that brought Liverpool, and the River Mersey, worldwide fame.

World War I saw the river awash with boats and ships of every size. Although constantly menaced by U-boats (the *Lusitania* was early prey), Liverpool was a great and major port, and even today every picture of it features the Liver Building and its birds that, by a bizarre set of circumstances, were responsible for my creation. It wasn't a miracle of ornithology; it simply meant that, during World War I, my exotically named mother, Hannah Evelyn DeValve, was currently working for the census department in Liverpool and paid a visit to the Liver Building. There the very sight of her dazzled and bewitched a visiting purser of the Canadian Pacific. The young merchant navy officer's ship was at the landing stage nearby and, after crossing the Atlantic in convoy, he reported in to check paperwork at head office, where he was instantly overcome with attraction for Hannah Evelyn. But these were conventional times and he was forced to watch, frustrated, as my mother, her business now finished, turned to go. Then fate, sublimely, gave him an opportunity, which to his eternal credit he took with both hands. An official needed my mother's name and business address and, using steel nib, and in the neat and tidy calligraphy of the day, she dipped the pen in the ink, duly wrote her name and office address and blotted it, then left, apparently never to be seen again. How small events colour life. My father, with singular shrewdness, pocketed the blotting paper, decamped to the gentlemen's lavatory and there, by using a mirror, deciphered my mother's name and office address. I always held him in some regard for this simple manoeuvre. He never seemed to me to be a particularly romantic person, yet there I had a picture of him jiggling that blotting paper and finding the address of my mother. It was the action of a Hollywood hero. Within days, they were in contact. Within weeks, they were married.

Mother was 25, and it was a wartime marriage in 1917. It may have been the healthy sea life but the children came rather quickly. First son Stuart was born in 1919, six months after the horror of the trench war had ground slowly to a halt. The end of the submarine menace lifted seafarers' morale and second son Peter was born 18 months later, in 1920. Hannah Evelyn then changed her name to the less exotic Ivy, at the same time giving birth to her third son, Graham, in January 1922. Prams in those days were giant carriages rolling along on huge wheels, the babies almost in midair. It shows something for our family's fairly secure social place that a special pram, taking all three of us at the same time, had to be ordered. This masculine trend obviously came from my father's family, as he was one of five sons brought up in Edinburgh. In future years, attempting to curry favour from any Scotsman, I merely had to tell them that one of my father's brothers, Bertie, was the goalkeeper for Hibernian, one of the great soccer teams of Scotland, and instant respect was assured.

My mother had been born in the small town of Wallasey – neat, upper class and on the opposite bank of the River Mersey. Daily, the ferryboats took the chief clerks, bank managers and minor industrialists across the river to their work in Liverpool and at night got them safely back again to sleep the sleep of the well-off and contented. That was now where we lived. The greatest virtue of Wallasey was the promenade. This ribbon of beautifully maintained macadam, the golden sands of the shore nesting up to it, was the social centre of the town. Rather smugly aware that the working class of Liverpool was safely on the other side of the river, on a fine day the female residents could stroll up and down, exchanging pleasantries, gossip and check up on the latest in the fashion world while their husbands dutifully toiled at their desks across the water. The oohing and aahing at their respective babies in the prams (the men safely back from the wars made sure the birth rate rapidly increased) was of course tripled in my mother's case. Quite soon the three Stark sons became minor celebrities, if only for the cascade of fluffy toys that was hurled onto the promenade as we made our daily progress.

Mother had a fixation that she would never live opposite anything that could be built on. The rest of our lives with her were in houses opposite parks, golf courses, or land that was sacrosanct, and in Wallasey she made sure our house faced the river, with our front garden gate opening onto the promenade. Fifteen paces and there were steps down onto the beach. Our childhood was idyllic – a glorious time playing with bucket and spade while all the great ships sailed past us on the way to the landing stage: the Blue Funnels from China; the glamorous *Reina Del Pacifico* from South America; the Union Castles steaming up from South Africa; the great rivals Cunard and White Star, soon to be merged; and of course our own ships (as we called them), the Canadian Pacifics – the *Montcalm*, the *Montclare* and of course the *Montrose*, which gained everlasting fame as the ship on which the infamous Dr Crippen and his mistress, Ethel le Neve, were arrested while fleeing the country. (The sad and apparently genteel doctor had not allowed for the fact that, in 1910, the *Montrose* was one of the earliest ships to be fitted with wireless telegraph.) Also in the fleet were the *Duchess Of Atholl* and all the other drunken *Duchesses*. (This alliteration was kept very quiet, as the title was earned because they rolled so much.) Finally, the pride of the fleet, one of the most beautiful ships ever launched, there was the *Empress Of Britain*.

But it was the two small ships that made the short run from the Isle of Man that were our favourites. No one ever explained why, but they made the run up the river at a much higher speed than any other ship and we would time it to perfection, making sure we were in our bathing costumes at the water's edge as they ploughed past. The waves seemed to us to be on the level of the mighty surfing waves off Hawaii.

Mother never seemed to have muscular arms, but the strain of pushing that pram must have cost her dear. Father was a distant figure, reappearing for a few days every month, a glamorous figure in his chief purser uniform, gold rings halfway up his arm. His ship did the weekly run to Canada and, like clockwork, he duly reappeared every third week. Mother was an extraordinary woman as – with a mainly absent husband, three sons born very close together and a house to run – she dealt with every situation. With toughness and a fiery temper she had a quality that would make her overcome almost any problem. Eventually she grew disillusioned with my father, seeing in him a person who wanted to go through life with the minimum of fuss and bother. He had found his *métier* on the ships he voyaged on, and his position and uniform gave him all the respect he ever wanted, but there was really no limit to Mother's ambition, and her ability to get things done was remarkable. She juggled with the upbringing of her sons, the running of her home, the business (which, in her husband's absence, she was forced to deal with), all with considerable flair plus the ability to become, in her time, quite a fashion plate.

Sunday morning in the summertime was the great parade on the promenade. Every lady of the town strolled there with the express intent of souring the day for all the other ladies. Stores in Liverpool were raided weekly to make sure their clothes had enough style and flair to put them in the front rank of fashion, and I must say Mother was up there with the best of them. Once we had made it out of the pram and graduated to our little sailor suits (the height of boyish fashion in the '20s), we toddled along the promenade with Mother, who never let three sons in any way detract from her style and fashion. She caused a major sensation in the town by becoming the first platinum blonde of Merseyside. Opposite the house, the council had been very thoughtful in providing a staircase down to the beach, and we were able to play in front of our little striped windbreaker tent while Mother, ever glamorous in her white bathing suit and with the sunlight glinting on her blonde hair, lay back sunbathing in her deck-chair. Two old ladies of the town, wearing the conventional black, looked down at her from the promenade above. "Showing all God gave her" was the verdict.

At the tender age of five, my two brothers and I were immortalised by having our photograph taken. Peter and I, wearing our sailor suits, with Stuart (recently promoted to the equally fashionable stiff collar and Eton jacket), stood in the salon of photography of Mr Priestley. Actually, it was a small studio, with glass roof for daylight photography, at the bottom of Falkland Road. I grasped the equally moist hand of Peter while gazing, petrified, at the strange five-legged monster that stood before us. Its huge single glass eye held us in terrified thrall when suddenly, as if by magic, two of the five legs separated from the others and stepped sideways. A large black cloth flapped wildly and a human face popped out. "Could we manage to make ourselves just the *teeniest* bit angelic for just the briefest moment, children dears!" Mr Priestley was our local photographer and he did guarantee a faithful likeness of one's nearest and dearest. While one limpid hand squeezed the rubber ball shutter release, the other held a small zinc tray aloft, a trigger was pulled and a blinding flash of magnesium powder almost set the studio on fire. We screamed with terror and dissolved into tears but the framed photograph soon had pride of place – along with the obligatory fringed, draped shawl – on our mini-grand piano.

Very close, with a safe route along the promenade, Vaughan Road School welcomed all three of us in turn and we dutifully struggled to make sense of the little red paper-backed schoolbooks. On summer days in the playground we greedily drank water from the heavy metal cup that dangled on a chain from the drinking fountain. It's difficult to think of a more unsanitary arrangement. With some surprise I fell sideways one hot day in class and, after an examination by the school doctor (and to my great delight), my desk was placed outside the window in the playground, as it was discovered that the heat gave me fainting fits. Naturally, I was labelled "Sneaky Stark", but it was all quite genuine. I steadily fainted at odd times right up to the end of the war, when I fortunately grew out of it.

Suddenly there was a cloud on the horizon. The frightening Depression of the late '20s hit the world and everything changed. Bankers threw themselves from skyscrapers and the shipping lines had to retrench as the world's harbours were too full of businessmen jumping into them for ships to be able to navigate.

Mother took it all in her stride. "We," indicating Father, "are off to

America." The facts became clear. Ships were being laid up in hundreds and Father was to be given a shore job by the company in the City of Brotherly Love, Philadelphia. "I have arranged," continued Mother, "for all three of you to stay in a convent while we are away. Just a few months. The nuns will guard you." As the youngest (just turned seven), I had no idea what we were to be guarded from, but Mother did try to make it as easy as possible for us (not that we had much option), and off we went to Boscombe Spa, near Harrogate. I can remember the nuns were kind, firm and strict, and daily told us that as soon as our mother returned we should let her know that we all desperately wanted to convert to Catholicism. We resisted this blandishment, but to this day I firmly press back the flesh above my nails with the towel every time I wash my hands, as the nuns insisted we all had beautiful cuticles, and the habit has never left me. The other pupils of the school treated us as strange unbelievers, but the strength of the three of us being together got us though fairly painlessly. The day of Mother's return (seven months precisely) was typical of her. In a room where the mother superior lay, very old and very bed-ridden, Mother had her suitcase open on the bed and, to squeals of shocked delight, she flourished all the underwear she had bought in America. The watching nuns busily crossed themselves as the mother superior held a pair of lacy camiknickers on high. "Do you mean the poor creatures walk about wearing these? Sure it's the constant pneumonias they're having."

Back to the promenade and the house we had rented out, and it was once more joy on the shore. But schools had to be attended. We had outgrown Vaughan Road and now it was to be Wrigley's, a small private school in Seabank Road which had quite a snazzy uniform. This may have been the reason that decided Mother to send us there, but it was a disaster, a disaster which came to a head rather quickly. In our new, neat, pristine outfits, Stuart, Peter and Graham Stark presented themselves at the school on the first day of term and we dutifully sat in our respective seats until the break at 10.30am, then streamed into the small playground, which fronted onto one of the main roads of Wallasey. Unfortunately, there was a bus stop right by the playground and within a few minutes passengers waiting for their public transport watched a school fight which set some sort of record for its ferocity. I, needless to say, was the reason. I never knew his name but there's always one at every school: the large boy who took one look at the midget in front of him and shouted, "New boy!"

Several other Neanderthal friends, knuckles scraping the playground surface and grunting with pleasure at the thought, all dived on me. Within seconds I was up against the wall and, with the expertise of all bullying schoolboys, in moments they had my arms twisted up behind my back. The tears flowed, the pain increased and I opened my mouth and screamed, "Peter, Stuart." The adage that blood is thicker than water could never be better illustrated, as my two brothers, hell incarnate, came around the corner and leapt at the boys who had me trapped. It was a free-for-all never before witnessed at Wrigley's. In moments, the boys of that academy had decided that we, as a family, were much too uppity and should be taught a lesson – after all, I was a new boy and new boys, in true *Tom Brown's Schooldays* tradition, were always fair game. So the demarcation line was simple: the Starks versus the rest of the school. My brothers equipped themselves well while I, small as I was, tried my best. Suddenly a loud crash of glass and, acting like a bell at a boxing match, all action ceased. The headmaster appeared speechless and apoplectic, gazed at the large broken window and the glass littering the playground and then, in a few terse words, informed us that we were not welcome at his academy and were to be summarily expelled.

Straight back to home we trooped, and that morning our mother reached a height in our respect that was hardly ever equalled. In a scene, set in my memory as firmly as an insect trapped in amber, we watched, enthralled, as she flung around her neck her fearsome foxfur. This animal was always brought into use when Mother was in one of her embattled moods. The half-open jaw showed bared teeth, and the ferocious yellowed eyes gave the sense of an animal about to spring. With it clipped in place, her hat adjusted, she led us back to the school where the headmaster, a helpless creature, trapped in his study by the demon face of the fox and the fury of my mother, backed away as she informed him that no boys of hers would *ever* bear the stigma of expulsion. "I am removing them from your school and they will receive a *proper* education at the Wallasey Grammar School." This was said in a tone of voice that would have done credit to Edith Evans as Lady Bracknell. The headmaster, suitably cowed (the Wallasey Grammar School was in a far superior league to Wrigley's, and well he knew it), retired hurt, and off to the grammar school we went.

The welcome there was of quite a different order and we settled in with pleasure. The Jesuits boast that, give them a child up to the age of seven, that child will be theirs for the rest of their life. The headmaster of the Wallasey Grammar School may not have been a Jesuit but he was passionate about the theatre and that passion was to infect me for the rest of my life. Mr Wilkinson was all that a headmaster should be. He moved amongst us with godlike authority, occasionally descending from Olympian heights to make earth-shaking announcements, such as the results of the end-of-term examinations and to let us all know that there was no greater beauty than the English language. He promoted literary events, and the end-of-term school plays were mounted with an almost professional zeal. I was quite young when I won my first prize in a poetry competition. I stood in class and spouted the short piece and was bound to win simply because I was the only one who had actually learnt it.

From then it was a short leap to actually appearing in a school play – a rather turgid comedy in which, because I was small, I got the female role playing the Weather Clerk's Wife, desperately plucking a goose to make sure we had lots of snow. Boxes of sleet, wind and hail surrounded the Weather Clerk and I, and a local photographer was there recording for posterity my demure and alluring appearance in a costume Mother had cut down from some past party dress. (She seized on this opportunity, as raising three children had smothered her own theatricality.)

And there was even more to come. The greatest provincial repertory theatre in the British Isles was the one in Liverpool, and heading it was the legendary figure of director William Armstrong. It was a foregone conclusion that every London critic would attend a Liverpool Rep opening, and the list of star actors who began their careers under Armstrong's direction was endless. Noël Coward made his first appearance there. He and our headmaster were close friends and, in a spirit of obviously extreme charity, Wilkinson got him to attend one of our school productions, mounted this time at the large and imposing Tower Theatre in Wallasey. I had been given a promotion and extended my range – still playing a female character, a comedy version of Queen Boadicea – shooting about the stage in a chariot. God knows what came over Armstrong, but evidently he muttered to Mr Wilkinson, "Now, there is a born actor." This remark Wilkinson passed onto my mother, and my life (and hers) totally changed.

In the early '30s, Shirley Temple had fired the hearts of a million theatrical mothers by becoming a major film star, as she looked divine, was ever such a goody little girl and vaguely tap-danced. The ringlets helped a lot, of course. Dancing schools for children mushroomed in every town and, not to be left out, Mother carted me off to the Wallasey dancing academy run by a Miss Molly Dick. In a small room she enjoined her classes to be future dancing stars, but in my case she very soon gave up the ghost. I was sent home with condemnation ringing in my ears. "That boy," Miss Dick declared, "has not an *ounce* of rhythm in his body!"

Not in the least put out, my Mother realised we would have to go further afield. In Bold Street, Liverpool, I was sent to a dancing school which was of a much higher quality, run by Miss Audrey Butterworth, who obviously had more patience. Gradually, both my left feet deserted me, and soon a dancing medal came my way. Being a boy – a rarity amongst hordes of females – did help. Hundreds of little girls in identical tutus does get a bit boring, and leaping on in tights a boy got more attention. But I did enter the strict world of ballet dancing, and what a world it was! Olympic athletes could never have such discipline. The bare studio with the wooden barre running down one side became the centre of my existence and sweat-stained hours were spent practising. The dedication of dancers is legendary but very infectious, and it never occurred to any of us children to complain. Mother, ever a perfectionist, found a huge, wall-sized mirror, which was mounted at the end of a room in our house and, stripped of furniture, with linoleum covering the floor, it became my practice room Every evening, back from my day at dancing school, I would be in there, conscientiously doing my hour at the barre, then into the centre for the real dancing, watching in that mirror to make sure every gesture, every stretch of a limb, was correct. Any idea that a male dancer equals limp wrist and lack of masculinity would vanish should anyone spend time as a pupil at a school for dancing.

Then William Armstrong reappeared in our lives. The director, who had been so responsible for Mother's enthusiasm, was mounting a very prestigious production of *Macbeth* at Liverpool Rep in 1934, with Wyndham Goldie and Ena Burrell playing the murderous pair, plus a splendid cast, including myself in the small but very telling part of Macduff's son. An ingenious set of rails above the stage made full-length curtains act as the set, and transformations could be made in moments. The opening night, as usual, had an audience packed with all the local dignitaries, plus the majority of the London critics. This Liverpool Rep William Armstrong production was a production to be noted. As the lights lowered, gloomy music swelled and the audience settled in for an emotion-racked night. That is, until I came on. The production was Early Britain in look and my costume was a short linen toga, minuscule pants and sandals. My mother, Lady Macduff and I went through our scene, then she and the newly entered Messenger went downstage to play their dialogue. Armstrong had sensibly sent me upstage out of the way, giving what he thought was uncomplicated directions to this boy actor: "There's a cot up there with a baby; just look at that for a couple of minutes." Lady Macduff went into her speech and the laughs started. Convinced her skirt was falling off or some such horror, she turned to see an even bigger horror. There I sat on an Early British stool, facing an Early British cot, keeping an Early British baby amused by pulling comical faces at it. On her exit to the wings, she swore she would kill me. And worse was to come. The Murderer uttered the famous line, "What you egg. Young fry of treachery!" and stabbed me. My small figure fell to the floor and, as the music once more swelled to a crescendo, the lights closed down to a spot effect, focusing on the tiny dead body alone on the stage. The music swelled all right, the lights were fine, and then I discovered my little toga was above my medieval knickers. Without a pause, the dead child firmly pulled the toga down. The laughter could be heard the other side of the Mersey.

There were 14 cinemas in our modest-sized town, which gives you some idea of the power and influence that films had at the time. One drop of rain in the afternoon and, like locusts, every schoolchild swarmed to their local fleapit, as every cinema was jokingly labelled. It was not always a joke, of course. MGM, its slogan "More stars than in the heavens", ruled the roost, and even today memories of their movies remind you they seemed to have the great common touch. Signing Johnny Weismuller, swinging through the jungle and giving the cry that every schoolboy imitated, was a masterstroke, and through the years he quite rightly earned them millions. Wallace Beery hopped about on a crutch as Long John Silver in *Treasure Island* and became our idol, as villains invariably are to boys. As some sort of homage, my brother Peter and I went home and ceremoniously cut half one of our teddy bear's legs off, then stuck a piece of wood up inside it to represent the wooden leg.

Then came Fred Astaire. Every film of his I saw time and time again. My own attempts to be a dancer gave me every excuse to watch this magical performer, and to try to understand just what it was that made him so much better than anyone else. He was perfection in every routine, and later, when it was revealed just how hard he rehearsed and how insistent he was that no cutting took place during his dances, you realised it was sheer endeavour and that indefinable thing called taste. I can screen in my mind even today sections of *Follow The Fleet*, which I saw at the Capitol Cinema in Wallasey no fewer than 13 times in one week on its first release (films ran continuously in those days and all you had to do was pay your admission at the matinée and stay in your seat until the last screening), and the film contained what I still think is the most perfect dance routine that Astaire and Rogers ever danced. The wonderful art-deco set of (presumably) the casino at Monte Carlo was the background for the sad, moving and beautifully orchestrated 'Let's Face The Music And Dance'. Surely Irving Berlin, forbidding any changes in his music or parodies of his lyrics while he was alive, must have spun like a dervish in his grave when that song was used in a television commercial.

The great steamship companies now came up with a splendid idea, as well as a financial bonanza. In the early '30s, summer holidays abroad were only for the chosen few. The Union Castle ships took the wealthy to South Africa for the winter and that was about it. The Mediterranean beckoned and, before you could say "Up anchor and aweigh", summer cruises became all the rage. For what today seems like the unbelievable bargain price of £14, you could go on a two-week cruise, which worked out at £1 a day. That included your accommodation, all your meals, the luxury of the floating hotel taking you to glamorous ports, as well as the fun and excitement of possible shipboard romance. They were a sell-out. As the wife of an officer of the CPR, Mother was entitled to a cut rate, so off she and I went on a cruise. A wife was never permitted to sail with her husband, as in an emergency it was felt that there could be divided loyalty (a quite sensible premise), so we sailed on a sister ship of my father's.

It was a wonderful holiday. On the island of Madeira, I remember shooting down the cobbled hills at breathtaking speed on wooden sledges, the men leaping off at the corners and pulling on the ropes to get us round the hairpin bends. On that same island, we realised what a privilege it was to be British and have half the globe pink. Mother shopped for Madeira lace, found a wonderful tablecloth, plus all the serviettes, and then told the shopkeeper we would have to go back to the ship – moored in the harbour – for the money to pay for it. He instantly wrapped it up, gave it to her, and then told her to go back to the ship and return with the money.

"The ship sails tonight," said my mother. "We could stay on it and never come back."

The shopkeeper gave us a smile. "But you are British. You will come back."

2 I Feel You Are Not Quite Right As Hamlet

In November 1935, via my dancing school, I was booked for my first professional engagement and the chance to be in one of the most famous pantomimes in London, at the Lyceum Theatre. These pantomimes, a tradition in England since the days of Grimaldi the clown, were played at Christmas time in most theatres and were the deviate's delight. The hero was always played by a girl (she had to have great legs as her costume was always miniskirt, pelmet length) and was called "principal boy". The heroine, usually a princess – or, in Cinderella's case, a serving wench – was known as the "principal girl". To add to the fantasy, the mother of the heroine was always played by an elderly comedian, and he was the dame. The plot was always one of the many fairy tales, such as *Dick Whittington* or *Mother Goose*, and the script was full of double entendres, which fortunately the children – who comprised at least 50 per cent of the audience – didn't understand. But they screamed with delight as custard pies were pushed in faces, long strings of sausages were used as skipping ropes and wallpapering a room by the comedians meant gallons of paste were sloshed all over the stage. The audience were invited to join in, and this singularly British form of entertainment packed every theatre it played at. Every artiste had their own speciality, and a memorable moment came in one pantomime when Cinderella, abandoned in her kitchen, loudly proclaimed, "Never mind, I shall console myself on my saxophone," then opened a cupboard, took out a shining brass instrument and played several choruses of a currently popular tune. Our pantomime was *Ali Baba And The 40 Thieves*, in which I was wheeled on in a pram in the middle of Monsewer Eddie Gray's act, got out of the pram, did a solo dance and then was wheeled off again. I never found out why.

The fact we lived in the North did not trouble my mother for a moment. I was booked into a private hotel in Earl's Court, a section of London which was filled with sedate establishments that catered to the rather sad and lonely people who had no home to call their own. Separate tables, with your own silver napkin ring, was the order of the day, and, satisfied that no harm could come to me, Mother left me there just a short Underground ride away from the Lyceum Theatre. The rest of the cast were all big names, including Monsewer Eddie Gray, Naughton and Gold, George Jackley, but the star (as far as I was concerned) was a large, florid, bubbly lady who was a source of constant delight both onstage and off. Florrie Forde was a great music-hall idol in every sense of the word. 'I'm Forever Blowing Bubbles' was the song that had made her famous, and she possessed that magical quality that made every member of the audience adore her. Her smile radiated round the huge, ornate auditorium. Like all performers she loved her theatre stories, and she made a habit of sitting me on her knee in the wings reminiscing about the great music-hall days of her youth: "He was young, very handsome and very rich. Filled my dressing room with roses but I wouldn't marry him. Not for all the tea in China. Said he'd shoot himself, he did. Packed house, middle of my big song, he was in a box watching, when there was a big bang. I fell on the floor, screamed blue murder. It was pandemonium, and then we found it was a light bulb gone off. Talk about laugh." Her whole body wobbled like a giant jelly.

The Melville brothers, the producers of the show, wandered about the theatre like two tramps, as they didn't believe in spending money without reason. Andrew always wore a battered homburg and complained about the heat when he wore it, so realising it lacked ventilation he took a red-hot poker and burned holes in the top of it. But they were very generous when it came to Christmas presents for the cast, and asking for what you wanted was the tradition. "Anything within reason," said the manager. Records were all the rage, so I summoned up courage and asked for a wind-up gramophone and there it was, the dog listening to his master, on the cover. No records, of course, but the company went through their collections of records and gave me a couple of dozen, including several by La Quintette Du Hot Club De France. They would be priceless now.

We carried on playing to packed houses until the day of my 14th birthday, 20 January 1936, when London closed, the streets were bare and black armbands were de rigueur. The father of England passed away. George V, when it was suggested he could recuperate at the seaside, uttered the immortal words "Bugger Bognor" and expired. The cry "The King is dead, long live the King" echoed throughout the land, and from a flat roof at the back of the theatre, overlooking the Strand, we watched his successor, the disastrous

Edward VIII, plus seven fellow monarchs, walk stiffly behind the gun carriage bearing the coffin. All the London shows restarted the next day and the run of the pantomime took us well into the spring, when it was back to Wallasey, the seashore and the dancing classes.

The next year, the summer of 1937, I went on the same type of cruise that I'd done with Mother, this time with my father, and he looked very impressive walking about the ship in his uniform with the gold bands up his arm. We spent a day in Barcelona harbour and saw the twin towers of the overhead cable railway. Father was quite happy to take me ashore, but I preferred the freedom of the ship, as it was very hot and I happily splashed about in the children's pool on deck. An outraged crew member who worked in the shop on board made me get out of the small pool and into the big pool with her, and within ten minutes had me swimming. Three weeks after that cruise, the Spanish Civil War began and I believe the twin towers were destroyed. The day we landed back in Liverpool, Father casually said, "No need to mention that blonde girl, eh?"

Always one for one-upmanship, Mother now acquired a car. This elegant tourer, a Swift, was parked in the cul-de-sac at the rear of the house and attracted admiration and envy from all in the neighbourhood, thereby fully justifying the price paid for it. A very delicate green, the soft top was held in place by a collection of struts that could have come out of a Meccano set. It took hours to put up and could cost you a few fingers if you weren't careful, but with the mica windows in place it was a joy to ride in. Sadly, it didn't stay long. Taking some fellow members of her local bridge club for a spin, Mother drove round a bend, meeting a cyclist head-on, who somersaulted over the soft top and was relatively uninjured. Mother was found blameless for the accident but suffered too much of a shock to carry on driving, and the car was returned to Mr Appleby, local motor dealer, garage owner and swain to my mother. He was always known to my brothers and me as Uncle Frank, which gives one some idea of their relationship. Our father's absence at sea did make Mother somewhat of an attraction, and several gentlemen hovered, but Uncle Frank got priority. Portly, chain-smoking, with cigarette ash permanently covering his waistcoat, he often gave us joyrides in his large, black Rolls-Royce and excited us beyond belief by once driving us down the long, straight Leasowe Road at over 100 miles per hour.

But these were all flirtations until something rather serious came along. It was typical of Mother that the something serious was the impossibly glamorous gentleman called Jock Macfee, who was a big-game hunter, straight out of romantic fiction. He didn't actually walk about wearing a solar topee but he was tall, good-looking, with a permanent suntan, and had spent time in the Dark Continent polishing off rhinos, elephants and any other luckless creatures that came in range. I believe they met when Macfee had been a passenger on my father's ship and he had obviously waited until the husband sailed again before just happening to bump into her somewhere. There was always something of the night about him, to quote a famous remark made later of a politician. Everything was just too good, too smooth, and one can only presume the absence of Father, and the sumptuous meals that she cooked him, kept him (for a while, anyway) at our door.

The Butterworth School was part of a large matinée show at the Empire Theatre, a vast auditorium opposite St George's Hall, in the centre of Liverpool. Part of the Moss Empire circuit, it housed mainly variety shows but this was a special performance, the cast solely children from all the local theatrical schools. When we weren't onstage, we found we could go into the auditorium and watch. In the toilet at the back of the stalls, a tall, thin, manic boy of about 16, speaking with a put-on American accent, suddenly confronted me. He was with an older man, whom I gathered was his father. "I want you," his finger stabbed at me, "to tell your parents that you should be a member of the Hughie Green Gang! You gotta lotta talent, son!" This confrontation in the toilet would be very suspect today but, as the boy later became famous for impregnating any female that came near him, siring several illegitimate children, there was no need to worry. Hughie Green, who became a nauseating television personality after the war, was running a group of youngsters round the music halls and presumably he and his father were talent-spotting. His father, a self-appointed Major Green, gave me a card to give my mother, but fortunately she never pursued it.

Wallasey then became a backwoods, as far as Mother was concerned, and in late 1937 a migration to London took place. I think the trips she had taken to the capital to see me had fired her imagination and suddenly we were living in a flat in north London. Naturally she had done her homework and from the front window we were able to look out onto Highgate Woods. My brothers happily continued their respective trades (Stuart was apprenticed to an advertising company, Peter was in a bank), I got a new dancing teacher and Father did what he was told and reported to the flat in London instead of the house by the sea.

The new dancing teacher was the formidable Shelagh Elliott Clarke. She had swept though the dance scene like a whirlwind, proving that pretty toe dancing and childish whimsy were things of the past. This lady proceeded by cajolement, terrifying discipline, bullying, a lot of cane-banging and (most of all) a great deal of affection to turn me into quite a reasonable dancer. The box of medals she won for me over the years is still one of my proudest possessions. Daily, after my hour of concentrated agony at the barre and dressed in my obligatory tights, I twirled in my *tour en l'air*, beat my legs in *entrechats*, and leapt in *grands jetés*. Gradually the legs strengthened, the leaps got loftier and Shelagh Elliott, like a demented James Mason, whacked the floor with a cane and screamed, "You will jump higher!" Sadly, success bred even greater heights of ambition in my mother. The pinnacle of fame to a child dancer was the All England Cup, for which three sections in costume were danced: Classical (frothy tutus for the girls, black tights and white blouses for the boys), Character (anything suitable for what you were dancing) and Musical Comedy (garish and colourful). It was very serious, very competitive, and months of preparation and training went into it. Every child dancer in England entered the competition and it was held in aid of the Blind Children of the Sunshine Homes, whose headquarters were at the head of Great Portland Street, near Regent's Park. Children and their parents, by the dozen, were there on finals day in 1938. We few, we very precious few, segregated after weeks of judgment in the semi-finals, waited for our music to tinkle from the piano. Suddenly, her face flushed, the silver fox rampant, my mother was on her knees in front of me.

"Anything! You can have anything if you win that cup today!"

Just as suddenly, Shelagh Elliott, with a dextrous move, propelled me down the stairs into Great Portland Street and hailed a cab. She directed it into Regents Park and, as we quietly chugged round the outer circle, this lady of the forbidding countenance and bright-red dyed hair, a cigarette jutting from her lips, gently and very surprisingly took my hand. "It doesn't matter a bugger if you win this cup or not. You're a good dancer. You'll do well. Just don't take any sodding notice of your sodding mother and enjoy it." The taxi took us back to Great Portland Street, I was handed back to my parent and not another word was spoken. I didn't win the cup, but I did come second.

One Sunday lunchtime at the flat, my elder brother Stuart announced that he'd seen Jock Macfee the day before, walking down Piccadilly. The effect was rather frightening. Mother went demented and I'm quite sure Stuart was sorry he'd mentioned it.

It was about this time that it was decided that, if I was to be an actor, I should lose my Liverpool accent. That accent – now cherished, then an abomination – had to be got rid of. The metal frame of the lift clattered upwards every day as it took me up to the Kensington flat of the greatest vocal coach in the country, Elsie Fogarty, who was as imposing as her name. Every stage actor of merit went to her and I got just as much attention as Laurence Olivier, who always gave her the credit for giving him his superb diction. She bullied the Liverpool accent out of me over several weeks: there was a lot of "How now brown cow" and Peter Piper picked enough peppers to keep every chef in London happy for years.

Early in 1939, the still-novel and very efficient Underground train took me all the way to Uxbridge station, where it was a short bus ride to Denham Film Studios. Alexander Korda had built this enormous, stylish studio complex after he had talked the Prudential Insurance Company into lending him several million pounds to (as he put it) internationalise British films. He succeeded with *The Private Life Of Henry VIII* and many other distinguished films. Everything he made had the elegance that became his trademark, and *The Spy In Black*, a World War I submarine thriller, had a very notable pedigree. It was the first Powell-Pressburger film and starred Conrad Veidt. I walked across the set in the first scene as a pageboy. My very first screen appearance totalled about six seconds, but it was a moment I never forgot, as to watch Veidt, the consummate actor, acting was to watch years of film experience. From the *Cabinet Of Caligari* on, every screen appearance was memorable. Walking out of the scene, having been asked by Bernard Miles as the hotel concierge how many ships he had sunk this trip, he merely, with his back to camera, casually held up two fingers. Describing that today sounds nonsensical, but it was a lesson in underacting I never forgot, and I got a clear and distinct reminder when I was asked to give a memorabilia lecture at the National Film Theatre a little while ago. They supplied, and screened, quite a few clips from past movies I had appeared in, including this brief sequence. Evidently, at some time I'd mentioned Denham and the film and they had gone to great lengths to find it. It got a big laugh as, even wearing a pageboy pillbox hat, my comical face was unmistakable.

A long, dusty room with tall windows, through which the red bricks of Waterloo Station could be seen, was quite empty apart from an upright piano, at which sat a rehearsal pianist. Sitting in one of the furthest window seats was the formidable figure of Ninette De Valois, undisputed queen of the British ballet world, and elegantly draped by her side, in an artistic pose, was Robert Helpmann, then the leading male dancer of the country. Standing by them, not quite so artistically posed, was Tyrone Gurthrie, who was then one of the foremost stage directors in the country. Faced by this formidable trio, and dressed in rehearsal black tights and white blouse, I scuffed my feet in the rosin box and then, as the pianist fumbled her way through the piano piece, I danced. This audition at the Old Vic Theatre, home of the Sadler's Wells ballet company, had been arranged by my dancing school and, dutifully, I jumped and twirled, spun and leapt, finally ending in what I hoped was a correct and engaging position. A small bow, then I went back to the other end of the long room while the three legendary figures, heads arched together, went into conference. A gesture from Ninette De Valois and my mother came in, followed by Shelagh Elliott Clarke. "We should like," De Valois said with perfect diction, "for the boy to accept a two-year scholarship with our ballet school, and then to join our company." She gave a graceful bow of her head and, followed by her two companions, left the room. Shelagh Elliott clasped her hands in ecstasy, my mother gave a smile of bliss and I said, "I don't want to be a dancer."

There was a famous cartoonist called Bateman who specialised in drawing consternation. Waiters askance with horror surrounded the man who asked for chips at the Ritz. The reactions Bateman drew were nothing compared to the look on Shelagh Elliott's face, and I thought Mother was going to have a good old-fashioned swoon. Nevertheless, even at the tender age of 17, I was quite adamant. The years of toil in the dance classes I knew would physically end one day. Surprisingly, Mother never put up any resistance.

In the same year, I was enrolled into RADA (Royal Academy of Dramatic Art). This splendid edifice in Gower Street, just across the road from Oxford Street in the West End of London, was the mecca of all would-be actors, as well as being a finishing school for some of the glamorous debutantes, who used it as part of their coming-out season. While fishing for the odd earl or viscount with a large des res in the country, shooting and hunting a must, they had lots of giggles and laughs at the Academy, but there were also lots of other young ladies who took it seriously, including one in my class, a small, dark-haired girl called Harriet. I was 17, with a very high level of untampered-with testosterone, and she was obviously partial to the art of initiation, so I was invited for tea at her flat near Olympia and, in the privacy of her apartment, she uttered the immortal words, "I shall change into something more comfortable." She then returned wearing black velvet pyjamas. I never got the tea but was given a tremendous amount of sympathy. My lone 134 bus ride back to Highgate was euphoric.

In the middle of the '50s, a letter was forwarded to me via the BBC. It was a short but very charming note from Harriet, telling me she had heard a few broadcasts and was glad to see things were going well and, as a telephone number was enclosed and the letter had a wistful note, I phoned. She had never become an actress but obviously wished she had. It was only a brief talk, but at the end, very sweetly, she suddenly said, "Sorry you didn't get your tea."

It was standard at RADA that we had an end-of-term acting production for the class. The choice was of *Hamlet* and once again the bard was my undoing. To test us thoroughly, we were given two parts each, and in the first half I played the gloomy Dane and in the second the doddery Polonius. The principal of the Academy, Sir Kenneth Barnes, gracefully hit the nail on the head: "Very good as Polonius, but I feel you are not *quite right* as Hamlet." At the end of the summer term, July 1939, he stood on the stage of their small theatre to give his usual speech, then suddenly said, "I do not envisage us meeting here again for some considerable time. There will be war." He gave a small bow and left the stage.

3 What Happens If The
Tappet Clearance Falls In The Sump?

There was a lot of sinister digging in the Royal Parks and talks of this German upstart Hitler. The cartoonists had a field day with his little black moustache while hundreds of demented fascists in black shirts marched into the Jewish area of the East End of London, screaming anti-Semitic slogans. The Jewish boys, in the best traditions of Daniel Mendoza and Kid Berg, did a little bit of flash shadow-boxing, then gave them a bloody good hiding. My mother felt, with a masterpiece of bad timing, that it was necessary for us to have our own house, and so, in August 1939, exactly one month before World War II started, we moved into our new home in Friern Barnet, a little further out of London. To nobody's surprise, it faced one Friary Park. Very lovely, very detached, but my brothers spent only three weeks in it before being called up by the army. They were both volunteer reservists (patriotism was sweeping the country) and, as I was too young, Mother and I became sole occupants of the new house. She faced the gathering storm with two of her sons and her husband away from home.

When the war did come, quickly and ruthlessly, I, like everybody else in the country, remembered exactly where I was at the moment the dry voice of our prime minister, Neville Chamberlain, came crackling out of every loudspeaker in the country. The nation tuned in to hear him saying, "We are now at war with Germany." With my best friend, Ernie Cochi, I stood on that sunny Sunday morning on 3 September, on the corner of Holloway Road and the Seven Sisters Road (two major roads in north London), listening at an open window. Ernie's family ran a small restaurant opposite the Tube station at the top of Holloway Road and the area was our playground. Chamberlain's final words were spoken and a bus driver, his vehicle stationary to hear the speech, suddenly called out, "I don't know about the rest of you, but I'm buggering off home. North Finchley, and anyone can cadge a lift." We both leapt aboard and half an hour later I was home, doing my best to be the only man about the house.

Although my father was still doing the Atlantic run, my brothers in local camps, the Phoney War meant things stayed very quiet. Wellington bombers flew leaflet raids over Germany telling the naughty Huns that Hitler was a baddie and they ought to get rid of him and Anderson shelters (named after some politician) were dug in every garden with a sheet of corrugated iron bent above you to protect you from the bombs that Germany was bound to drop on us. But nothing happened. Apart from the strict blackout, life stayed very normal and I got a job in a factory close by, piling enormous timbers into stacks. Mother ran everything with her usual flair until her father, a glorious throwback to wild Victorian days, dropped dead in Wallasey on 5 January 1940.

Henry Richard DeValve was a tiny bantam cock of a man, with wild, fiery eyes that gave you a clue as to his past behaviour. Son to a wealthy family, he was made a ward in Chancery as he was born after his father had suddenly died. His inheritance, which included the four largest public houses in Birkenhead (the large town next to Wallasey), a carriage yard plus a sizeable fortune, was placed in the hands of lawyers and, with wise investing, the value of his inheritance increased. It was Victorian days, and with the inheritance came almost unlimited credit. People nudged each other, pointing him out as someone who would, one day, come into a fortune and sadly, at the age of 16, it all went to his head. Wishing for the high life but unable to inherit until he was 21, he went on a gargantuan spending spree using his expectations as currency. One of his simple solutions was to order six tailor-made suits. Then, as soon as they were finished, they would be collected and put straight into the pawnbrokers' next door. Everything was bought on credit and, just as rapidly, sold at a much cheaper price. At 21, he met and married Annie, my grandmother, and although a great deal of his wealth had gone, he still rode in a carriage and lit cigars with a banknote. Grandma DeValve once admired a small dress shop, so he walked straight through the front door and bought it for her. It was no surprise that at the age of 23 he was flat broke and had to go to sea as a steward. Then he became a piano tuner. With an absolute fetish about his shoes shining like mirrors, he would sit in his armchair holding one of them in his hand and, giving it an occasional spit (mingles with the blacking, gives it that extra sheen, he explained), the polishing brush would go to and fro like a pendulum.

It was Tuesday when Mother duly caught the train north. Two days later, my father turned up (his ship had docked early) and naturally followed her up north for the funeral. Then Peter came home for the day on Saturday. Well trained to keep the larder full, I duly went shopping and returned to find him, still in his army uniform, washing a cup in the kitchen sink. He never turned around when I opened the front door. "Telegram on the table," he said. "You'd better read it."

Irritated, and busy stacking the shopping, I snapped at him, "Come on, tell me what it says."

He noisily stacked the dishes. "Read it," he said. Telegrams in those days always came in their yellow envelopes, with the messages typed out on strips of paper and then stuck onto the telegram form. It was quite brief, addressed to me, and might have been better worded. "Your mother died this morning. Funeral Tuesday. Let Peter and Stuart know. Signed Father."

It lived up to the expectation that all telegrams were bearers of bad news. The Great War generation were brought up to dread the sight of the telegraph boy bearing the small flimsy envelopes but, thinking Mother had wired to tell us of her return, Peter had opened it. "It's a mistake," I said. "He means Grandmother's died." But I was wrong. By coincidence, my elder brother had phoned earlier and was given the news, so the next morning we three joined a train from Euston and back to our home town we went. Grandma DeValve was the real loser, as she had lived with her husband for over 50 years and Mother was her only child. To lose them both inside a week was a tragedy worthy of Greek mythology.

I never understood why I was chosen to accompany him, but Father felt he ought to check on the funeral arrangements so he and I were solemnly led into a small, tin-roofed shed owned by the undertaker at the top of Falkland Road, where Grandma lived. With the sycophantic excess of sympathy that seems to go with their calling, the undertaker proudly showed us the coffin selected for my mother, the brass handles that were fitted and also pointed out the quality of the wood. It wasn't easy to concentrate, as Mother was in the coffin and the lid was open. She lay there, a tiny forlorn figure, and my father said, "Can't we shut her mouth?" With a practised movement the undertaker smoothly closed it, the lid was placed on the coffin and that was the last I saw of her. She was 49 when she died.

At the cemetery, the gravediggers dug out the newly turned earth that covered her father and her coffin joined his in the grave. At the Victoria Hotel we sat on stiff-backed chairs, were given cups of tea and fruitcake, then shook hands with a few relatives, most of whom I'd never seen before. A few days later it was my 18th birthday, and back in the empty house in London (my brothers had returned to the army) Father looked about. "Can't live here on your own," he said. "I'll sell it all up. You'll be all right, won't you?" I was just too young to comprehend properly and, within two weeks, at the hastily arranged auction, there I stood and heard seedy-looking dealers making arrangements not to bid against each other while every stick of furniture in the house was sold. Every toy we had possessed, every stitch of Mother's clothing, was bought and stuffed into tea chests. Father had gone back to sea a much-relieved man, pausing just long enough to press a £5 note into my hand. I moved in with a local landlady that Dickens would have had a wonderful time describing. Mean and grasping, she hated her husband, she hated her baby and she hated me, because all three of us had to be fed just enough to keep us alive. The misery was just too much, and after a few weeks I moved back to Wallasey and lived with Grandma DeValve.

I think I was some sort of solace for her after her loss, and she was a sweet, kind and lovely lady. After every meal in the tiny back kitchen, she filled the white tin basin with hot water to wash the dishes, giving a whisk with the small metal cage filled with scraps of soap to get some foam. Then from a hook on the wall she took a large black velvet hat, decorated with false cherries on the front. From this she pulled a long steel hatpin, put the hat on, then pushed the hatpin back through the hat and her hair, fastening it firmly in position. This routine was constant and never changed. One day I suddenly asked her, "Why the hat?"

She looked at me and spoke as if to a child. "It keeps the steam out of my hair."

The move to Wallasey was an unfortunate coincidence because it was just about then that Hitler decided the Liverpool docks should be put out of business, and the Germans sustained fierce and prolonged attacks with incendiary bombs, which set Merseyside literally aflame. I'd volunteered for the RAF and, while waiting to be called up, the Porter family – pre-war friends who owned a huge building on the dock road – gave me a job firewatching. With the youthful conviction that you bear a charmed life, I and another firewatcher spent nights kicking the small incendiary bombs off the roof of the tall building. Then the pattern changed. The incendiaries had done their job lighting up the way, and now the ribbon of the Mersey was a delight to the Luftwaffe navigators, who used the shining water to guide their Heinkels so they could unload their high explosives precisely on the docks. The giant overhead railway, a fixture of Merseyside as long as I could remember, ran along the dock road, and a busload of firemen – called out to cope with the raging fires that threatened to obliterate the entire area – came roaring down the road and pulled under the overhead for them to clamber out. A bomb landed exactly on the girders above, and the huge mass of the railway collapsed on them. The other firewatcher of the night and I managed to cross the street to use the police call box to summon help, but there wasn't much anyone could do.

Aerial mines were also used. Giant canisters floated down on parachutes, but a prevailing wind made sure they all drifted slightly south and landed on Wallasey. One of them blew the rear wall of my grandma's house off, but luckily she had gone to the cellar a few minutes earlier. A lump of concrete the size of a table went straight through the back of the armchair she had been sitting in.

Then my papers came through and I was sent off to basic training in the RAF. It may have been a terrible change from civilian life, but to wear the uniform of the RAF separated you from the boys and you walked with an unconscious swagger down the promenade. (I drew a long straw and did my training on the seafront of the holiday resort of Blackpool.) It gave you all the ego support you ever wanted, as it was the autumn of 1941 and the RAF, after the Battle of Britain, had a glamorous aura. Very unfair to the army and navy, but that's life. However humble your rank (there wasn't anything lower than mine – aircraftman, second class), you got that little bit more attention and admiration. But war was never far away. While doing some drill on the promenade, a distant roar of engines made our squad look up, and there – above our heads, clear in the blue sky – were three Hampden bombers in formation. Slowly, in unison, they made a crossing of the sky and, just as slowly, one of them turned and flew straight into the side of the plane next to it. A small puff of smoke. A second later, the delayed bang. Then, with half a wing gone, one of the planes spiralled to the ground. A train packed with holidaymakers pulled into Blackpool station as the now wingless body came through the roof. Over 30 people were killed.

I volunteered, like many others, for aircrew and confidently took my medical. Dancing had kept me fit with flexing my muscles, taking in deep breaths, coughing while doctors checked my testicles and urinating into jars with the utmost confidence. Fully dressed again I was presented with a large book filled with lots of tiny coloured dots. "Just read out the numbers," the doctor said, and 50 pages later I had read out four of them correctly. "Christ," said the doctor. "I wouldn't let you within 20 feet of a plane. What do you do about traffic lights?"

Colour-blindness stopped all thought of bravery in the air, so I was given a posting to an aerodrome called Woolfox, neatly hidden away in Rutland, the smallest county in England. This was my home for the next 18 months, during which time I attained the magic of my 21st birthday. I celebrated by myself in a public house in the nearby town of Stamford, drinking several pints of one of the most horrific liquids that the British have ever invented. It's called mild beer and it's always served warm. The eight-mile drive back to camp by the local bus was a disaster, as halfway back the driver had to stop to let me off and be ill in a hedge. Then having to walk the remaining four miles to camp, it wasn't really the best way to celebrate.

For a while, they stuck me in the kitchen of the sergeants' mess, giving me what was undoubtedly the worst job on the camp. Even today the words "tin room" can make me feel nauseous. A large galvanised tank, filled with very hot water and soda, was where all the large greasy dishes used in the cookhouse were tipped and, without any protection for your hands, you had to hack away at the remains of roast potatoes or try to clean off the soggy left-over lumps of Yorkshire pudding that stuck remorselessly to the baking tins. The steam and heat was overpowering and my fingers became like white bananas. I only wore a pair of air-force-issue dungarees over my air-force-issue underpants and sloshed about in gumboots. Grease caked my hair, sweat ran in streams down my body, and I left the dungarees unbuttoned down to my waist to let some air in.

A corporal cook, whose face I can see to this day, was a practical joker and he felt that the idiot airman in the tin room was fair game. It seems a dead mole had been found and, creeping up behind me, he dropped the mangled and bloody creature down the front of my dungarees, smearing my bare chest and soaking my underpants with its blood. I gave a cry, turned and, through a curtain of red mist, I saw the laughing face of the cook. I pulled the dead mole from the front of my dungarees, grabbed a butcher's cleaver from the side of the tank and threw it at him. It missed his head by a fraction, going straight into a wooden rack of dishes on the wall behind him. As the rack and dishes shattered onto the tiled floor, the door opened and the station warrant officer walked in. Warrant Officer Grogan, who ran the station, was an air-force regular who came from Northern Ireland. Strict but very fair, he seemed to sense exactly what had happened. The mangled corpse of the dead mole lay on the floor; my chest, underwear and dungarees were soaked in its blood. He kicked at the cleaver on the floor, kicked at the dead mole, gave a look at the white-faced cook, and then looked at me. "You've been in that tin-room job too long, Stark. Go and have a clean-up. Take the day off tomorrow, then report to the fire section." We all knew that, had that cleaver been an inch closer, I'd have probably spent the next ten years in a military prison.

The fire section was fine, teaching all and sundry how to operate the fire extinguishers and pumps, and everything went smoothly until the WAAFs came to the camp. All male for months, the camp was suddenly invaded by a contingent of female members of the air force, and they in their turn had to be taught what to do in case of fire.

Fifty young ladies sat in serried rows, with one airman just turned 21 standing in front. I started the standard explanation: "You see, the male coupling of the hose has to be fitted into the female coupling of the hose and..." This routine had been performed 100 times, but the inquiring female mind had to be satisfied. "Could you tell me..." with hand raised high the young WAAF had an expression of extreme innocence. "Could you tell me why that is called a male coupling, and why that," she gave a gesture, "is called a female coupling?"

Fifty pairs of feminine eyes gazed with delicious anticipation at the young airman and, walking straight into the trap, I confidently picked up both ends of the fire hose and explained. "Well, you see the male is called male because it's a bit smaller and can fit into the fe—"

That is as far as I got. A loud cough from behind me and the fire section sergeant gently beckoned. "I feel, Stark, that this would be as good a time as any to send you up to the crash tender on the airstrip. They could do with an extra hand."

And they did welcome me up there. In fact, they were very effusive. The corporal in charge walked round me several times, making noises of approval. "Definitely the right size. Very definitely." There were also murmuring noises of approval by the other members of the crew that I was definitely the right size. We stood by the DP41 Crossley crash tender, the fearsome vehicle that they were the crew of. This huge diesel-engined vehicle would roar down the runway alongside any plane either taking off or landing and, should disaster strike, the crew, like outriders on a Western stagecoach, would leap off, hoses at the ready, and pour water or foam on any fire that might occur. They also had, riding at the front alongside the driver, the key member of the crew. He was attired in asbestos suit and helmet and, armed with a long, fearsome metal rod, with claw attached, he would fight his way into the damaged aircraft attempting to rescue, amidst the flames, any of the aircrew still trapped in the wreckage. The suit was not very large and needed someone of slight build to fit inside it. "Definitely the right size," repeated the corporal and, whether I liked it or not, I climbed into the thick claustrophobic garment.

Our squadron at the airport was number 64, equipped with Lancaster bombers, and almost every night these huge planes, engines roaring, taxied into position, waiting for take-off. Our crash tender stood ready beside each plane as the crew members looked down from the tiny windows high above us; then, at the signal, they lurched away down the runway and slowly climbed, loaded with fuel and bombs, up into the sky. The Lancasters soon proved themselves to be some of the most efficient flying machines of the war and had an elegance which one could never expect of something designed exclusively to rain death and destruction on the ground beneath. But they were magnificent planes and the part that the crews that flew them played in winning the war has never really been recognised. The young men we watched every night clambered clumsily aboard, then sat cramped in their tiny, claustrophobic seats, flying for many hours into the nightmare of German anti-aircraft fire.

The scandal that no medal was ever awarded to bomber crews rankles even now, as their loss ratio was higher than almost every other branch of the armed forces. Even after their return from hours of terror, they still had to hope that they could land safely. It's fashionable now to complain of the destruction they rained on Dresden, but why this town should bring forth such waves of sympathy I have never understood. To bomb a town (a major rail depot, incidentally) with a population that managed to slaughter six million unarmed, defenceless men, women and children I always felt was quite justified. I lost too many friends among those aircrew, including Archie Mitchell, my best friend from my teenage days. Archie, already in the air force, volunteered for aircrew duty after his brother Bobby, in the merchant navy, went down in the engine room of his ship off the coast of North Africa. They got Archie over Rumania, while he was bombing the oil fields of Ploesti. I met their mother again in a public house in Wallasey one night, some years after the war. Through a haze of liquor, she peered at me then, mascara running down her cheeks. She flung her arms about me. "Those bastards, they got them both. My only children!" she said. "Both my sodding sons!"

After every operation, we sat waiting by the runway, the crash tender engine always running, counting off the planes that had made it back, and if the number fell short we knew some more of the aircrew weren't going to be having breakfast in the sergeants' and officers' messes that morning. Only one plane, a Wellington – not of our squadron but desperately needing somewhere to set down – crashed on landing. We couldn't get anyone out.

I stopped wearing the asbestos suit because of a hole in the runway. Doing a practice run, we hit it at speed, I catapulted through the air, and landed very hard on the tarmac. I staggered to my feet and looked at our corporal. "What about my hand?" I said. "It's in the wrong place."

The corporal gave an irritated tut-tut. "All you've done is dislocated it. I'll put it back for you." He grabbed my hand and pulled it and I passed out. The X-rays showed I had a double fracture of the wrist, which the putting-back-into-place hadn't exactly helped. After my arm was set – then broken again, because of the extra damage by the friendly corporal – I got two weeks' sick leave. I came back to find an order was posted that 250,000 flight mechanics were needed. This enormous number could only be found through the rank and file, which included me.

With no mechanical knowledge whatever, I found myself at a grim peacetime station called Cosford, about to start a six-week course learning how to completely service a Rolls-Royce Merlin engine. This monstrous, complicated mass of tubes, cogs, pistons and hundreds of ancillary pieces of machinery stood before us while a sergeant instructor began his lecture. "This end 'ere is the timing chain," he said. "This 'ere is where the petrol goes in, and this bit 'ere at the front is where you lot make sure the screws are done up tight cos that's where the propeller goes." I was already fighting heavy lids. Wearing overalls, we marched in our heavy boots each day to our lecture, and each day I marched back knowing less and less about Rolls-Royce Merlins.

One night, tired and dejected, I stood in my squad outside my hut waiting to be dismissed, aching to lie on the three biscuits on my bed that the RAF laughingly called a mattress when suddenly there was a raucous bellow. "Right, now pay attention!" The bellow came from a small, ruddy-faced flight sergeant of indeterminate age whose whole manner and appearance told you he was a regular in the RAF. Buttons polished, boots gleaming, uniform pressed, he gazed at us with a tense, searching look. "Fall out all men over six feet." Several men left the squad. "Fall out all men under five feet five." Just a couple this time. "All men on sick parade." No one moved. "Finally, hands up any man who thinks they cannot do a 15-mile route march through Wolverhampton next Saturday in aid of War Savings Week!"

My hand went up almost as a reflex action. That bloody engine, my dirty overalls, the flight sergeant shouting, the 15-mile route march, it was all too much. The flight sergeant came very close; his eyes narrowed further, his voice much quieter. "Just tell me, sonny. Just tell me why you can't do that march. Just tell me, eh?"

The rest of the squad strained to hear. To me, my voice sounded rather far away and distant. "It's my feet, Flight Sergeant," I said. "My feet hurt."

His face got nearer, his voice even quieter. "Have you seen the medical officer?"

I gave a brief swallow. "I'm going tomorrow morning."

He barked an order and a corporal was at his side. The flight sergeant's fingers trembled as he pointed at me. "Corporal, you will take this man's name and number, you will check he sees the medical officer first thing tomorrow morning and then you will bring me the medical officer's report!" He glared at me once more. "Fall out." In the barracks that night, I carefully examined my feet. There was absolutely nothing wrong with them. I tried kicking the radiators a few times, but it didn't seem to help.

The next morning, the doctor tapped my bare right foot with a rubber mallet. "Seems to be all right. Rather good condition, your feet. Still hurt, eh?" I gave a nod. "Better take your other boot off." The lump of leather hit the ground with a thump. He peered closely, then said, "Ah!" and wrote on a piece of paper. "Take this to the chiropodist. Other side of the parade ground. She'll see to you."

The chiropodist was a very pretty, blonde WAAF. She looked at the paper, took out a long surgical knife and said, "Boots off." Once more they hit the floor. "Thick skin, that's what's doing it. That, and those bloody boots." A thin skim across the balls of my feet and she signed the paper. "You got a pair of shoes?" she said. Well, every serviceman in every branch of the armed forces has got a pair of shoes, the last relic of his past civilisation cherished and stored safely. "Come on," she said, "you can have this." And with that she signed an "excused boots" chit, a document that stays with you for the rest of your service life and means you never wear boots again and are excused every parade and is probably the most prized document any serviceman can ever be given. I mumbled my thanks and the WAAF gave a smile. "You should all have them," she said.

The corporal passed the papers to the flight sergeant, who examined them and then looked at me. "All right, airman, you will not be on the route march and you can fall out from this squad as well, and you will be wearing shoes from now on." I swear there was almost a slight smile on his lips. He knew I'd got away with it and I knew that he knew.

There was release from the flight mechanics course, as well. Our instructor's question was clear and concise. "Tell me, Stark. What would you do if the tappet clearance fell in the sump?"

Vainly I looked about for inspiration as the instructor patiently waited. "Well, Sarge," I began. "I suppose you'd have to unscrew—"

He gave a short sigh, and then beckoned me to follow him. In the office upstairs we stood in front of a flight lieutenant. "He really 'as tried, sir, but this airman is a mechanical idiot. Much too dangerous to let him near an engine." The flight lieutenant signed a paper, the sergeant gave me a sympathetic pat on the shoulder and I was free. And from the horror of the engine shop came the bliss of the ration wagon at Halton.

Halton was the home of the RAF School of Cookery, situated in the beautiful Vale of Aylesbury, and it was a paradise posting. Here was the home of the experts who made sure the airmen of England were well and sufficiently fed, and I was in charge of the wagon that made certain that all the departments received their correct allocation of food. Actually, there was a warrant officer in charge, but he wanted an easy and contented life and, while he rode in front, I busied myself at the rear of the truck sorting out who got what. Butter by the box, sides of bacon galore and eggs by the crate. They were all loaded aboard every day and we trundled round the camp issuing them. It would have been too easy to start a discreet black market, but I resisted temptation and the only bending of the rules came when every other week my warrant officer appeared at the back of the truck to inform me nonchalantly that he had a weekend pass and would be going home. Giving me that information, he would then place on the rear platform a very small brown attaché case and walk away. Twenty minutes later, the case, slightly heavier, would be collected. Of course, it was all too good to last.

The pilot officers who piloted planes were heroes of the war. Pilot officers who ran the administration of the camps were often a pain in the arse, and there never was a bigger one that the PO who came to the station in late 1943. It was new brooms sweeping clean with a terrible violence. I stood in front of his desk, trying to image what infringement of the rules I was guilty of while he peered at a document. Then, in a high, nasal voice, reeking of minor public school and snobbery, he said, "Goin' through your records, I find you have been on general duties for over two years, what?" I shifted slightly, not knowing what was being asked of me. "You should have a trade. You know that, don't you?"

At last, a direct question. "Well, I failed aircrew sir – colour-blindness – and I wasn't any good at being a flight mechanic."

My failure at two careers in the air force – one for a physical reason, one for a mental – seemed to bring on a mild seizure as he tugged at his collar, went rather red and then gave me a savage look. "What were you in civilian life, eh?"

As I more or less knew what his reaction was going to be, I shifted some more. "I was a dancer, sir."

His face got redder and his voice became icier. "Oh, I see." Vaguely he looked about for inspiration, and then it came to him. "Righto. Supposing you have an accident and lose both your legs. What then?" He sat back, having made his point. Something warned me it would not be tactful to mention Wing Commander Douglas Bader, who *did* lose both legs but went on to become one of the most feared fighter pilots of the war, so I stayed silent.

He gave me another glare. "Think over what I've said and be here Monday morning. Then we'll decide what you're going to be and where I shall post you."

4 We Were Sitting On Vesuvius
And We Never Even Knew

And that strange, lunatic conversation was one of the turning points in my life. The brainless, chinless idiot of a pilot officer was a blessing in disguise. Back in the barracks, filled with gloom and depression, I realised I was once more being placed on the treadmill of yet another posting and, while all the other airmen were off to Aylesbury for the Friday night booze-up, I sat alone, filled with self-pity. It was then that I saw a small air force magazine lying on the table. There was nothing else to look at, so I leafed through it and there, on a left-hand page, was a small boxed announcement asking for volunteers for the RAF gang show. Gravely, it warned that this was not a fall-on-your-feet posting – pre-war experience in the theatre was essential and a signed recommendation from your entertainments officer had to be sent with your application to the Air Ministry.

Luckily, I'd already done a couple of cabarets at the camp for the entertainments officer, and he signed at once. With some delight, I informed the pilot officer that I had sent off my application to Air Ministry and, as they were unassailable magic words, he could do nothing. Three days later, I was summoned to the London School of Economics (the building still stands in Houghton Street, at the bottom of the Aldwych), which had been taken over by Air Ministry Intelligence and, as it had its own small theatre, was being used as the headquarters for the gang show. Squadron Leader Ralph Reader was the brains behind it all. He ran gang shows before the war, mainly for the Scouts, and as they were immensely successful all-male shows someone had the bright idea that they would slot into the RAF. They were an instant success. At a time when service shows had the reputation of playing down to the troops (dirty jokes, lawnmowers chasing girls in grass skirts), Reader insisted nothing like that should be in the gang shows and their popularity soon proved him right. Soon there were 13 all-male shows and two all-female shows playing in every combat area of the war. Fingers sore from polishing the buttons on my uniform, I stood rigidly at attention in front of Squadron Leader Jack

Cracknell, who ran the gang show office (Reader was abroad), hoping that smartness was what they were looking for. He gave a tolerant smile, told me to relax and handed me a script.

He laughed a lot at my reading, and then it was all back to normality as I was given the standard rejection. "Very good, but there just aren't any vacancies. However, if there is one in the future, we'll let you know." On the train back to Halton, I could only picture the face of my nemesis, the pilot officer, picking out some derelict station for me to spend the rest of my time in the service.

Sure enough, I stood in front of him the very next day, but the glare he gave me was of frustration. An Air Ministry signal lay in front of him. "They want you back." His voice was thick with fury but, as Air Ministry signals were the holiest of holies, that signal had to be obeyed.

Squadron Leader Cracknell smiled benignly. "Well, Stark," he said. "Gave you my word about vacancies, and there is one." John Blatchley, a member of number four show, had failed his medical and was not permitted to go abroad; the rest of number four unit had not failed their medicals and were going. "Would you like to go with them? You can think about it, if you like." My reply was instant, and without further ado I was member of the gang shows. Two and a half solid years of stamping my foot to the ground, two and a half years of bringing the arm smartly up to the buttons of my forage cap, two and a half years of automation, were now over.

The world, and my time in the RAF, changed instantly. The little stage of the theatre in Houghton Street was littered with the theatrical skips that have always been the heart of the strolling player through centuries. Made of wickerwork – to withstand the thumping and banging of trains, planes and automobiles – they would become our most cherished item, to be guarded wherever we went, as everything we owned, plus costumes and make-up, would go in them. Any nervousness I may have had as the new boy vanished at once, as the unit were far too busy hurling into those skips what they thought could keep them alive in foreign parts to worry about new blood.

Then came the RAF's own personal form of torture. The Inquisition of Torquemada's time had some very nasty means of persuasion, but I can tell you, from personal experience, that nothing in their terrifying catalogue comes anything near what the RAF inflicted on you the moment they knew you were posted overseas. As the gang show weren't too precise as to where we would be going, the medical orderly's eyes lit up. Here was his chance to inject every known serum he had in stock and check the results. "This one 'ere," he held up a syringe that I would have thought was only used on elephants, "this one 'ere is in case you fall in the Nile, while this one 'ere is for your monsoon swamps in Burma." As each of the giant needles sank into my rear, I gave a groan and, as what I thought was the last of the empty syringes clattered into the stainless steel trays, I sat up with relief. "Got a few more," the orderly said. "Beriberi, tsetse fly and our old friend malaria. Got to look after you, you know." Finally the fiendish ritual was over. That entire weekend I spent alone on a camp bed, arms swollen, head throbbing, with every kind of feverish reaction possible.

Number four gang show (one flight sergeant and ten airmen) finally boarded the SS *Maloja*, a 20,000-ton converted troopship, and with our skips and kitbags stored we lurched down through a rough and stormy Bay of Biscay. Fortunately, the U-boats ignored us and we landed safely in Algiers on Christmas Day 1943.

The stumbling troops, coated with blue woad, that shuffled behind the chariot of Queen Boadicea, attempting to stem the might of the Roman Empire, had one. The British Army, struggling to make the first dent in the bastion that Napoleon had made of Europe, forcing the Duke of Wellington to make that classic statement ("They may not frighten the enemy, but by God, they frighten me!"), had one. In fact, the noble duke was probably looking right at him when he made that famous remark. There were undoubtedly several of them that spent many nasty, uncomfortable years dodging German shells and bullets in the quagmire of the Western Front in the 1914-18 war, and you have my personal guarantee that there was one in North Africa in the months leading up to the final assault by the Allied Troops upon the Third Reich in Italy. I say this because he happened to be the driver of the three-tonner truck that took myself, and the rest of the show, off to our first camp in North Africa.

Yes, the Ginger-Headed Corporal has been an integral part of the British armed forces since the beginning of time, and I feel certain that a large section of the female populace of the world has reason to be grateful for his continued existence. The Ginger-Headed Corporal, obviously named because of the two stripes he wears upon his arm and the shock of red hair on top of his head, usually has other physical characteristics – quite short in height, wide shoulders, freckled and with a tendency to be bow-legged. Not, you would think, endowed by nature with too many physical advantages, and yet this legendary figure has proved himself down the ages to be one of the world's greatest lovers.

We clambered onto the back of the truck and bumped our way to the transit camp, aptly named Blida. Any hope we were going to some glamorous Beau Geste fortress, with foreign legionnaires standing nobly on the ramparts gazing at the shifting sands of the Sahara, were quickly dashed. The camp of Blida was chiefly mud, very damp, dotted with decrepit bell tents, and the only stone building was a very large, and very smelly, gents' lavatory. However, the camp did boast something from the dark days of the legion and that was a flight sergeant who made anyone from the PC Wren novel look like a fairy on a Christmas tree. He obviously had an intense hatred of anything to do with showbusiness and, as an entertainment unit, he had made quite sure our tent was right next to that nasty-looking stone lavatory.

It was at this crisis moment that we discovered the talents of our red-headed driver for the first time. He was called Charlie and was the original dyed-in-the-wool Cockney. His head just about reached the medal ribbons that festooned the chest of the terrifying monster NCO who was in the position to rule our lives, but, undaunted, he looked up into that stone-aged face. "Quite possible they could be poofs, sir," he said. "Might well be a disrupting influence of the rest of the camp. Take my advice – bung them out there under them palm trees." He gestured to a hillock, which at least had shade, as well as being above the mud level.

The knuckles of the flight sergeant twitched. "They do look a bit nancified, I must bloody say. Right, tent 27!" He strode away with that odd jerk of the body that 25 years of service had instilled into him.

We moved in a tight circle round our ginger-headed friend. "What was that about being poofs?" we asked.

The freckles moved even closer as he gave a grin. "Get your bleedin' gear into tent 27 quick before some other crafty sod knocks it off. It's the best one on the bleedin' camp."

We could only presume that Charlie was a bit stagestruck himself, as (without any reward) he took us under his wing. I think he could have given the Admirable Crichton a few lessons. There didn't seem to be anything that Charlie couldn't arrange, knock off, scrounge, and he had a line in flannel that would have put Baron Munchausen to shame. As the days went by, hourly we raised our eyes to heaven to praise both the good Lord and the Air Ministry for appointing him as our driver. However, clever as he was at the fiddle, we didn't realise the full talents of our Charlie until it came to our first social outing. We'd already done a couple of shows at local camps, and now came our first night off and the chance to savour the sensuous delights of North Africa. There *was* a local village, it *did* have a dance hall and, yes, there *were* lots of girls in the locality. To men who had just spent a month on a troopship, the thought of getting near a girl made all the appalling discomfort of that camp worthwhile – and French girls, at that! It conjured up pictures of petite mademoiselles, saucily winking and throatily telling you, in the accent that drives all Englishmen mad with lust, "I am obliged to say you are the most attractive man I have evair met..."

Of course, it wasn't like that at all. The so-called dance hall was a long, converted barn which had a platform at one end, where the orchestra (comprising an accordion player and a drummer) sat. There was no twirling mirrored glass ball, just two naked light bulbs and, if that wasn't bad enough, sitting around the room the full terror. We saw plenty of petite mademoiselles, all right, and considering the circumstances they were rather pretty, but each and every one of them had with her a chaperone. Like the dreaded Madame La Farges, who sat at the foot of Madame Guillotine, these harpies, all dressed in black, dared us to approach their precious daughters. Better men than us had given in before such odds and a dreary night lay ahead, but Charlie licked his lips, glanced around the room and said, "Stone me, look at all those darlings!" We looked at the girls, we looked at the chaperones and finally we looked at Charlie. Even in his best blue, with brass buttons shining and half a bottle of Brylcreem plastered on that red hair, he hardly looked the answer to a maiden's prayer. The accordion wheezed, the drummer ran tatty brushes across his snare drum and the chaperones glared at the sheepish group of airmen huddled together at the end of the hall.

Without a pause, Charlie walked down the centre of the hall, his shiny boots clicking on the wood floor, and stopped in front of a pretty girl, his body jerked forward at an angle of 45 degrees and he muttered something to both the girl and the woman who sat by her side. God knows what halting French words Charlie used, but suddenly the girl rose and he took her in his arms. "Christ, he's done it," someone said. With all the confidence of a ballroom champion, he began to waltz her round the room. At least, I think it was a waltz – with that accordion player, you couldn't tell.

Charlie's girl didn't stay with him. She abruptly left. Completely unabashed, he at once danced with another, and as she too left him he took yet another. With the sense we were watching a seasoned campaigner, we watched his movements. The latest girl stayed quite a while longer and cunningly he steered her to the door nearest the exit. She was plump, dark and pretty, and her eyelashes demurely lowered as she and Charlie vanished into the night. By now the accordion player, determined to show L'Air Force Anglais he knew what he was doing, started a Glenn Miller medley. It wasn't too easy to discover what tune he was playing at any given time, but the drummer caught on and practically had a hernia thumping his bass drum. The plump girl reappeared and went back to her seat. Charlie stood behind us, mopping his brow. "What a goer!" He clutched his pocket. "Christ, I've still got her knickers!"

Open-mouthed, we gazed at the wonder boy. "What did you do, stand on a box?!" someone said.

"No need," said Charlie. "She was on top."

As we gazed with feelings of frustration, jealousy and admiration at our little friend, we heard the accordion player and his fellow assassin on the drum give the final *coup de grâce* to the French national anthem. We climbed into the back of the truck and trundled back to camp, and in tent 27 the oil lamp burned while cigarettes glowed. "It's no good, Charlie, you've got to tell us. How the bleeding hell do you do it? How come you have such a girl when you look like the back of a bus? And not a very pretty bus at that."

Charlie smiled and drew on a cigarette and, as if we hadn't had enough, he then curled his tongue and blew a perfect smoke ring. "It's easy if you've got the bleedin' nerve," he said. "Once round the floor, then you tell them straight out what you're going to do to them. Three of them leave you, right? But finally one *doesn't.*"

Someone tried the smoke ring and failed. "But you can't be sure, Charlie. Not absolutely sure."

Charlie blew another perfect circle. "If it's not the third, it's the fourth, and if it's not her, it'll be the one after that. I'm telling you, there's always one."

Faithfully, for the rest of our time in North Africa, Charlie drove us to all the little stations with the makeshift theatres, draughty tents, sometimes just a pile of packing cases, where we slapped on our make-up and did the shows. The golden rule was that, the further from civilisation you got and the worse the living conditions were, the better the audience. Ralph Reader had rejected suggestions we should all be made up to sergeants, so we stayed ordinary servicemen like our audiences. We slept in the same accommodation, ate the same food and thankfully met corporals like Charlie.

Finally, sadly, we said goodbye to him on the same quayside where we'd met him, and embarked on a storm-tossed crossing of the Mediterranean to the Bay of Naples. This time we could forget the tents. Billeted in a former brothel, taken over by ENSA, we had a real bed, and we played the jewel of Neapolitan opera houses, the Petrizelli. This beautiful theatre had a gilded horseshoe circle of boxes, the pit nesting beneath them, plus acoustics of perfection. We played a week at the theatre and it was great success, as another golden rule of Ralph Reader's was that all material in the show – the songs, the sketches – had to be purer than driven snow, and of course he was right. The day after finishing that week we had a day off and were invited to see the ENSA show that was following us in at the same theatre. We settled in our seats, the curtain went up and all hell broke loose.

The comics of the ENSA show, civilians sent out from London, decided that the troops abroad were of the lower classes, so their material ranged from dire to filthy and was greeted with silence. We cringed in our seats as the jokes got dirtier, and it was the troops in the back of the pit who settled matters. There was a squeaking of rubber, a blowing of air, then suddenly, above the back seats, appeared a whole row of inflated condoms. These were then tapped slowly forward, row after row of the audience taking over and, as the army of inflated rubber dumbbells advanced towards them, the cast broke and fled. The show was over.

On our last night in Naples the housekeeper ran in. Hysterically, she called, "Vesuvio! Vesuvio!" We told her we had climbed it only four days earlier, sitting on the warm rocks, drinking bottles of Lachrima Christi, but her repeated cries made us go up to the flat roof where, 15 miles across the bay, we saw Vesuvius in full eruption. Vast streams of molten lava ran down its sides and suddenly all the bombardments of the war seemed puny. Three days later, after crossing the spine of Italy, we drove into Bari, on the Adriatic, the skies above us black with volcano dust, and when there was a sudden cloudburst it rained mud. The pride of Bari was its opera house, the largest in Europe. Our little show seemed comical upon the vast stage but the troops, as always, were a great audience. We dodged about the south of Italy – Brindisi, Taranto, Foggia and, finally, the palace at Caserta, where we had a welcome from the troops as well as the Italians themselves. They had only too willingly surrendered and the Italian cook who was seconded to us summed it all up. This ex-soldier had been sent to fight at Stalingrad; the Russians had captured him, taken one look at him and then sent him unharmed back to Italy. Small, fat and very excitable, his hands flourished with extravagant gestures as he explained our relationship. "You don't-a dislike me. I don't dislike-a you.

Whatta we fight for?" Starstruck, he watched our show every night from the wings and pleaded to stay with us wherever we went but, as the signal had come through posting us to India and Burma, it was out of the question.

Once more the baskets were repacked and a Dakota flew us via Malta down to Libya, and then, through the night, we flew along the North African coast towards Egypt. After years of total blackout in England, it was a shock to see the blaze of light in the distance that was Cairo. We rode a camel, climbed a couple of stones on one of the great pyramids and gave up, did a few more shows and then, quite happily, flew on to the Far East. Spartan Britain had changed us and none of us liked the ostentatious style of living that was Cairo. The refuelling stops, where we also played shows, were names from the legendary Empire flying-boat routes – Basra, Jawani, Sha Ja – with buildings made from hundreds of petrol cans. The plane finally dipped onto Karachi Airport and our passage to India was over.

5 These Proceedings Are Closed

The Indian customs officials circled our skips warily, convinced that they were full of rare silks and satins, exotic jewellery and gold coins of the realm being cunningly smuggled into the country. Passengers at the airport were delighted to see us having to put on some of our costumes just to prove we were actors. Before heading north, we played some shows in Karachi (the make-up had to be kept in bowls of ice) and then climbed aboard the train to travel across the dreaded Sind Desert. Huge blocks of ice, slung high in the carriages – while fans blew the iced air down on us – was the very basic air conditioning. A towel shifted in the night and within days I was in hospital in Lahore with pleurisy, but I met up with the show again in Delhi and then we were off again into the foothills of the Himalayas, over a 12,000-foot pass, to the hill station of Chakrata. As the clouds cleared from underneath us we saw a vista of what seemed to be the whole of north India. From then on, everywhere we travelled we faced monumental climbs, skirmishes with the jungle, and monsoons in Chittagong that made Manchester look like arid desert, until finally we came to what we had really come for: the jungles of Burma.

In that jungle were the British forces fighting the Japanese army, which had made such a terrifying advance right to the borders of India. This nightmare battle, fought in conditions which beggared belief, was at that time centred round Imphal, where the Japanese had laid siege to the town, and in a decrepit Dakota plane we set off to do a show there. Clambering aboard to hitch a ride into Imphal (very brave under the circumstances) was Jack Hawkins, who later became such a big star in Hollywood. We worked together later on in the film *Guns At Batasi* and reminisced how lucky we were to survive that flight in such a beaten-up plane. The airstrip was so rough that both tyres on the plane burst when we landed, but the welcome was incredible. Even though they were surrounded by the enemy, the troops whooped and laughed, gave huge rounds of applause for every performer and cheered us to the echo at the curtain, all in the little theatre they had made themselves. Perhaps the noise irritated the Japanese, as that night sticky bombs were attached to all the British fighter planes that stood on the runway. Fortunately they hadn't stuck one on the Dakota, as next day our plane did just manage to get off the ground safely.

Then it was across country to see how the British Raj was coping, and where better to go than Poona, home to the pukka-est of pukka sahibs? That was when personal tragedy struck. The ravages of the Delhi belly – or Montezuma's revenge, call it what you will – caught me just before boarding a plane. The gentlemen's lavatory (a small grass hut) beckoned, and diving inside I hung my faithful camera, the Kodak Autograph 120, on a peg. A few moments of relief, then the roar of the twin radial engines made me rush to the aeroplane, and only as we were halfway to Secunderabad did I realise my camera was still hanging on that peg. A tragedy, as it was one of the few objects that I'd salvaged from those dealers who had bought up our home. The next show we played should have been photographed, as it was such a fantasy.

We had been travelling for nearly six months and were starting to show signs of exhaustion – styes on the eyelids, boils in nasty places. We were given three days off in Ceylon as a reward for our efforts and the thought of bathing on Candy Beach was bliss, but an entertainments officer came to spoil things. "You see," the young pilot officer twisted his cap nervously, "there's this small island, about 400 miles out in the Indian Ocean and on it are 30 airmen who have never had any entertainment of any kind. Ever! Been there for 18 months and one *does* feel a bit sorry for them." We all knew what was coming, but after the siege of Imphal none of us were really in the mind to say no.

That young officer may have knocked our three days on the head but he did do us, and those 30 airmen, proud. A huge Sunderland flying boat was commandeered (the log book said it was going on submarine patrol) and they even took the side off it so we could get a mini-piano on board. The eleven of us, the pilot officer, our sacred skips plus the mini-piano were then flown 400 miles to Kelai, one of the Maldives, which, from the air, looked exactly like a Dorothy Lamour atoll. The huge flying boat spiralled slowly down above the island, made a perfect landing in the horseshoe lagoon, and every one of the 30 airmen, plus their officer, came out on an iron barge to greet us. The poor buggers were there purely as a refuelling base for any flying boat on patrol. and the show that night, in a large grass hut, was extraordinary. A hand-painted notice displaying the legend "The only show to brave the danger of the Isles" was fastened above the entrance and their officer, a very imaginative flight lieutenant, then broke open the rum ration, raided medical supplies for whisky, put in a couple of tins of boot polish and mixed it all up in a large zinc bath, making a brew the witches of *Macbeth* would have been proud of. The bath was placed at the back of the audience and every airman was told to bring his tin cup and dip into it during the show. Halfway through, the entire audience were as pissed as a newts and in the morning all 30 ashen-faced airmen, plus officer, staggered onto the beach to say goodbye. We had a refreshing dive into the water of the lagoon from the wing of the giant flying boat, then the bow wave whitened as the Sunderland picked up speed and from the air we saw the tiny figures still waving goodbye.

At a hill station somewhere, we'd heard the news of D-Day, the famous 6 June, and realised it was just possible we might see the end of this bloody war. We endured endless days and nights of second- and third-class travel on the railways (our record was seven days non-stop) or bounced our spines to jelly on the three-ton trucks, covering almost every RAF station in India. We admired the secretariat in Delhi (a building for the viceroy which made Buckingham Palace look like a seaside bungalow) and for a week were stationed at the other end of the giant avenue, in the Irwin stadium. The fixture, known to every serving man in India as the char wallah (the tea man), was already sitting there to greet us. The grapevine that told these gentlemen that new troops were arriving still stays a mystery. All we knew was that, moving into any barrack room in India for the first time, you would see one of these venerable gentlemen squatting on the floor, the vast urn of boiling water by his side, and a row of cups, jars of tea and bottles of milk at the ready. On the hills of Simla, on the sunbaked railway stations of the Sind, on the sweaty verandas of Chittagong, they would be there waiting to serve you as you arrived. As usual, we made the standard inquiry, "Good char?", and in the heaviest Scottish dialect I have ever heard outside of the Glasgow Gorbals he announced, "This is the best char you will ever taste in the entire continent!" This char wallah had spent 50 years serving the Black Watch regiment and, short of wearing a kilt and playing bagpipes, he was a native of the Highlands.

At last, at the gateway of India, on the seafront at Bombay, we boarded the sister ship of the boat that had taken us to Algiers, the *Mooltan*, and we were off back home. The trip back stoked the resentment of the servicemen that resulted in the landslide election of 1945, when the Labour Party swept to power. Crowded like cattle at the bottom of the ship (I think we were below the water line), conditions for the ordinary servicemen were appalling. During rough seas, a constant stream of them staggered into the cubicles, where the toilets were, and were sick as dogs; the washing facilities were laughable, as thin trickles of tepid water were all we could coax from the showers; and, lying in our hammocks, bodies bumping against one another all night, you realised that, should a U-boat launch a successful attack, we, down in the bowels of the ship, could never get up the stairs in time. The horror of being trapped down there never left us. They did mount pathetic lifeboat drills, but as we sheepishly lined up on the decks we knew there wasn't a dog's chance of salvation should we get hit.

At the rear of the ship, right above the churning propellers, was a small crescent of deck allocated to the serving men, and on this we took what exercise we could, boldly striding ten paces forward, then ten paces back. Looking up we could see the officers and their wives glancing down at us from the spacious decks that they were allocated. Three weeks later we arrived in convoy at the mouth of the peaceful, and placid, River Mersey. Peaceful, that is, until the several hundred troops we had on board, veterans of years in the Burmese jungle, realised that the ship that had brought them back from those almost unendurable years was stationary. The convoy had been large, as the submarine wolf packs were still roving, and being jammed like sardines below decks had been nerve-racking as we constantly awaited a torpedo attack. Finally, we were safe and sound, but absolutely still. No movement at all. To me there was the added gall of seeing my home town, sharp and clear across the narrow river, but stationary we stayed...and stayed.

Mutterings from the soldiers grew as, savagely, they gazed at the land. Their wives, mothers, girlfriends were there. Some of them had spent four long years abroad and now only a strip of water was the barrier between them and their families. Herded below decks in hammocks, slung wherever there was an inch of room, the first night was the worst. The next day, tempers rose and there were threats of jumping over the side and swimming for shore. Four bleedin' years fighting and can't go home! Then, out of the blue, the captain appeared on the bridge. Clean and smart in his merchant navy uniform, he proved a master diplomat with his opening words: "May I have your attention gentlemen, please." As most of the men had not been called a gentleman for some years, it certainly did get their attention. Sullenly, they stood, wary of the officer class who would surely see to it that they (who did all the dirty work) would get the short end of the stick. But, to his eternal credit, that captain kept up the diplomacy. Quietly and calmly, he explained the convoy tradition. "We have 16 ships, but only two can go up the river at a time. I do assure you the turnaround at the landing stage is very fast, and four ships a day will be taken care of, but…" The pause was just a little too long.

From the back came a strong Yorkshire voice. "I knew there'd be a fookin' 'but'."

Over the laugh, the captain persisted. "The chief pilot has a hat in which all the ships' names are placed. They are then selected purely by chance. First name comes out disembarks first."

But the white rose wasn't having any. "Booger off," he said. "My wife's waitin' in Sheffield. Been waitin' three year. I've been waitin' three year!" Another laugh, and then a slightly embarrassed silence.

In that silence, the captain put his hand in his pocket and took out a piece of paper. "I now intend," he said, "to read the Riot Act," and he did. "'If twelve or more persons assemble unlawfully to the disturbance of the public peace, a magistrate or official may read a proclamation ordering them to disperse; if the rioters nevertheless continue together an hour after the reading of the proclamation, they are guilty of a felony and may be dispersed by force.'"

Passed into law in 1714, the Riot Act is often quoted but not often understood. It has all the terror and majesty of English law behind it and, as the words "may be dispersed by force" were spoken, the sailors standing either side of the captain brought their Lee Enfield rifles into view and drew back the bolts. As we heard the ominous clicks, it was pin-drop time. Nothing like a bit of live ammunition to quieten things down.

There was a lot of shuffling feet, and a few truculent murmurs, but our captain had things under control. "Sorry, gentlemen," he said. "Nothing personal." For two more days, we looked at Liverpool. Then the fussy little tugs came out to escort us to the landing stage. The Liver birds had a good look at us as we clambered onto shore.

A week's disembarkation leave, a chance to deliver to Grandma the precious box of oranges that I had manhandled all the way from India. Then, in June 1944, off to Germany. All through my teenage years, I'd seen pictures plastered on the front page of newspapers of the rise of the invincible Third Reich. Grim-faced solders, wearing Darth Vader helmets, lifting the striped bars that marked the frontiers they marched through, with a few obliging onlookers giving them flowers. Servile diplomats grovelling to the champagne salesman Ribbentrop, Goering waving his *Felt Marechals* baton so everybody could have a good look at it and Hitler making sure he wasn't in the stadium when Jesse Owens took every gold medal in sight. How did we ever take them seriously? Tragically, we had to.

Now it was our chance to see it close up and we started in relative luxury. No dreaded three-ton trucks bouncing over unmade roads as they flew us into Brussels, which had only been liberated by the Guards armoured division a couple of weeks earlier, and it was good-to-be-alive-and-a-British-serviceman time. Dancing in the streets day and night, and public transport was free and gratis to every Allied soldier, sailor or airman. Dazed and dumbfounded by their release from occupation the population fought with each other to make us welcome. The huge bar cafés were bursting with people celebrating freedom and, sitting one night with one of our pianists, Tommy Pollard, a fantasy came true.

Tommy, plump and plain, was a miracle at the keyboard. He had been the winner in the *Melody Maker* poll at the start of the war as the best young jazz player in the country, and after the war Benny Goodman chose Tommy to play with him at the London Palladium. We listened to the band playing (jazz was always very popular in Belgium), and Tommy said, "What would I give to sit in with them." He'd been playing our ranky-tank numbers forever, so I grabbed him by the arm, went straight to the bandleader, and said, "My friend would like to play a number with you." There was a mixture of agony and fear on the bandleader's face. He couldn't bring himself to be rude to a member of the British Royal Air Force, but how could he let some unknown airman sit in with his musicians? Slowly and carefully, the bandleader asked what my friend would care to play. Tommy didn't hesitate. "'Rose Room' in C," he said.

Instantly, all the tentative looks vanished as he had spoken words that meant he had both taste and expertise in the world of jazz. The piano was vacated, but the bandleader signalled the accordion player to vamp alongside Tommy just in case, but within six bars he never played another note. It was the Hollywood movie coming to life as all the customers gathered around to hear the British airman give them music they'd never heard before, and the band wouldn't let Tommy stop playing. The story had a sad ending as, after the war – and his post-war jazz success – Tommy got among villains and ended his days a drug addict.

★

Back to the dreaded three-ton trucks, but this time we had the luxury of the autobahns they'd built in Germany. We crossed the Rhine at Wesel, and with satisfaction I saw the flattened buildings that some of the Lancaster crews we had lost from 64 Squadron had helped to flatten. I don't remember any of us particularly crowing until we got to Celle, where the RAF had pitched a huge theatre tent. A very hot summer, but with the flaps at the back of the tent opened it was bearable, and all day long sad, derelict creatures wandered about, starved and emaciated, desperately hoping to find their families again. Two little girls watched, fascinated, as I put on my comical make-up. They both had long lines of numbers tattooed on their arms.

Upset about my loss in the gents' lavatory in Poona, I had bought another small camera in London and was already showing alarming signs of my love affair with photography. I suppose we covered every major camp in the north German area, from Cologne on the Rhine to Lüneburg in the north. I'd just discovered the books of Dashiell Hammett and stayed in the barracks one afternoon especially to finish *Red Harvest*. The huge room, with some 40 or 50 beds in it, was completely empty apart from myself lying on a bed reading, and I was just trying to work out the body count from all the gangland slayings when a door opened at one end of the long room. In the doorway, shafts of sunlight framing him, was a fully uniformed German general, minus of course medals and Nazi insignias, as well as his hat. He bowed, clicked his heels (in the empty room it sounded like a rifle shot), held up a broom in his hand and said, "You will permit?" The accent was cultured, with only a slight accent.

I wasn't going to click my heels back at him, but I did manage a small nod and said, "Yes, I will permit," and out of the corner of my eye I watched the bizarre ritual of a captured German general, who had been told to clean up, go along every section of the room and meticulously sweep, while the lowest-ranking airman you could imagine lay on a bed reading. Not an inch of the floor escaped the general, and at the far end he clicked his heels again, gave a slight bow and vanished.

Once more, with impeccable timing, we finished our tour of Germany to get back to London for the start of the V-2 campaign. These terrifying rockets, which fell on civilians without warning, were in a strange way less frightening than the V-1s, which gave a lot of action to the bowels when the motors cut out just above you, and you had to wait for what you presumed was to be your certain death. Well, we survived the V-1s and went off round the country doing more shows, while the certainty that the war in Europe was coming to an end grew in our minds. When it did come, on V-E Day, we all did the obligatory dancing in the streets, but remembered we had the nasty Japanese business in the Far East to deal with. Fortunately, the Americans, totting up the horrendous casualties that could take place on the island-hopping campaign, showed a great deal of common sense by dropping two bombs on Japan, which settled the matter. General MacArthur spoke as the Japanese surrender documents were signed. It was a magnificent understatement: "These proceedings are closed."

Piccadilly Circus on 15 August 1945, the war declared officially over, was once again a wonderful, yelling, laughing, leg-kicking night of revelry spoilt only by my having one of my fainting fits again. It says a lot for the great British policeman that, seeing me sitting on the kerbside and hearing about my problem, he merely gave a little smile: "Get your head down between your knees, son, and then get out of that uniform as fast as you can. You'll feel a lot better." Many wives, who were forced to accept that their husbands would be away for the duration, now realised they could be coming back up the garden path again, and sadly there were a lot who knew they wouldn't. Demobilisation was the word on every serving man's lips, but we knew that the older, married men (there were several of them in my unit) would get priority. They gradually disappeared to collect their civilian clothes.

The squadron leader, whom I had to thank for putting me into the gang show, called me into the office. "Get three stripes put on your arm," he said. "You are now Sergeant Stark, and you're off to run number nine show at Abingdon."

Through the gates of RAF Station Abingdon I marched and the sentry called out, "Papers, Sergeant, please!" I kept walking until I realised he was talking to me. The show had performers in it that became household names, chiefly Tony Hancock. A Stirling bomber flew us to Gibraltar, where we played in the cave theatre. It was the start of a working relationship, and friendship, that lasted many years. Back at Houghton House, I started another friendship – this time with Leading Aircraftsman Peter Sellers – that lasted until his death.

With no family, I was living in a serving men's club opposite Victoria station and Peter was horrified, especially when he knew I had to sleep every night with the legs of the bed down inside my shoes. It was the only way to stop them being stolen. At once he took me back to north London, where he lived with his parents, and got me a spare bedroom in the flat beneath him, and from that night on Peter and I were out together dating (if possible) all the WAAFs, ATS girls and Wrens we could find. Finally there was a visit to a large, depressing building in west London, where I produced a piece of paper; then a gentleman, behind a long counter, produced a civilian suit. It was all free and gratis. In addition, as my reward for being a good serviceman for five years, I was given the sum of £35 as my gratuity payment. I was a civilian again.

6 Sir Thomas And The Old Pantomime
One, Two, In

It might have been freedom, but trying to get back into the theatre was long and lonely, traipsing from agent to agent. The sight of the chalk-stripe suit put them off, as this was the standard demobilisation outfit issued to every ex-serviceman. There was an alternative offered but the chalk stripe was the popular choice, as we all wanted to look like Humphrey Bogart in *The Maltese Falcon*. The money started to run short and I lingered one day outside the back of the Regent Palace Hotel, where a small hand-printed notice on a piece of cardboard told all and sundry that dishwashers were required. "Well, that's it next week," I said, and started to walk down the stairs to Piccadilly Underground station as John Blatchley, the boy whose failure to pass his medical had given me the chance to join the gang show, came walking up. We stopped, face to face, the usual hellos, and then he said, "I've just left the Midland Theatre Company in Kidderminster and they're doing *Alice In Wonderland* for Christmas. You'd be perfect. I'll give you the address."

The Midland Theatre Company, run by the Arts Council, was based in Kidderminster but played right throughout the Midlands. They *were* doing *Alice,* and after the interview I was booked to be in the production. Even better, before *Alice* opened they asked me stay on, as I think they liked the business I was doing in rehearsal with my tail while I was playing the Gryphon. I went for one play and, unbelievably, stayed for four years, playing every character part ever written. There were a couple of Shakespeare productions, but luckily they made sure I only played the parts that were meant to be funny. I spent every summer, during the break in the season, in Wallasey staying with Grandma, and it was always a happy time as she looked after me, and I felt that, in her loneliness, she was always glad to see me. The time came for me to leave the company (now based in Coventry), but I could never be more thankful for the experience they'd given me. Then I had even more reason to thank them.

★

At the Edinburgh Festival in 1951, the Arts Council mounted one of the most opulent productions ever seen in the British Isles which incorporated all three of the major arts. First, the Molière play *Le Bourgeois Gentilhomme* with a cast of English actors headed by Miles Malleson. The third act of this was removed and replaced by a one-act opera, *Ariadne Auf Naxos*, by Richard Strauss. The Ballet Rambert were the dancers and Oliver Messel was brought in to design the costumes and sets. Photographed by the dean of stage photographers, Angus McBean, the whole production was under the direction of Carl Ebert, who headed the Glyndebourne Opera Company participation. What more could they possibly want? The Arts Council thought about that, then, throwing all caution to the winds, decided to gild the lily by putting one of the most famous conductors in the world, Sir Thomas Beecham, and his Royal Philharmonic Orchestra in the orchestra pit.

Once the news of this production was announced, the entire run in Edinburgh at the King's Theatre was completely sold out and each section of the production began rehearsals separate from the others. I joined the play section as the Dancing Master. The Arts Council (who ran the company in Coventry) suggested me, as I'd had an apprenticeship as a classical dancer and we duly rehearsed in a broken-down hall, as actors have done since the beginning of time. The Molière play, a satire, had one very comic (we hoped) section early on. Miles Malleson had to be taught to dance by the Dancing Master and Richard Strauss had composed a delicious little piece of music for this, containing certain words written by the librettist Hugo von Hofmannsthal. These were my dance directions, which had to be spoken very precisely in time with the music. At every rehearsal, a young gentleman from Glyndebourne waved a pencil in time with the rehearsal pianist and eventually seemed reasonably satisfied with my performance.

We travelled down for the dress rehearsal in a luxury Pullman coach and found ourselves backstage at the Glyndebourne Theatre. This jewel of an opera house, set in the beautiful countryside of Lewes, was the mecca for the champagne-drinking, strawberry-eating audiences, who liked their opera in the atmosphere of a high-class English garden party. The audiences were the social register of Britain. A bewildering mixture of actors, singers and ballet dancers clustered onstage while – with the curtain still raised – we awaited the real star of the show. Then, down the centre aisle, came Sir Thomas himself. Beecham, in person, was small and plumper than one imagined, but his perambulation down the centre aisle, giving an occasional gesture in acknowledgement of the applause (we had a small audience of devotees), was that of a superb showman. Known as one of the great wits of the century, his orchestra adored him, relishing every sardonic remark and hoping for some error, however slight, so that the fiendish Sir Thomas could leap. They didn't have to wait long. The curtain descended and we few actors, who opened the play, stood waiting for the overture we'd heard so many times tinkled out on the upright piano. Suddenly, from the other side of the curtain, came a wall of sound as the 70 musicians that made up the Royal Philharmonic launched into the Richard Strauss overture. It was breathtaking. It was overpowering. It was Germanic music at its grandest. We were still recovering as the curtain finally disappeared up into the flies and Sir Thomas glared at us. He'd lowered his baton as the overture had finished and now dared us to enunciate Molière's boring lines, while he obviously itched to get on with the serious matter of the opera.

For a little while, ears still ringing from the musical assault, we duly went through our rehearsed dialogue. The audience smiled and gave polite laughs while the 70 musicians, seated just below us, imitated Sir Thomas by giving us tolerant looks, at the same time checking their music for future cues. Then the moment I had been dreading was upon me: Miles had to have his dancing lesson. I spoke the cue line I had spoken so many times before in that seedy rehearsal room, but this time there was no tinkling piano, and no vapid youth making small, delicate movements with his pencil. Now it was Sir Thomas Beecham, slashing downward with his baton and, once more, the blast of Richard Strauss at his most energetic. Miles and I stood completely petrified, motionless!

The baton whipped down once more. In an instant, the orchestra, drilled to perfection by Beecham, was totally silent. Every eye, including those of Miles' and myself, was focused on the short, stocky man. The dry, caustic voice was succinct and very much to the point: "You gave the cue. I brought in the music. What happened?" From somewhere in the brass section came a snigger as the orchestra scented blood. These were the moments that made the long hours of rehearsal worthwhile. Then Miles Malleson did a terrible thing. In rehearsal (the time for invention), I had made the fatal error of thinking of a comical moment, and now, to explain why we had been late on the cue, Miles looked hard at me. After all, I had thought of the joke! My footsteps as I moved to the footlights echoed with doom-laden hollowness.

Like a bad impression of Richard III, I bent, crooked, over the footlights, shielding my eyes from the glare. "Well, you see, Sir Thomas, when Mr Malleson and I were rehearsing…" And then the enormity of what I was about to say made me pause.

"Please continue, Mr, er…?" said Beecham.

"Stark," I said.

"Right, Mr Stark. Please continue." Several musicians lowered their instruments and leant a little closer.

"Well, as I knew you and the orchestra would be in the pit, I intended to place Mr Malleson in a comic posture, then give you a nod, stamp my foot, and you would have the old pantomime one, two, in!"

Not a sound. Not a snigger. Just a rapt silence as 70 musicians gazed at Beecham. He did not disappoint them. The majestic head turned solemnly and looked at them. "Did you hear that, gentlemen? Mr Stark is going to give us the old pantomime one, two, in. Personally I can't wait."

Without another word, he raised his baton, I scurried back to Miles, put him in the comical position and then, with an abject sense of disaster, nodded at Beecham and stamped my foot. Whoosh! went the opening to the music, which bore no resemblance to the rehearsals, but terror so filled me I stumbled on. The dance was fine and, watching the baton of Beecham like a hypnotised rabbit, I think I got most of the words right. The brief dance sequence finally ended and now, on autopilot, Miles and I went on with the dialogue. We should have known better. The baton tapped on the music stand, we stopped talking, and then a miracle took place. The sternness had vanished from the face of Sir Thomas and in its place that indefinable look of someone about to make a suggestion that might not be favourable.

"You may have noticed," he said, "that during the piece the music is sometimes *fortissimo*, sometimes *pianissimo*." His arms raised and fell to illustrate. "Well, it just occurred to me that you *might* – and, of course, you don't *have* to use the idea – move your body in some similar fashion." Give an actor some good comic business and there's no stopping him. Gratefully thanking the great man, that piece of business went in from the first performance in Edinburgh. Up and down I went like a Versailles version of Groucho Marx. It was an immediate hit, with huge laughs at every single show.

The joy I got was doubled as every night, without fail, during the laughs Beecham looked joyously over his shoulder at the audience and then, also without fail, turned and winked at me. We were sharing that applause and laughter, and he knew it. He came backstage after every performance to take his curtain call, and every night he would pat me on the back saying, "My boy, we certainly gave them the old pantomime one, two tonight!"

Photography fanatic that I am, I smuggled my own camera into the dress rehearsal hoping I could get an odd shot with Angus McBean's lighting. Well, you know the old saying – the bigger they are, the nicer they are. Not only did he let me take some shots, but he even suggested I should have a record of my own make-up and costume. Without a pause, he took my camera off me and shot a single of myself, therefore giving me the chance to develop and print it in my own darkroom. It rates as the most venerated photograph I own.

Being in the festival at Edinburgh gave me a chance to visit, sadly for the last time, Grandma DeValve. This wonderful old lady had lived in Pilrig Street, at the top of Arthur's Walk, for most of her life, and had had five sons, including my father. She had always been kind to all her grandchildren: every birthday I received, as did my brothers, a crisp, crinkly £1 note with a birthday card. She never, ever forgot. Now bedridden at the age of 91, she was so thrilled I was in the festival, especially as one night she heard the broadcast that was made of the production, particularly as the dear Queen Elizabeth was in the audience that night. She passed away some time later, and back in London the even sadder news arrived that Grandma DeValve had died in Wallasey. I travelled up for her funeral and found making the arrangements almost unbearable. It was decided that she would be buried with her husband and daughter and, in a far corner of the cemetery, standing on some wild, uncut piece of grass, I looked vainly for their grave. The cemetery official consulted a piece of paper. "Here somewhere," he said, then kicked with his foot, uncovering a small white stone bearing a number. He checked the paper once more. "DeValve and Stark. Is that right?" We did have the burial and I placed a suitable stone to record that my grandfather, my grandmother and my mother were buried there.

Showbusiness is a home for fantasists. With no particular talent, and unwilling to learn lines, rehearse a song or go through the rigours of a dancer, they happily latch onto a profession which promises a world of excitement and glamour. Providing they have a glib enough tongue and are willing to fabricate a private life that hints at power, money and influence, they may well go far. There are quite a few of those on the periphery and, worse than that, quite a few in the centre of our profession. Many a performer has suffered at their hands. "Wouldn't it be better if...?" they are heard to say, when every experienced actor, dancer and musician knows perfectly well it wouldn't. Unlike a bricklayer, who has to lay a level course, or an accountant, who has to add up correctly, these charlatans constantly pop into offices and with unctuous tones assure the managing director everything is under control. The early days of television bred them like bluebottles and they buzzed up and down the corridors of both the BBC and ITV, creating havoc wherever they alighted.

Peter Eton, a shrewd BBC producer whose credits included *The Goon Show*, among many other programmes, explained that teaching someone *how* to cut to camera five would take all of ten minutes. Teaching someone *when* to cut to camera five would take a lifetime. But the bluebottles flitted to and fro in the profession and, by and large, were a bloody nuisance. The theatre had them as well. Cecil Landau did have one enormous plus to his credit, or so he used to claim. "I discovered Audrey Hepburn" was his constant cry, and there is no doubt than she always seemed to be with him, but the truth is that, once she made her appearance onstage in *High Button Shoes* at the London Hippodrome, every critic in London noted and promoted her.

He first appeared backstage in 1952 at the Garrick Theatre, where I had taken over from Walter Gore during a production of a Molière play with Elisabeth Bergner. I'd been promoted to a star dressing room and Cecil, plus Audrey Hepburn, swept in to see me. While she sat demurely, not speaking, he expanded on the cabaret he intended mounting at the Washington Hotel. "You and Johnnie Hewer will be the stars – no expense spared – and Eleanor Fazan will be doing the choreography." Terms were agreed and into rehearsal we went, and quite early on Eleanor (a very brilliant choreographer) and I became allies against the lunacy of Landau. With overcoat draped over the shoulders, in true impresario style, he reclined in a gilded chair and described what would be a highlight of the show. "We have a stage," he said, "made of sheets of emery cloth and, as Graham dances, the flints which will be attached to his shoes will give off sparks!"

Eleanor stood up quietly and said, "I take it you will be informing the fire authority of this." The idea was dropped.

Trying to add something of style, I asked Alan Simpson and Ray Galton (soon to be the greatest writing team in radio and television) to help, and they wrote a lot of material. It was all a waste of time, as the production was so amateurish the show never had a chance. On a tiny stage at the Washington, we battled the diners and their bread-roll fights – a standard amusement for the well heeled at the time – but worse things reared their head. A small West Indian group of musicians played behind us, but it was made quite clear they that used the back entrance of the hotel only. We were only too happy for the show to end. Several years later, Alan and Ray, now the highest-paid writers in the country, saw Cecil climbing out of a taxi outside his flat, directly opposite the Ritz. They had never been paid for the work they had done and the sight of Cecil, still with the overcoat draped round his shoulders, the ever-present flower in the buttonhole and riding in a taxi in Mayfair, made them confront him. "About that money, Cecil," they began to say.

Dramatically, he faced them. "Dear boys," he said, "I had *such* faith in you both. Whatever *happened* to you?" With that, his key was in the front door, it closed behind him and they never saw him again.

It's a sad fact that, the moment a famous figure passes away, men start launching their attacks. Typewriters merrily tap out their vitriolic anecdotes and the almost obligatory character assassination takes place. Churchill was a despotic, brandy-swilling drunk, partial to calling natives "wogs", and was almost solely responsible for the disaster of the Dardanelles, Eisenhower was far too busy gaining carnal knowledge of his lady driver to give too much attention to the launching of the Second Front while General de Gaulle was an unbalanced megalomaniac. We all now realise that it was only the incredible ineptitude of A Hitler and his acolytes that made it possible for the Allies to win World War II. Clearly, it had nothing to do with any ability our wartime leaders may have possessed.

Which leads, of course, to Monty. The moment the famous two-badged beret was no longer with us, every armchair pundit was only too happy to tell us that the noble viscount needn't have bothered to be at El Alamein at all. What none of us had realised was that Field Marshal Rommel had absolutely no intention of going near Cairo at all. He just fancied a bit of a stroll over the sand dunes so that he could nip back to the old Friedrichstrasse and flash his suntan to a few adoring Fräuleins. But that naughty Monty insisted that our lads went and fired their guns. Needless to say, the British Tommy was so upset by this that every year after the war he turned up at the El Alamein reunion to cheer Montgomery to the rafters.

One memorable night in the early '50s, Humphrey Lestocq (of Flying Officer Kite fame) and I were among the 8,000 ex-servicemen who packed the arena at Earls Court Stadium. Humphrey and I had been engaged as comic relief. Dressed as the Two Types, wearing desert boots, khaki shorts,

Mother, circa 1925

The Stark brothers. Graham (five), Peter (six), Stuart (eight). 1927

My first appearance on the stage. Wallasey Grammar School, 1933

Mother and I, Lisbon, 1934

Mother and I aboard a cruise ship, 1934

Mother on a cruise ship, 1934

Hannah Evelyn (Ivy) Stark

"A pupil of the Butterworth School, Liverpool, danced two solos at the Park Lane Cabaret and is now booked for solo work in the Lyceum pantomime." From *Dancing Times*

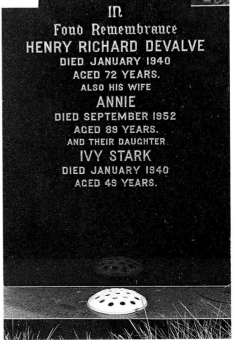

Leading aircraftsman Stark surveys the north-west frontier of India, 1944

Miles Malleson and I awaiting the baton of Sir Thomas Beecham at the Edinburgh Festival, 1951

Sophia Loren. *The Millionairess*. MGM, Elstree Studios, 1960

Peter Sellers and I. *Only Two Can Play*. Shepperton Studios, 1962

The great Stanley Kubrick, 1963

And Cinderella fell in love with Ringo! Telling fairy stories to Vivienne Kubrick.1963

Sean Connery: shaken, not stirred! Pinewood Studios, 1964

Shirley Eaton having just washed off the gold paint! Pinewood Studios, 1964

Elizabeth Taylor and Richard Burton. *Beckett*. Shepperton Studios, 1964

Mia Farrow. *Guns Of Batasi*. Pinewood Studios, 1964

Peter and his high-speed Ferrari. Elstead, 1966

The Wrong Box. Pinewood Studios, 1966

Britt Ekland. Pinewood Studios, 1967

Yul Brynner. Pinewood Studios, 1967

Ursula Andress. *Casino Royale*. Pinewood Studios, 1967

"This is going on my mother's piano." Sidney Poitier. Pinewood Studios, 1967

Ron Moody as Fagin. Shepperton Studios, 1968

sweaters with the officers' pips rampant, and the weather-beaten Australian-type hats, we were exact replicas of those officers who were wonderfully drawn by Jon, and published as a strip cartoon in the *Crusader*, which was circulated all through the Middle East during the desert war. They personified the dash and élan of the young subalterns who took on the Afrika Corps. We lurked in one of the entrances to the arena and waited for the speeches to end.

Prince Philip, sitting on a small rostrum, said a few words, made a few jokes and, considering he was in naval uniform, got some surprisingly good laughs. A short speech from the American General Gunter and then the great roar went up as the slim, khaki-clad man wearing the inevitable black beret that sported those two badges rose to his feet. The nasal voice was as firm and direct as ever and the packed audience loved every word.

Then came the clowns. Humphrey went on first, beaming at the audience, and got a great reception. The fact that he was sitting on a camel didn't do him any harm. Then the fact that the said camel, no doubt nervous at the roars of laughter, dropped his load – as the service jargon politely puts it – right in front of the dais on which Philip and Monty sat, got them in a good mood, to put it mildly.

I had to come on then. I thought I might be an anticlimax, but I needn't have worried. I got just as big a laugh as I carried on a huge, outsized mine detector. Every poor sod in that audience had been lumbered with that job in the desert at least once and, as I circled the floor, headphones fastened to my ears, the large metal disc skimming the floor, they hooted with laughter. They hooted even more when the disc hovered over the pile the camel had just deposited. How I blessed the animal. Then the fates were even more kind. I don't know to this day what inspired me to do it, but I looked at Monty and saw the gleaming mass of medals that hung on his chest, the medals that everyone there knew were his pride and joy. Gawd knows how many there were. Without a pause, I waved the mine detector across Monty's chest, looked at Humphrey, and said, "Never mind that lot on the floor. There's an even bigger load up here!"

I've heard of the Hampden roar (that wall of sound that comes from Scottish football supporters on a good day), but the laugh that went up after that line would have shamed it. The British soldier loves to take the mickey out of people he most admires. Considering the circumstances, Monty behaved very well. The smile *was* a bit thin, but at least he did smile. Prince

Philip didn't smile. He got hysterics, and if there hadn't been a rail behind him, he'd have gone backward off the rostrum.

Yes, the knocking brigade has had Montgomery well and truly in their sights in the past, but personally I was glad he was around at El Alamein. I never had any illusions what would have happened if the Afrika Corps had ever managed to get a quick paddle in the Nile. It would be nice to think that in the future the story will be told of the night a mine detector was stuck on the chest of Viscount Montgomery of El Alamein, thereby causing Prince Philip to experience an advanced attack of hysteria and that – even more remarkable – the person who did the sticking lived to tell the tale.

Almost overnight, the BBC suddenly became the most powerful medium in the country. Every comedian fought to be on it and an avalanche of comedy shows, backed by BBC expertise, became overnight sensations. Scriptwriters – no longer hacks to be thrown ten-shilling notes for the odd joke – now became sought-after, and comedy actors whose voices suited the microphone were quickly rounded up. Tony Hancock, struggling round the music halls, hit the jackpot with his breathy pomposity and, booked for a series, he came to see me in my basement room in Holland Park, where I had perfected the cheapest possible way to live – a sack of oatmeal, a tin cup and cold water. Take this mixture every two hours and you never felt hungry. The only window was a small, curved, half-moon-shaped one at street level through which, even though it was heavily barred, I could see ankles pass by me all day. Tony had a fit when he saw it. "The only way you'll get out of here is in a coffin," he said. Two days later he arranged for me to join him in a new radio show starring Derek Roy, as members of a scout troop – my broadcasting career had begun. I was one of the lucky people who could put on voices, and soon I was doing four or five shows a week. Peter Sellers was one of the very best with comedy voices (a talent he never lost all his life) and, carrying on the camaraderie of the gang show, he spoke on my behalf to the star of *Ray's A Laugh*, Ted Ray. Overnight I was in that show, too.

Ray's A Laugh made huge sections of the British public laugh, and rightly so. Without any pretensions to satirical humour, it went straight to the beach at Blackpool – seaside rock, cleaning ladies with a nice line in double entendres, fat ladies in bright-red bathing costumes, and men's handkerchiefs, knotted at four corners, worn on the head. The show was full of catchphrases that held the audience breathless with anticipation until they were spoken, and then greeted with roars of laughter. If they didn't hear "Ooh, it's agony, Ivy!" every Thursday night, all was not right with the world. Ted Ray himself was that rarity, an ever-optimistic performer. No introspective shadow of gloom ever crossed that puckish face and to see him work an audience was a joy, and his philosophy was simple: the audience were lucky to be sitting there because they were about to see, and hear, the greatest radio show ever. He was also another rarity. To upstage your fellows is one of showbusiness' greatest clichés and sadly practised since the days of Sir Henry Irving, whose version was to have his own pink spotlight (the choice of colour might raise an eyebrow or two today) follow him every moment he was on the stage. Another knight of the theatre, Donald Wolfit, king of the provinces in his own productions, could easily be picked out, as he was invariably the only actor on the stage who didn't have his back to the audience.

Ted would have none of this. He never cared where the laugh came from, providing it came. In one of the earliest shows I did with him, knowing I had the comedy lines, he quite deliberately moved so he was looking upstage at me, making sure I got all the audience's attention. After *Ray's A Laugh* eventually ended (that kind of show just went out of style), Ted was reborn as one of the wittiest ad libbers in the business. Tommy Trinder, Jimmy Edwards, Arthur Askey – all had great reputations for the snappy retort, as quasi-American reporters had it, but Ted was number one. And it was in a restaurant that he solidified that position for all time.

Ted had been voted King Rat by that most famous of theatrical charities, the Grand Order of Water Rats, and there was a luncheon arranged to honour his election. The Café Royal was the venue and the long table was crammed with every well-known comic in the business, as Ted was very popular and no fellow entertainer could imagine not being there. They all fell on each other with stories of terrible digs in Attercliffe, the chambermaid they'd seduced in Bolton, what really happened that night at the Palace Manchester when the safety curtain got stuck, and did Dorothy Squires *really* say that to the audience in Sunderland? A frenzy of nostalgia, until the deafening bellow of the red-coated toastmaster cut through the buzz demanding silence. "Your King Rat of the Year, Mr Ted Ray, will now say grace!" Two hundred star comedians obediently pushed their chairs back, shuffled to their feet, and bent their heads.

Ted did the same. With the layman's natural embarrassment concerning religious matters, he mumbled the standard address. "For what we are about to…"

The deafening bellow came from behind him as the bemedalled red-coated toastmaster arched and stiffened, veins thickening in the neck as his foghorn voice echoed round the room. "Speak up, Mr Ray. Can't hear you!"

Without a moment's pause, without any delay and in a voice quite clear and audible, Ted raised his head, looked at the toastmaster and said, "I wasn't talking to you."

I had the ultimate booking in June 1953, when the BBC produced *The Coronation Goon Show*. *The Goon Show* had become the intelligentsia's delight. Written by Spike Milligan, it broke every convention of radio comedy and soared in the critic's approbation. Even the ordinary listener eventually realised what joys were to be had by tuning in, and they became enormously popular. To this day, they are comedy classics, listened to worldwide. I still possess my copy of the *Coronation* script and there, to my delight, on the cover is the billing, "The BBC proudly presents *The Coronation Goon Show*, starring Lord Peter Sellers, Lord Harold Secombe, Lord Spike Milligan and Dame Graham Stark." Today, when titles seem to be distributed in Britain at an alarming rate, it's nice to think that we four performers beat everyone to it.

A fellow comedian, Clive Dunn, later to achieve immortal fame as Corporal Jones in *Dad's Army*, was producing a summer show at Cromer, a famous seaside resort in Norfolk. These summer shows, an institution in Britain, gave you wonderful opportunities to perform almost everything in the comedy field and Clive persuaded me that I should do it and guided me all the way. Every bit of tried-and-trusted material he passed onto me, and it was an experience to match all the years I had spent performing in plays at Coventry. The three-month season, at a seaside resort which time and again holds the British record for sunshine, ended very happily, as I was given the Bucket and Spade Oscar. This silver-plated statue – an orange surmounted with a starfish playing a spade as a banjo – was given to me for being the best comic in summer shows. Inset in the base, a small silver bucket is inscribed with the words, "Graham Stark 1954". I have it still, standing in a place of honour in my study. It may not have been presented in Los Angeles, but it's an object I shall always cherish.

★

The great bonus of working so much on radio was that the audience, the fickle public, couldn't get tired of you, as you were just a voice. Apart from *Ray's A Laugh*, I played in *The Arthur Askey Show*. Arthur was a very brave and funny little man and, like Ted Ray, was a master of ad libbing. At the age of 80, both his legs had to be amputated, as gangrene had set in. Being measured for his false legs, he asked if, seeing as he was only five foot two inches tall, they could be made a bit longer this time!

I had been doing a very successful radio series with Tony Hancock, written by the two future giants of radio and television, Alan Simpson and Ray Galton. These two amiable gentlemen, both six foot four, had become (and still are) close friends. Now proudly owning my first little car, a minuscule Standard Eight drop-head coupé, I ran around London in the days when there was virtually no traffic and, with gallantry, I gave all my friends lifts. I often drove Alan and Ray down to south London where they lived, but the rides over the cobbled streets got bumpier and bumpier – so bumpy, in fact, that I had to take the car into a garage, where the mechanic lay on the little platform with the miniature wheels, then slid underneath the car, reappearing almost at once. "Christ," he said. "The bleedin' springs is totally flat. Wot you been carryin' in this motor?"

Guessing the combined weight of Alan and Ray, I said, "About 28 stone."

By that time, Tony Hancock had started building the wall between himself and the rest of his fellow performers. A brilliant comic, he idolised past performers who had not only been eccentric funny men but also shared a love of the bottle. Whether Tony felt he too should become addicted (so as to match them) I never knew, but suddenly the mistiming started, along with the inability to learn lines. The heavy drinking became standard, which resulted, tragically, in his suicide years later, a sad, tawdry ending to someone who, in the days just after the war, had been a very close friend and who attained a level of popularity on radio and television in Britain that has hardly ever been matched.

Then, of course, there was Archie Andrews. A million children (and several million adults) worshipped this wooden ventriloquist's doll who had one of the peak spots on radio, and Peter Brough – who stood elegantly at the microphone, his hand stuck firmly through Archie's back, manipulating his eyes and mouth – was a very astute businessman who very sensibly cashed in on the enormous popularity of Archie by touring the top vaudeville theatres of the country. As I was one of the resident cast, I thereby I found myself playing the ABC Cinema, Aberdeen, during the week of 11 July 1955.

Touring with Brough was a Rolls-Royce affair. We only played once nightly, at all the best resorts, and we were treated in the grand manner. After the Monday-night show in Aberdeen, he faced myself, harmonica player Ronald Chesney and our two singers, The Tanner Sisters. Sounding as if he was about to tackle the north face of some ice-ridden peak, he pronounced, "Tomorrow Balmoral!" Having a connection with "the Palace" (he arranged the Christmas cabaret each year for the royal family at Windsor), he rather smugly told us he had contacted "certain persons" and had been given permission to take his small group of strolling players on a conducted tour of the highland honeymoon home of Queen Victoria and Prince Albert. We were, of course, given to understand this was a *private* home and we were privileged to be looking over the premises. Peter drove us through the glorious heather-covered scenery, the memory of which incites expatriate Scotsmen dotted all round the globe to drain their whisky glasses dry while trying to blot out memories of some of the most glorious scenery in the world.

Then, suddenly, there it was. Encrusted with intertwining V and A initials, Balmoral stands as a monument to Victorian kitsch, but in reality it puts the picture postcards to shame. At the entrance, and with an incline of the body just one degree off perpendicular, as befits a member of the royal household, our appointed guide greeted us.

Tall and beautifully suited (perhaps just a trifle tight at the waist and with the rear pleats a shade too ostentatious), our guide glided across the hall as if on royal castors. His hands made delicate, wafting gestures, indicating features that we should gaze upon. While the dulcet tones of his voice spoke of the magnificent oak beams that arched above our heads, I was more aware of the sad, pleading eyes of the stags whose heads were fastened to every wall in serried rows. Beneath each one a small, elegant brass plate, meticulously labelled and dated, told me whose finger had squeezed the trigger that had put that head on the wall.

The wafting gestures continued as the conducted tour continued and the interest and – dare one say it – the excitement mounted as we came closer and closer to the royal bedchamber. Our guide, realising he was approaching a *coup du théâtre*, flung back a bedroom door (well, actually, it was not really flung back, as the door was much too heavy for that; it was more of a rapid open) and gave a waft towards the window. "Notice the glorious view. The

Queen Empress herself planned the whole building. *Everything* was her idea!" His fingers caressed the dark wood of the giant built-in wardrobe that ran along one side of the bedroom, and the smirk that had constantly lingered now became a triumphant smile.

"You've not seen it, have you?" An eager jerk forward of the head went with these words, and the smile widened. Faced with the unanswerable question, we all went dumb. "We are talking about *the toilet*!" He was steadily building to his climax. We were professionals enough to realise this was a set routine which, as yet, did not merit an interruption and, appreciative of our silence, he began a rather alarming crablike move along the huge wardrobe towards the window, the smile still set on his face.

An elegantly manicured hand rested on the final wardrobe doorknob, clasped it firmly, and one almost expected "Abracadabra!" as he pulled it open. And there it was, the Imperial throne itself, concealed behind that door, in a small tiled room that was home to a porcelain water closet that Mr Crapper himself would have been proud of. Simple, unassuming, workmanlike. Continuing his routine, the voice now had a hushed secretive quality. "No one", he said, "could *ever* be allowed to see Victoria Regina proceeding down the corridor for her ablutions. *En-suite* bathrooms were unheard of, so this delightful feature was incorporated!"

Satisfied by our reaction, which was in its turn an affirmation of his performance, he carefully ignored the large double bed which stood against the rear wall and gestured to a small room off to the right. One would have expected, possibly, a space for a dressing table, but to my pleasant surprise there was a DIY-type electric drill mounted on a stand with a fair number of wood shavings dotted about. One sensed that HRH Prince Philip had given strict instructions to leave alone whatever he was involved in making.

As the latest waft had turned into a beckoning gesture, we turned to leave, and it was then that the most delightful secret of Balmoral was revealed. By the side of the double bed stood a small, bedside table, quite bare apart from a book on it. The book was open, face down, obviously half-read and, placed carefully, it had the same "Do not touch" appearance as the drill. The colourful, glossy book cover was still intact.

It would have been rather nice if the errant, bombastic, boorish Randolph Churchill had been with us at that moment. He had recently been accusing a newspaper of printing excerpts from this bestseller, calling it arrant pornography, and his reaction to finding it on the Queen's bedside table would have been something to see. *Forever Amber*, written by Kathleen Winsor, had been a lusty, bawdy, historical novel, top of the bestseller list for weeks, and it was later filmed as a somewhat bowdlerised version. I have to admit that the wood shavings and the sight of *Forever Amber* did make that forbidding Victorian pile a little less forbidding. Unfortunately, it didn't do anything about those stags' eyes, but then, you can't have everything.

7 Oh Well, If You're Going To Cheat

My friendship with Peter Sellers, first established when we were in the RAF together, continued while he, Harry Secombe and Spike Milligan recorded *The Goon Show* every Sunday. Why it was called this has much been argued about, but all we knew was that, thanks to the amazingly comic and inventive scripts by Spike, it set a new standard of radio comedy that soon passed into mythology. It also had an influence on every comedy show of the future. Apart from the script, Peter, Harry and Spike were all very good performers, and with the production quality the BBC gave the show, it blossomed.

In 1953, Great Britain was awash with patriotic fervour as the young new Queen, Elizabeth II, was due to be crowned. A dramatic moment of TV history as the entire nation, nails digging into palms time, watched a doddering elderly cleric, suitably enrobed, nearly cause the dissolution of the British Empire as he found difficulty locating the whereabouts of the head on which he was to lower the diamond-studded crown. Vague movements, desperate promptings: finally the deed was done and Her Majesty embarked on her long reign. The BBC leapt on the bandwagon and one of my proudest possessions is my original script of *The Coronation Goon Show*, dated 1 June 1953. With patriotic zeal, the BBC proudly announced that Lord Peter Sellers, Lord Harry Secombe, Lord Spike Milligan and Dame Graham Stark would be appearing. The accolades bestowed on Harry and Spike by the BBC did eventually, in fact, become true: Harry was made a Knight Bachelor in 1981 (splitting his trousers while bending over the day before on the golf course, he had them reinforced, then rehearsed the sword on the shoulder with his lovely wife, Myra, utilising the carving knife as a substitute), while Spike had to make do with his honorary knighthood as, in a fit of pique at the Passport Office, he had taken up Irish citizenship. Peter sadly never got beyond the award of CBE. In the meanwhile, I am still practising my curtsy in case I get the call to the Palace to collect my damehood.

Spike had depressive attacks and couldn't always record the show and so I and Dick Emery deputised for him. Spike was a tortured soul who, if he suffered, made sure a lot of people suffered with him, but they understood the torments and, on form, he could be the most wonderful and exhilarating company.

"But you must go down to the sea again, the lonely sea and the sky!" The morning phone call from Spike had a note of hysteria in it. "Hancock's done a bunk and I've got to get this boat back to Tower Bridge by Friday night!"

"You may have a tall ship," I said, "but have you a star to steer her by?"

"As you're paying for this call, Stark," said Spike (he had cunningly reversed the charges), "don't waste time proving you can quote Masefield. Just let me know if you're going to help. Anyway, you don't need a star." I gave a non-committal grunt and Spike felt I needed more information. "As I said, Hancock's done a bunk. He emptied all the pubs on the way up the river and now he reckons he can't face all those locks on the way down." Gradually, the truth emerged. Spike and Tony Hancock (a bizarre crew, worthy of Jerome K Jerome) had negotiated a hired motor cruiser all the way up to Oxford and dear Tony, with an eye to a possible inclusion in a future edition of *The Guinness Book Of Records*, had indeed moored the boat at every riverside hostelry, insisting they knock a few back at every stop.

Honey dripped off Spike's tongue. "After all, you're good at this sort of thing. I mean, you were born on Merseyside. You're not bothered about drinking. And you can wave at all the girls sunbathing on the riverbank."

"I leave without delay," I said. By a small quayside at Abingdon, I clambered aboard the *Crystal Queen*. "We're not going to have any trouble about that name?" I said.

"Let's face it," Milligan replied, "if anyone looks at us and thinks were a couple of poofs, they don't know much about life." It wasn't exactly Donald Campbell going up Coniston Water, but at least there was that lovely white churning wake stretching out behind us, the water fiercely slapping the banks as we passed through the narrower stretches. The rather off-key voices of Milligan and Stark roared out, "Old Father Thames keeps rolling along, down to the mighty sea!" and equally loudly a voice shouted back from the towpath, "You'll go down to the bleedin' nick if you don't slow down!"

Spike gave me a look. "Trust us to find a policeman fishing on his day off!"

Kenneth Grahame wrote the immortal line "There's nothing like messing about in boats", and he was so right. Three magic days chugging down the river, three nights moored by the bank with the oil lamp burning in the cabin, a bottle of red wine on the table and the very best beans on toast *à la* Milligan. Moments of bizarre beauty, too. The first dawn, woken by a strange and sinister grating noise, we climbed on deck to find a solitary cow trying her best to chew through the mooring rope, which was tied to a nearby tree. Hurling a mixture of abuse and empty baked bean tins, Spike and I realised the animal was not alone. The clatter of tins woke other cows and, in unison, they slowly arose like magic through what had looked like an unbroken sea of mist. Spike gazed in awe. "Imagine what Tommy Cooper would have given for that trick!"

A small mountain of empty baked bean tins littered the cabin floor by the time we reached our first lock and, following the river tradition, helped push open the huge gates. As we were leaving, the lockkeeper's wife thrust a small cup of sugar into our hands and we were about to mumble our thanks when the good lady nodded firmly. "You give that to Mrs Hardcastle next lock down. Thank her kindly and tell her she can have the sewing machine next week." At the next lock, we took on two rabbits to be presented to Mr Thomas' twin daughters at the next lock down. Gradually, it dawned on us that here was the most delightful free postal service in England. Up and down that river, messages and goods flowed in an easy stream.

Not until the last lock but one did another side of human nature rear its ugly head. As we finally started to move off, the lockkeeper gazed down at us. A slim, gypsy-looking man, with black curling hair and tattoos on his brown arms. He spoke slowly. "Big dark-haired fellow at the next lock."

"Oh yes," I said.

He spoke again. "Little red-haired woman there, too."

"Oh yes," said Spike.

"If he's there," said the lockkeeper, "you don't say anything."

"Oh yes," I said.

His eyes narrowed slightly. "But if she's there by herself…"

I looked at Spike. "It's your turn."

"Oh yes," said Spike.

"You tell her Jacko say's it's all right for Thursday."

We chugged away. Silence. "Just think what Somerset Maugham would do with that?" I said.

"Bit more DH Lawrence," said Spike.

A hundred feet away, we could see the red hair glinting in the sunlight as she watched us come nearer. "You get through the last lock all right?" She looked at us hard.

Spike and I, like Tweedledum and Tweedledee, nodded in unison, but Spike was braver. He gave a slight cough and opened his mouth and a large, dark-haired man stepped out of a door. Spike gave another cough and closed his mouth. The man stood about six foot four and was built like a wardrobe. "You were about to say?" he asked. Once more, Spike and I went into the mute Tweedledum routine. The wardrobe looked at his wife suspiciously, looked at us, and then glanced at the name of the boat and a slow smile came over his face. "Got no women on board, I see!" He gave a pointed leer, then looked again at the redhead. "We'd better open the gates for these *gentlemen*. They might hurt themselves!"

In silent fury, Spike and I watched as they dutifully closed one lock gate behind us, then opened the one in front. Spike carefully passed a tin of baked beans to the woman. "Just to say thank you, and make sure you keep it the right way up!"

I roared up the engine and away we chugged. "Cheeky bastard!" I said. "I wouldn't have given them anything. And anyway, there's no right way up for a tin of baked beans!"

"There is when you've scratched a message on the bottom." Spike said. He folded up the pocket knife and gave me a smile. "I do hope I've spelt 'Jacko' right."

Some get-rich-quick entrepreneur was responsible for Peter Sellers and myself getting into films. His name is past history, but I'll always be grateful. In what he hoped would be a cunning scheme, he bought up a collection of vintage Laurel and Hardy shorts, then screened them. Oliver Hardy coyly wiggled his tie at the camera, Stan Laurel scratched his head and gave a childish grin, but not one word did they utter, as there was no soundtrack. Frantically, the gentleman scrabbled around for two actors to put the voices on, and Peter and I got the job. We watched Stan and Ollie, who were years ahead of any other comedians of the time. Their elegant pauses, the subtle looks, the insistence on character coming before the pratfall – it was an object lesson, and I know Peter and I learnt a lot. In his penultimate film, *Being There,* Peter based that wonderful performance as Chance the gardener on Stan Laurel. Even more important, I got to meet them.

I was visiting Tony Hancock, who was playing pantomime in Nottingham and hating every minute of it. The stage door of his theatre in this provincial town opened onto a small alley, which was not unusual. On the other side of the alley, a mere six feet away, was another stage door, which *was* unusual. The two face-to-face stage doors meant social life between both theatres was busy and you could wander between them at will. "You ought to pop in there," Tony said. "Gordon Craig is the stage manager." In the RAF, he was Corporal Craig, a member of the first gang show that I'd gone halfway round the world with, and so, while Tony struggled through the matinée, I crossed the alleyway and asked for Gordon, and for 15 minutes we swapped wartime reminiscences. Suddenly there was a great storm of applause and Gordon signalled the curtain to fall, then said, "But you must meet the boys." Coming offstage, Oliver Hardy was finding it difficult to walk. Ponderously, he looked at his partner, Stan Laurel, and with his courteous Georgia accent said, "I think I'll have a little lie-down, Stanley," and moved off. They were topping the bill and had just finished their performance. Stan Laurel turned to go and then Gordon introduced me, for which I shall always be grateful. Then he mentioned our time together in the RAF, said I was an up-and-coming comedian, and I died with embarrassment several times. Laurel, much taller off-screen that one would have imagined, politely talked for a little while, then gave my hand a shake and, in that extraordinary Ulverston Los Angeles accent, told me it had been a pleasure. He gave his bowler hat a little raise, on his face the squeezed-up smile, and then he disappeared.

Peter and I soon managed to get minor parts in very minor films. Jackie Collins – then an actress, now one of the greatest-selling authors of her time – still reminisces with me about those oh-so-unbelievably-small-budget pictures we appeared in together. There was very little traffic and the police had other things on their mind, so cameras were set up wherever possible and large black cars with dummy police badges on them raced about the streets pretending to chase villains who were to be filmed later, somewhere else, committing the crimes for which they would be eventually chased. At eight o'clock one morning, I was still in bed when EJ Fancy called. He was the producer of one of these epics I had just made. "No time for breakfast," he said. "Get down to Leicester Square right away. We've got your costume here." I gathered the film was under time, so it was back to the Keystone Kops days and, with hidden camera rolling, I dodged about the street avoiding traffic, pretended to make a phone call in a call box, then (overacting very badly) bought a newspaper. He gave me a £10 note and slapped me on the back. "We've got the extra three minutes," he said and off I went back to bed. Nobody really rated EJ until, in an astute move that would make the rest of the Wardour Street producers gnaw their accounts books with envy, he made a deal with a small French film-maker for an equally small sum and got the English rights for a so-called naughty French film called *Emmanuelle*. I believe his share of the English market hovered round the £1 million mark.

In the summer of 1957, I was booked to appear as principal comedian at the Hippodrome Theatre, Eastbourne, which is considered to be one of the more elegant summer resorts on the south coast. Hoping to repeat the success I'd had in Cromer, when I won the Bucket and Spade Oscar, I leapt onto the stage, confident that all would be well. The numerous wheelchairs in front warned me that there could be problems, and with loud cries of, "What's he saying? Can't hear a word!" echoing around the auditorium, I realised deaf-aids were rampant and I was in trouble. It never got any better, and I had eight weeks of what is known as dying the death. Fortunately, salvation lay with my father, of all people. He reappeared, accompanied by his second wife, who was a delightful lady by the name of Billie. They lived in a nice, small house on the outskirts of Eastbourne and at once suggested that I stay with them. Such a lovely woman, it would have been churlish to say no and, bursting with maternalism, she looked after me as if I was her son. Many years later, she too passed on, but my father, apparently taking after the longevity of his mother, lived until he was 89, dying peacefully in the Mariners' Homes, on the banks of the Mersey River.

The '50s spawned a glut of new post-war performers eagerly rushing from TV studios to theatres, taking in a few film studios on the way. Flushed with both youth and success, they had the energy, and ebullience, to join in the current craze: sport! The beautiful game seduced the majority, as the sheer physical effort entailed burning up testosterone, which was very much needed as these were not yet the swinging '60s. The Showbiz Eleven became the team to join and most Sundays in the season a group of young actors, singers and musicians gathered in Hyde Park, or any other greensward, racing about the grass emulating the current soccer stars. We happy band of brothers were ready to take on anybody.

A constant player was Anthony Newley, already a budding leading man (he starred with Peter Ustinov in *Vice Versa* [1947], and had held his own as the Artful Dodger alongside Alec Guinness' Fagin in David Lean's *Oliver*

Twist [1948]). Rubbing salt in the wound, he made several successful and very original pop records, and as if that wasn't enough, in 1958 he excited publicity by going to Brixton jail for a month, as he insisted on driving even though he'd lost his licence. Quite unabashed, he wore a sweater with the legend "Brixton '58" emblazoned across the front and garnered even more publicity when he later married the stunning and ageless Joan Collins. Just as a sideline, he wrote a couple of songs, including 'What Kind Of Fool Am I?"

One day in 1958, we got the exciting news that the following Sunday morning we were playing (for charity, as usual) the reserve team at Arsenal and, even more exciting, we were to be permitted to play on their second-eleven pitch. The hallowed turf at Arsenal was not to be kicked about by a motley band of mountebanks, but it was sufficient that we were to play at one of the greatest soccer venues in the history of the sport. With the ban on his driving still in force, Newley begged a lift, so there we were that fateful Sunday morning, gliding along in my new Mini, entering the sacred portals of Arsenal. None of the having to pull on shorts modestly behind a nearby clump of bushes – this time, white-tiled luxury changing rooms, hot and cold showers and the after-game giant communal bath, able to cope with two teams at once.

Even though it was the second-eleven pitch, it was still imposing, with serried rows of seats surrounding it, plus a reasonable turnout of lots of teenage fans to cheer us on. The Arsenal reserves trotted out, giving us the indulgent smiles of professionals to amateurs, and soon proved they knew what they were up to. Doing the decent thing, they realised it was a charity game and didn't press us too hard. Some of our team may not have had that much skill, but they made up for it in passion and Harry Fowler (as centre forward) played like a demon while Newley and I did our best to help him on the right wing. The odd congratulation of the two players opposing Tony and I was quite nice, and very sportsmanlike we felt. Rather difficult to understand, as they were both Hungarians, but there was lots of good-hearted shouting and occasional applause. Steaming, perspiring, with hearts pounding, we trotted off after the first half feeling we had kept up our end.

It was about three minutes into the second half that we spotted the bowler hat. Black, placed squarely on the head, it stood out in the crowd as the owner sat himself down, about four rows back, and smilingly watched with interest. Well, it wasn't every day George Allison, the legendary manager of Arsenal, got the chance to watch the reserves have a knockabout, and the idiot actors and musicians were a bonus. To say his appearance had an effect was the understatement of the year. It was Nelson treading the deck of his flagship, Wellington trotting by on his horse before Waterloo, and the sunlight glinting on the two cap badges on Montgomery's beret prior to El Alamein. None of those came near the effect of Allison's appearance on that Arsenal reserve team. Ever since their signing with the reserves, this was the moment they had all waited for – the chance to show the legendary manager just what they were made of, and to prove, by their ability, that *they* should be promoted, once and for all, to the first team. And no one believed that more than the two Hungarian players who directly opposed Newley and me.

The devious balletic footwork vanished, and the cunning and artistic dribbling became a thing of the past. A phalanx of Hungarian brawn was launched against us and Nureyev himself would have been proud of their Poltavian dance leaps as the two opposing wingers kept launching themselves skyward. With uncanny accuracy, they always managed to land on top of Tony and me, and it was no longer a question of playing for one's team; it was more a question of saving one's body from further crippling injury. Bruised and battered, we somehow survived the onslaught and later, in the huge, steaming hot communal bath, we both compared bruises that would have done credit to Picasso in his most colourful period. We never found out if those Hungarian gentlemen made the first team, but I can say that Tony and I soon realised why the Russians had to send so many tanks into Hungary.

The makers of commercial television, newly arrived, felt that they should avoid always putting on the obvious and did a brave thing. They commissioned, paid for and mounted *The Goon Show* on television called *Idiots Weekly, Price Tuppence*. Later, the title was changed to *A Show Called Fred*, but the format of anarchy stayed the same, and overnight it changed it changed the style of British television comedy forever. Up to then it was glittering nightclub sets in which, apart from the well-dressed extras circling the floor pretending to dance, there were equally well-dressed comedians telling oh-so-terribly-terribly upper-class jokes. These shows alternated with sets painted to represent seedy saloon bars populated by jovial fat men, perspiring profusely, wearing flat caps and holding sticks of Blackpool rock which equally fat women pointed at, screaming, "Ooh, aint you got a big one?"

To this day, the Monty Python ensemble pay tribute to the show and admit to how it paved the way for all their future work, while in America both Mel Brooks and Woody Allen speak of it with reverence. Our young director, Dick

Lester, went on to direct The Beatles in their films as well as mount *The Three Musketeers*. Spike, the creator of the shows, was in his element with the technical possibilities of TV as his creativeness never seemed to lag and he never accepted that the camera was just something to photograph actors with. He used back projection in a manner that had never been seen before, with the wake of a speeding motorboat streaming out from behind the announcer as he solemnly announced the next item. A sequence explained how out-of-work actors made a living by deputising for the animals in the zoo – Ken Connor went in with the monkeys and I swam with the sea lions while Val Dyall joined a vulture in a cage. Playing back this sequence, Peter Sellers had a fit of laughing watching one of the vultures nervously edge away as Val Dyall climbed in with it.

Without a doubt, the high spot of the series was the cod-Shakespearean scene in which Peter gave his uncanny impression of Laurence Olivier as Richard III. It went much further than an impression and made one realise that Peter really had become an actor. I felt my impression of John Gielgud as the Duke of Clarence, blond wig and nose prominent rampant, was quite telling, too. Spike wrote a very funny finish to the sketch, which was a shot of a lone spear carrier on the battlements who had stood motionless and silent throughout the performance. A close-up at the end would reveal it was Olivier quietly shaking his head, but nobody had the nerve to ask him. Olivier later admitted he would have loved to have done it. "If only they'd asked me," he said.

Life suddenly became a lot brighter when, wanting to eat one evening, I cut my hand badly on a stubborn corned beef tin, went to an actors' club for a meal instead, saw a beautiful girl, managed to get to get to know her, took her out a few times, met her parents, then finally proposed to her in that same actors' club just as she was off to the ladies'. I actually spoke the words "Will you marry me?" in the corridor outside the toilet, and I've often thought that she said yes because she was so desperate to go.

I was a great friend with singer Alma Cogan, who had just become the biggest record-seller in the country. When she saw me with Audrey one day, she took me to one side, gave a knowing smile and said, "You're never going to pull that one. Much too ladylike."

I gave her a smile. "Actually, we've just got engaged."

Alma gently shook her head. "Oh well, if you're going to cheat..."

Audrey and I married in the autumn of 1959, and my best man was the gentleman who guided what career I had for the rest of his life. (Acknowledged as the foremost film agent in Britain, Dennis Selinger also became our best friend, and godfather to our three children.) With memories of only seeing feet going by the window, and other assorted poky rooms, I was determined to start our new life with a house of our own and bought one not more than a few hundred yards from the last house I had lived in with my mother in 1940. Nothing symbolic, nor was I expunging any sinister memories, but it was a delightful area, including the park Mother liked so much, and Audrey and I have very happy memories of the ten years we lived there.

From the moment that the marriage vows have been made, the bride views her mate in a new light. No longer the courting gentleman alert to her needs, he now becomes the breadwinner, someone to be studied in depth, to be assessed carefully. In the long term, this person will, she hopes, one day be the father of her child or children. Nature designed it so, and the female of the species is a great believer in Darwinian theory. My own case is a classic example. A couple of weeks after our marriage my wife gazed at me with added interest. "You're limping," she said. "You've been doing it for some time. I've already called the doctor. He can see you tomorrow." Despite my assurances that a pulled leg muscle was nothing, it was made quite clear the appointment was to be kept.

"Does it hurt when I do this?"

As my doctor had my leg in a grip that would have done credit to a top-rank, all-in wrestler, I naturally said, "Yes."

The ballpoint pen scribbled on the pad. "Now, how about this?" The grip was even more complicated.

"No, nothing," I said. My leg hit the Rexine-covered table with a thump.

He gave me a look. "Definitely nothing?" I nodded my head. The ballpoint pen became feverish. "I think you'd better see Mr Cavendish. He's very sound."

Wimpole Street hasn't quite the cachet of Harley Street, but Mr Cavendish had all the trappings that put one at ease. I could have sworn the Rexine on the couch had been warmed. The repetition was exact – even to the raising of the leg. "Does it hurt when I do this? And how about this?" My replies were just the same, as was the scribble on the pad. Only *he* used a silver pen.

Then we got moved further up the medical scale. "I think you had better see Sir Ralph Marnham." I was informed that, as he was the Queen's surgeon, I would be getting the very, very best diagnosis. Also, needless to say, he was very sound.

There was no fooling around with Sir Ralph. We got not only Harley Street but the black jacket and the striped trousers as well. The leg-raising, plus the questioning, was just the same, but I had to admire the casual twirling of the horn-rimmed glasses as he then sat and gazed out at the passing traffic. That is, until I had the temerity to speak. "You see, I think—" I started to say.

The twirling stopped, as he swung round in his chair, looked at me, and made a terrible mistake. "I'm not interested in what you think," he said.

"You'd better be," I replied, "as I'm the one who's going to write out your cheque."

It was *Duel At The OK Corral*, both faces quite stony, but obviously I had won a victory of sorts. Sir Ralph rose to his feet and moved to the wall of books, a tiny stepladder with wheels was placed in position, mounted, and a thick, leather-backed volume pulled out. Briskly, he leafed through the pages, and then gave a small "Ah", peering down at me over his glasses. "I am not *absolutely* certain," he said, "but it is entirely possible you *may* have an opturate hernia." As if to add weight to this diagnosis, he added, "I don't suppose your doctor's even seen one." Triumphantly the book was snapped shut, and he descended the ladder. Then the slightest cloud flickered across his face. "However, I feel you ought to see Professor Fleming. He's very sound!"

Realising I was possibly becoming a *cause célèbre* in the medical world, I was ushered in to see Professor Fleming. Tall, elegant, with the long slim fingers of a surgeon, he performed the wishbone treatment once more upon my legs. Then came dissension. "Sir Ralph," he mused, gazing at the ceiling, "is, of course," and I knew perfectly well what he was about to say, "very sound, but, you do *not* have an opturate hernia. You have a Brodie's abscess."

I became a patient at University College Hospital, where Mr Fleming performed the operation, apparently successfully. However, with the post-anaesthetic hallucinations, I was convinced my leg was about to fall off and there I lay, eyes closed, stiff as a board, terrified to move. But help was at hand. A slight cough and I opened my eyes to see the arresting face of Jonathan Miller smiling down at me. Already famous for his appearances in *Beyond The Fringe*, this most academic of performers was, of course, a fully qualified doctor, resident at University College. "Heard you were here. Just thought I'd pop in and say hello." Within moments, I had all the assurances I needed as, with a bedside manner guaranteed to aid recovery, Jonathan assured me there was little chance of my leg falling off. "Ten minutes after the op, it starts healing. Only nature," he enthused, referring to my hip joint, "could grow tissue back upon something as smooth as a billiard ball. Besides," he gave a mischievous grin, "Fleming is a bit of an untidy bugger. Won't let them clean up too much after the op. 'Leave all that inside,' he says. 'Give nature something to grow on!'"

Reassured, I closed my eyes, but Jonathan was not finished yet. He leant even closer, his voice lowered. "You do know you were the subject of a bet?" All traces of post-anaesthetic left me as my eyes opened wide. "Oh yes," said Jonathan. "The other house surgeon here, Mr Wolfe, who had full access to your notes, disagreed entirely. He told Fleming you didn't have a Brodie's abscess, that you had a cyst." To say that Jonathan now had my full interest would be the understatement of the century. It was jaw-dropping time, and there was enough of the performer in Jonathan to enjoy the effect. "'Righty ho!' said Mr Fleming. 'We'll have a fiver on it!' And guess what?" said Jonathan. "Old Fleming was absolutely right. The moment the operation was over, he took the glass slide straight from the operating theatre to Wolfe's office and collected his money."

I spent some time pottering about on crutches, finally making an extremely theatrical entrance into Gerry's Club. This haven for actors, run by Gerry Campion, famed for his appearance as Billy Bunter on television, was in a basement in Shaftesbury Avenue. The entrance stairs were steep and I did get a minor round of applause as I negotiated my way down them. Satisfied I'd made a reasonable entrance, I sat at the table at the foot of the stairs and ordered lunch. My agent, Dennis, then made his entrance down the stairs and slid a pen and a piece of paper in front of me. "Just sign that," he said "and I'll be off." "That" was a contract for a revue in the West End, produced by Wolf Mankowitz, and starring myself.

"What about the, erm—?" I indicated my leg.

Dennis said, "You go to rehearsal and do it until you fall over." He then pocketed the contract I'd signed, grabbed my crutches and ran up the stairs. My fellow actors and their agents gave him the laugh his exit deserved.

Word had reached America about Peter's devastating impression of Olivier as Richard III, club foot and all, and he and I were booked to perform the sketch on a CBC TV show in Toronto. Peter was delayed and, thanks to the generosity of CBC, on 16 April 1960 I was allowed to fly, via New York, where I stayed the weekend. As Julie Andrews was an old friend, she arranged for me to stay at the same hotel as her and her (then-)husband, Tony Walton.

Currently the queen of Broadway as Eliza Doolittle in *My Fair Lady*, she also arranged for me to have the house seats (it was playing to capacity) as the show was the smash hit of the century. The cab driver that drove me to the Mark Hellinger Theater that night was furious. "How come you got seats for *My Fair Lady*, you bein' a limey and just orf the plane? Me, I been tryin' to see it for t'ree years!" When I told him Julie had given me the seats, his entire manner changed. If there's one thing Americans like, it's fame, and the fact that I was friend of a Julie was enough for my cab-driver friend. When we got to the theatre he uttered words that I had never heard from a cab driver before – or, for that matter, since. "You ain't payin'," he said. "She a real lady and, bein' a friend of yours, you gotta be a nice guy. So hands across the sea and all that sort of thing, old sport. God bless the British Empire!" He gave me a salute and drove off.

The TV show in Toronto was a big success, especially for Peter. We came back to England in even grander style, sitting in wooden deck chairs on the deck of the *Queen Elizabeth*. A smooth crossing and we both put on a lot of weight ordering from the largest epicurean menu in the world. I looked quite fancy, strolling the teak boards twirling my walking stick – still necessary after my encounter with the elegant surgery of Mr Fleming.

Six months to the day after the operation, I opened in the West End revue *The Art Of Living*, doing lots of dance numbers, apparently none the worse for wear. At rehearsals, I had fallen over a few times, but Mr Fleming had told me of the dried-peas trick. Two packets put into an empty sock and tied round the ankle, then on your back, lifting your leg 50 agonising times a day, soon did the trick. With some delight, I got Mr Fleming a couple of seats for the opening night. His eyes twinkled behind his glasses as he came to my dressing room after the show to congratulate me. "You must have got through an awful lot of peas," he said.

If ever two gentlemen proved that they were sound, they were Professor Fleming and Jonathan Miller.

8 Didn't You Used To Be Graham Stark?

I've never made a habit of lurking in Piccadilly Circus doorways at night-time and it took a fair bit of explaining to the policeman who shone his torch on me. Certain that he'd caught the Phantom Flasher of Fulham, I had to convince him that I'd waited many years to get my name above the title in a West End show and that now I quite fancied standing in Piccadilly watching it light up every night. My name, that is. I was now starring at the Criterion Theatre, right on Piccadilly Circus, and after good notices we soon settled down into a comfortable nine-month run, as each night I revelled in the luxury of the number-one dressing room.

Originally designed for the famous actress Dame Marie Tempest, it was none of your tiny cubbyhole with the peeling wallpaper; it was more your flock wallpaper, imitation-candlestick lights with dinky shades, large gilt-framed mirrors and a huge French Empire chaise longue. With this large, spacious room came the services of my very own dresser, who, apart from the alarming habit of changing the colour of his hair every Friday night, proved to be another Admirable Crichton in every sense of the word. Bobby was his name and, as I had about 15 changes of costume during the show, he certainly earned his money. Yes, a tower of strength, and I had no fault to find with him, but unfortunately he wasn't too happy about me. We'd only been running a couple of weeks when I noticed a definite frost in the air and there was a lot of banging of cupboards. The lips had also gone very thin.

"You do realise *we* are a star in the West End!" When Bobby said this, I looked over my shoulder, expecting to find someone else in the room, but I soon realised my occupation of the number-one dressing room meant I got the use of the royal *we*. "And," Bobby went on, "now *we* are a success, *we* may expect visits from other well-known theatrical celebrities, and what will *we*," his hand made a sweeping gesture around the splendid room, "be able to offer them in the way of refreshment? Just because *we* do not imbibe, it doesn't mean the rest of the acting profession has signed the pledge!" Ego destroyed,

I gazed at him with horror. It was true. Non-drinker that I was, it never occurred to me that friends, visitors, etc, might like a quick swig.

"Do what you like!" I told him, and Bobby took instant command.

"Right," he said. "I've got this bit of chintz. I'll run it up tomorrow. It'll go a treat over that table, then I'll pop out to the off-licence and stock up. You can settle with me later. And then my little white mess jacket that fits like a dream can go to the cleaners and before you know it *we* shall be the envy of the West End!"

Give him credit, *we* were done proud. Next night, the table was duly covered in the beautifully hemmed chintz, plus a dozen or so bottles, fronted by a row of polished and gleaming glasses, saucers of assorted nuts, boxes of cigarettes. Nothing had been left out. I was given a quick preview of the white jacket before the show and it did indeed fit like a dream. Perhaps a trifle tight across the rear, but the effect was quite fetching.

The show was a winner that night. Every laugh and round of applause came like clockwork and, after two hours of leaping about the stage, I sat in front of the gilt-framed mirror, drenched in perspiration, wiping the make-up off. A knock on the door and Laurier Lister, the director of the show, popped his head round and mentioned that someone had come backstage to see me. Without thinking, stripped to the waist and pouring sweat, I wandered to the door clutching an absolutely filthy make-up towel.

There, wearing a dinner jacket and looking, if possible, more distinguished off the screen than on, stood Sir Laurence Olivier. I looked at him and said, "Ah." At least, I meant to say, "Ah." What actually came out was something that sounded like a death rattle. He gave a charming smile and began to murmur congratulations, but unfortunately I couldn't understand a word he was saying as, owing to the state of shock I was in, everything started to sound as if it were underwater.

Finally, Sir Laurence stopped talking. Well, you couldn't blame him, as I'd never spoken a word, just stood there with my mouth open. I imagined him later saying, "Quite a talented lad, but obviously mentally retarded." There was a polite smile and he and Laurier vanished. I turned slowly from the door, shattered.

But there was worse to come. "*Charming!*" said Bobby. "Absolutely bleeding *charming!* Ran up the chintz, got me white jacket cleaned, polished all those glasses, and what happens? Only Sir bleeding Laurence at the door and you don't even ask him in. I could have had a gin in his hand before you could have said, "Now is the winter of our sodding discontent"! You could have had a little chat, I could have hovered politely in the background and who knows? He might have liked a handful of my mixed nuts."

He never really did forgive me. It was all very well having other theatrical friends round after that, but you couldn't top Sir Laurence. Thank God he wasn't Lord Olivier in those days! Yes, the arms were folded tight, the lips got even thinner and he paraphrased that well-known royal personage. "*We*," said Bobby, "were definitely *not* amused!"

However, thanks to gentleman in the next dressing room, we had lots of other stars to give drinks to. Hiram Sherman had been brought over from America to play Art Buchwald, the columnist, and I played most of the characters he met on his tour of Europe. Hiram, nicknamed Chubby, was a very deceptive man. On the surface, he was very sweet and charming, but in fact his history in the theatre showed another side, as he was a militant who did a great deal for his fellow actors in trade-union work in New York and was a great friend and confidant of Orson Welles in his Mercury Theatre days. He had helped Welles set up Mercury, and most nights his dressing room was full of actors visiting from America. Often he'd bring them into my room and, with the white jacket worn, the drinks and the bowl of nuts were in great demand. Boris Karloff came in one evening. Such a charming man, it was laughable to think he terrorised us as much as he did.

Actors, as a breed, tend to herd together. We do like to be within social distance of each other and any casting director would have had an easy time setting up shows from our neighbourhood. Spike Milligan was only a few streets away, as were Bernie Winters and Bruce Forsyth, and on a clear day Peter Sellers could be seen washing any of the numerous cars that he was constantly buying. But my nearest neighbour was Eric Morecambe, the comic in Morecambe and Wise, the most successful pair of entertainers in the history of British television. Every Sunday morning, small puffs of tobacco smoke like signals from the Indians in the hills came slowly down the pavement of Friary Road, Friern Barnet. His teeth clenching a favourite pipe, Eric came to savour the large mid-morning cups of tea that my wife, Audrey, and I would provide. This was an unbroken ritual. We would settle in the wooden-framed deck chairs on my small lawn and debate the state of our lives, and then he would complain about the lack of work, what an idiot his agent was, and ask if I'd heard the one about the lady being locked in the lavatory on the plane. In other words, normal everyday actor talk. Insular to an alarming degree, actors tread a narrow corridor of interest. They think about their profession, talk about their profession and, given the chance, single-mindedly perform it.

One Sunday, there was a longer pause than usual. Another message from the Black Hills of Dakota, then the pipe was removed. "We're packing it in, me and Ern. Getting nowhere. And I've got this offer to sell cars. Only posh ones, of course." Another puff at the pipe, another spiral of smoke and then the clipped statement was amplified. "Yes, definitely packing it in. No work these days. Friend's got this big car showroom up the road. Might as well." A television disaster in the '50s had soured things for them, but the thought that they would cease working came as a shock.

One week later, on 6 April 1960, a phone call from my agent: "*The Alma Cogan Show*, Saturday week. You're doing a duet with her. 'Fings Ain't What They Used To Be', as an old stage doorkeeper. Morecambe and Wise are on the show as well."

We had a week of rehearsals in a dingy broken-down church hall and then, on the third day, Ernie spoke to me. Delighted to get the show, he was still worried. "If you've got a minute, could you look at what we're doing? You've got a director's mind, you have." Flattery will get you everywhere, and I solemnly sat on a hard wood chair, watching the two go through their routine, a routine which later became famous. They called it "the get-out-of-that routine" and it was very funny, except... I pulled a face.

They crowded close. "What? What?" they said.

I pointed at Ernie. "You should be a woman," I said. "And you should have a handbag. Then you can slosh him whenever you want!"

Ecstatic smiles wreathed their faces as, with voices that would have done credit to Edith Evans, they exclaimed, "A handbag!"

The next Saturday night, we did the show live. My duet with Alma went quite well, then Ernie went through the routine of walloping Eric with the handbag and they stopped the show. Lew Grade – the ATV tycoon, the original lord of all he surveyed even before he got his title – watched the show, picked up the phone after the final caption and said, "Give them three London Palladium shows on the strength of that." He was, of course, talking of the greatest showcase for comics on TV at the time.

They did just as well. Within weeks, Morecambe and Wise were the hottest property on TV and signed for a full series. Then the BBC beckoned, they linked up with the writer Eddie Braben and the rest, as the cliché so truly has it, is history. New viewing figure records went into the books and their Christmas shows became national events.

In 1970, exactly ten years later, I managed to raise the money to direct a half-hour film called *Simon Simon* and, being a cheeky beggar, talked my friends in the profession into taking cameo roles. Even cheekier, I got them to do it for nothing.

One short sequence remained to be cast – two workmen, on the roof of a house, performing a comedy routine with a long ladder. Well, it was a Saturday afternoon, rain was pouring down, the house was very tall, had a very steep roof, and even getting the camera up there was tricky, never mind risking the actors' necks. It just took the one phone call and Eric and Ernie agreed to come over. Eric pulled on his overalls. "I really should be watching Luton," he said. Ernie bravely climbed the long ladder while Eric slithered about the roof, making sure not to look down, and the shot was in the film can in half an hour. With the rain still falling, I mumbled the thanks they both deserved for giving up the Saturday afternoon, for driving themselves to the location and for being two super gents.

Ernie gave one of his little-boy grins and looked at Eric, who grinned back. "But you see, we owe you," he said. "We haven't forgotten." Then, in perfect unison, like Tweedledum and Tweedledee, the two voices chorused, "*A handbag!*"

Restive soul that he was, Peter Sellers not only bought lots of cars but also anything else that caught his eye. He spotted a splendid manor house at Chipperfield, just outside London, and on the strength of getting his first major starring role in a film of George Bernard Shaw's *The Millionairess* he bought it. His star had been steadily rising, and now he reached a new peak by playing opposite one of the most desirable women in the world, Sophia Loren – at least, that's what the film's publicists called her, and for once they were absolutely right. I met her at a garden party at the new house and she was a delight. Then, playing her butler in the film, I had the chance to take a glamorous picture of her on the set, which many years later she signed for me. Sophia always called me "Bambino", but there was a lot of scandal about her and Peter on the film, as he would insist on telling everybody – including his wife, and me, and anybody else who would listen – that he was having an affair with her. Peter was a terrible sexual fantasist and it was totally untrue. Years later, he made an identical boast to me about another continental actress, Dany Robin, who later that very same day begged Audrey and I never to leave her alone with Peter, as he was just a silly boy.

Well, to some people he was a silly boy, but our joint agent Dennis made a sales pitch to the Mirisch brothers and, very partial to phone calls, Peter rang to tell me that he was flying to Rome to film with some American director, Blake Edwards. He knew he was taking over from Peter Ustinov, who had left the film before shooting began, but it didn't bother him – the money was so huge and the rest of the cast so glamorous that he was only too happy.

And so Inspector Clouseau was born. He took me to a private screening in London when *The Pink Panther* was finished, then looked at me afterwards with the worried look on his face of the actor who has just seen his full performance for the first time. I knew I'd just watched his elevation to international stardom so I wasn't bothered about his feelings and told him so.

There was a film boom going on in Britain and we seemed to spend all our days at Pinewood, Shepperton, Denham, MGM or wherever, with every studio going full blast. But the film that I enjoyed the most, *Only Two Can Play* (which gave Peter yet another hit), was made on location in Swansea, one of the major cities in Wales. Scurrying about the streets in a dirty raincoat, with several days' growth of beard, I had a lot of problems explaining to a local policeman I was merely an actor. I also had a problem with the director Sidney Gilliatt. Actors have an unfortunate habit of using the word "darling", usually when they've forgotten the name of the person they're talking to. I think I must have used it a few too many times on the set, as Sidney looked at Peter: "Your friend a poof, is he?"

American performers are very partial to London. In their own country, they have the choice of either New York or Los Angeles, which happen to be 3,000 miles apart, but in the Greater London area we had all the major film studios, both television channels, BBC radio in that temple of art deco, Broadcasting House, at the top of Regent Street, and in the West End there are over 50 theatres. In the early '60s, two major female recording stars from the USA came to record separate television shows, and I was in both of them. Patti Page, who had sold millions of records, did a show with ATV, while Jo Stafford, legendary singer with Tommy Dorsey, who had sold even more records, was doing a show for Lew Grade, and I had to sing with both of them. (My vocal experience had been songs on the back of a truck during my days with the RAF gang show. One day in India, while going over a pass on the way to the hill station of Simla, our pianist, Tommy Pollard, who had perfect pitch, gave me a look. "You do know," he said, "you are the only man in the world who could change key six times in one chorus of 'It Had To Be You' and not be aware of it!") On every floor of every television studio, there are marks put there by the cameramen so you stay in focus and can be heard properly. On both shows, I stood carefully two feet behind my marks, mouthing *sotto voce*.

But I did make a few records. If I wish to impress any of the local ladies that I meet at occasional garden parties, I merely have to drop into the conversation the fact that I am Squirrel Nutkin. Small delighted gasps result, as they all know this record (and have played it to their children countless times), which was made, with Vivien Leigh's narration, in the early '60s. Cyril Ornadel wrote the music, David Croft the lyrics and I sang 'I've Got A Tail' as Squirrel Nutkin. Oddly enough, as soon as I sang in the character voice of the squirrel, I gather that my pitch was perfect, and Cyril Ornadel was delighted as I recorded it in one take. There were other stories, including *Jemima Puddleduck*, and the production for children was delightful. Moulded in coloured plastic, the quality of the recordings was very high, and these Beatrix Potter records became instant classics.

Then I spent an extraordinary day with Peter Sellers in the sound studios at Abbey Road, recording what was to be a double-sided 45rpm record. George Martin, who later produced The Beatles' records, was in charge, and the first side, 'The Flat Earth Society', went very well. Peter was in good form as a tortured fanatic believing the world was flat and renouncing all things round and circular (including breasts). George suggested we went straight to the other side, which became a disaster. Peter was playing a wartime German bandleader, and within minutes he extemporised the character into a rabble-rousing, right-wing maniac, complaining that during the war all the smoke in the camps affected his saxophone playing. This side was never released but 'The Flat Earth Society' went out, backed by a Peter Ustinov recording, and sold very well.

The next time I passed Abbey Road, on the way to my dentist, I saw a sharp nose, supporting a pair of steel glasses, pointing at me. "Didn't you use to be Graham Stark?" said John Lennon and, relapsing into my native Liverpool accent, I assured him that I did used to be. The four Beatles were in the forecourt of the studio behind the railings having some photographs taken, with George Martin hovering in the background. He welcomed me in and, staying in the control room for the afternoon, I got the chance to watch and listen as the group, down in the studio, tried out odd sequences of music. They were all very nice and totally predictable: Paul the extrovert, a laugh, a joke and very dedicated; Ringo, squatting behind the drums doing his comical routines but not giving a lot away; George serious, quiet and equalling Paul's dedication; and John, who was missing nothing and constantly questioning everything, including was I who he thought I was, seemed to be a law unto himself. I'd love to say I was there at the birth of one of their classic songs, but it was a day of idle guitar strumming, odd thumping of the drums, and I wouldn't have missed it for anything.

"Well, you see, Kenneth Tynan got me a bit pissed and started me chatting about Elizabeth," said Richard Burton.

"I see," I said.

"And rather affectionately I said, 'She's got big tits and short legs,'" said Richard.

I wasn't sure what I should answer to this, so I simply nodded and said, "Ah."

"Then," said Burton, "the bastard goes ahead and prints it! Mind you," he added, "she has got big tits and short legs, but he shouldn't have done it."

Elizabeth Taylor looked at me, looked at Richard Burton, looked back at me and said, "I love a man who speaks his mind!"

I met Burton (not for the first time) while I was working in 1964 on the film *Beckett* at Shepperton Studios. As I walked on the set, playing the part of the pope's secretary and wearing my long monk's robes and a fringe haircut, Burton gave a burst of laughter. "Oh God," he said. "I didn't know it was going to be that sort of film!"

Loftily, I explained that I had been especially cast by the director, Peter Glenville, who had asked if, in the pursuit of reality, I would have my hair cut in a tonsure. "For the money you're offering me, I'll have it shaved off," I had replied.

Grinning, Burton watched me rehearse, being rather taken with the effect of my monk's robe touching the ground. As I scurried across the huge set, I looked like a religious hovercraft. Eventually, we did a take and, after I had glided silently, Dalek-like across the floor, Burton got up and glided across after me. The director was not amused. Burton apologised and simply said, "I couldn't resist it!" He was not a person you could dislike.

I, in my turn, watched fascinated as Burton effortlessly reeled off his long speeches. "Always had a photographic memory," he said, "Don't know why. Just have." The memory part was true, as within a few minutes of me appearing on the set he retold a joke I'd told him some eight years earlier in a pub in Camden. A group of us had been in there after a broadcast and the joke had involved a large brass tuba misused at a drunken party. He remembered it exactly, even to all the comical voices. I even think his version was slightly funnier than mine.

We had a break midmorning and then Burton gave me a nod. "Come on," he said. "Let's see how Madam is." As almost every newspaper in the world was making front-page news about the Burton–Taylor romance, which had started a few weeks earlier while they were filming *Cleopatra* in Rome, I didn't need a crystal ball to know who "Madam" was. Both identically dressed in our monks' regalia, Burton and I climbed to his first-floor dressing room. Contrary to popular belief, English film studios do not lay on much of a red carpet where actors are concerned – the room was really quite modest and definitely on the small size.

The living legend was wearing a white trouser suit and looked, if possible, more devastating offscreen than on. I stood like a paralysed rabbit, gazing at the thickest pair of false eyelashes I had ever seen framing the largest pair of eyes I had ever seen. Then I looked again and realised the lashes weren't false. Burton grinned at her. "Up off your arse," he said, "and get my friend a drink."

Her smile as she rose was catlike and very contented. "Such a gentleman," she purred. "And you will have?" An elegant hand gestured to the drinks cabinet.

I gave a slight shake of the head. As her eyes followed Burton around the room, you didn't have to be a mindreader to realise that she was just as mad about him as he was about her. Every day it was the same. A couple of scenes, then off upstairs to see how Madam was. The second day was quite exciting. One major paper made the mistake of printing a cartoon linking Elizabeth Taylor with a young lady who in the past had accepted money for her favours – a lady of the night! Lawyers appeared, there was a conference with Taylor and a charity was immediately the recipient of a very large sum of money, donated by that paper as a settlement for the libel.

Then came the nail scissors. Odd flickers of light came off the stainless steel as Taylor snipped at her elegant nails, her brow furrowed with the concentration such a task deserves. Jokingly, Burton made a reference to the girl paired with Taylor in the cartoon. "Not bad lookin'," he said. "I suppose if you had nothin' better to do…"

He got no further. The hiss from Taylor's lips would have done credit to the asp that eventually dispatched Cleopatra. The eyes flashed and her nose was inches from Burton's face. "Should that idea ever pass your mind, these scissors," they were flourished in his face, "would be used to cut your balls off." With heads lowered, every man in the room gave an involuntary wince.

It was about the middle of the third day when the subject of *Cleopatra* came up. The monster movie they had finally finished shooting in Rome had just been released and Burton made no secret of his disappointment at the notices he had received. "All that bastard Zanuck's fault. Poncin' about with that bloody polo mallet!" A vein throbbed in his temple and his voice thickened with anger as he spoke the name of the head of 20th Century Fox, who always ostentatiously carried a polo stick. "He saw the rough cut… Too bloody intellectual, as far as he was concerned… Got to have more bloody battle scenes… Cut my part to pieces!" His eyes searched the room as if seeking for some blunt instrument to strike down the midget tycoon. Then his eye alighted on Elizabeth. "Cut her bleedin' part, too."

Delighted to have sympathy, she gilded the lily: "And what about those clothes!" The thought of the outfits that had never been screened brought her to her feet. "That white dress, with all that beading!" Her hands fluttered across her body, making exotic patterns. "And remember that scene in the palace?"

On cue, Burton moved to her side. Remembrance of things cut out from the film filled the room. And so, sitting on the floor, still dressed in my monk's robe, I was given an exclusive and private performance by two of Hollywood's biggest stars (at that time, *the* biggest) of a couple of scenes that were never to feel the heat of a projection lamp.

If I thought I had reached some sort of apogee, there was more to come. On the last day of shooting, I tentatively asked Richard if I could have a shot of him in costume for my own personal picture collection. He knew I was a keen photographer and agreed at once. Grabbing Elizabeth Taylor's hand, he pulled her to her feet. "Come on, darlin'. Come and have your picture taken." Then he gave me a worried look. "I'm not being presumptuous, am I? You would like a picture of her as well, wouldn't you?"

I don't really know how I got through that picture session. The whole of Shepperton Studios was under siege by the world's press, frantic to get pictures of the world's most famous lovers (still officially married to other people), and there was I, Hasselblad in hand, while Burton and Taylor played a cod-love scene for me on the balcony.

As Burton bent Elizabeth backward in an over-the-top romantic embrace, he gave me a naughty grin. "£20,000, the *Daily Express*," he said.

"You know I never would," I said.

Another naughty grin. "Course. That's why we're doing it."

9 Well, You've Proved Yourself Now

1962 was another busy year of film-making. Olympic fencing champion, Hollywood leading man and film director Cornel Wilde came to Pinewood Studios to make another version of the Arthurian legend. Called *Lancelot,* it had faggots stacked around a stake, to which was chained a leading lady who had been a bit naughty at the top of the ivory tower. Tastefully gowned in a long, tight-fitting robe, she was rescued from the flames – which licked menacingly near to her designer dress – by an athletic knight swinging down from the castle walls by a rope. There was a lot of mead being quaffed from large tankards, huge haunches of venison sliced, and there were plenty of the actors' favourite food: roast chickens. These could be torn apart in moments depicting gluttony or hurled in rage at the serfs and varlets who scurried about the dining hall keeping the food supply coming. Roast chickens are an invaluable actors' prop and, should work be a little thin on the ground, help out with the food situation as well. Needless to say, I was one of the varlets. Or was I a serf? All I know is I wore a jerkin and a pair of very wrinkly tights, plus a scruffy wig. Born to play grovelling parts, as my friend Leo McKern so rightly put it. Actors like us never get to sit in the chair; we always stand behind it.

Strangely enough, my very next role, a few weeks later, was that of a very well-bred, rather superior army officer, and I was acting alongside one of the great gentleman of our profession. The picture I took of a winsome, flat-capped old gent may not seem to be the same person as that urbane, foppish character Osrick that appeared in Laurence Olivier's *Hamlet* (the film that dazzled audiences worldwide in 1948), but indeed it was. After many years acting in film, television and theatre, Peter Cushing finally went on to establish himself as one of the great mainstays of the Hammer horror films, laying wreaths of garlic on almost every film set he acted on. His appearance in all of these horror films was quite comical because, in real life, he was one of the gentlest, most tolerant and soft-spoken actors in the profession.

Surprisingly, he actually began his film career in pre-war Hollywood in *The Man In The Iron Mask* (1939) and then went on, in the same year, to play with two of Hollywood's immortals, Laurel and Hardy, in *A Chump At Oxford*. After the war came Osrick, and then finally he began his career with Hammer films. We first met in the early '50s, when we appeared together in a stage production of Molière's *The Imaginary Invalid* at the Garrick Theatre, starring Elisabeth Bergner, AE Matthews and Walter Gore. He proved that he was a true friend when, at an extraordinary matinée performance, Walter Gore (playing the mime role of Harlequin) collapsed. With only ten minutes to curtain-up time, they got me into Walter's Harlequin costume (luckily, we were the same build) and on I went. I had no words to speak, of course, but hundreds of complicated moves throughout the three acts.

Peter, playing an elegant courtier, calmly stood onstage telling me *sotte voce* just where I should be throughout the entire performance – "Over there to the corner, wait until she passes, then grab her!" – and graphically and elegantly, his hands moving in complete character, he directed my entire performance. Walter never came back to the show and I successfully took over the part for the rest of the run. Needless to say, Peter and I stayed great friends and at odd times I would go down to his house in the country, marvelling at the wonderful model theatre he had built at his home. His lovely wife, whom he adored, was always there with him.

We appeared together again in a BBC Comedy Playhouse programme in 1963, *The Plan*, in which, as Albert Fawkes, he tried to outdo his namesake by blowing up Parliament. He wore a marvellous make-up and I took a picture of him. A few years later, gentleman that he was, he rang and asked if he might use it in his autobiography. Sadly, his lovely wife eventually died and he took her loss very badly, but from then on until his own death he comforted himself with the thought that he would one day, to quote his own words, "be seeing my beautiful girl again".

How lucky actors are. Catching the 8.30am train every morning may bring security, and I'm sure that many friendships are struck up during the daily journey to and from work, but by and large the theatrical profession has more charmers than stinkers, and they do have, despite the gossip columnists' reports of bitchery, very big hearts (and pockets) where their fellow actors are concerned. Maxine Audley, a distinguished English actress, went with a friend to Paris at a time when there were strict restrictions on taking English currency abroad and, on her last night in Paris, their money almost run out, they watched Jean-Louis Barrault at the theatre. Backstage, congratulating another actor, they met Barrault by chance and, realising that they were English actors, he asked what other shows they were going to see. They briefly explained about the money, and with a Gallic flourish he pulled handfuls of francs from his pockets, telling them to stay on and see these other plays. "But you don't know us," they said. Barrault looked hurt. "I will be in London next year and you will find me. An actor will always pay back another actor."

Unfortunately, I met one who wouldn't. In 1963, I had a long run in *The Bed Sitting Room* with Spike Milligan in the West End while at the same time making a film with Cliff Richard at Pinewood. Alongside me in the film was Robert Morley and, as we were playing the two comedy villains, we had a splendid time. Unfortunately, one of the stuntmen's wives became very ill and I helped out. His brother, and fellow stuntman, Eddy, loomed over me on the set one day: "Wot you done for Arfur I shall nevah forget. Nevah!"

I assured him that it was nothing – after all, I wasn't the only one – but he persisted. "But me and Arfur 'ave gotta thank you somehow! Tell you wot. We got these 50 cans of emulsion off the back of a truck, know wot I mean?" He gave a wink.

"No, really," I said. "Don't want any. Thanks."

He looked frustrated. "Need any lead for the roof?"

I shook my head.

"Righto," he said. "The next time you want someone given a good thumpin', me an' Arfur will do it for free!"

In *The Bed Sitting Room*, someone else's wife was supposedly ill as one of the support actors came to me with an abject tale of woe. It seems a car had knocked down his wife, the children needed minding, and could I please help out? Copying Jean-Louis Barrault, I immediately passed a bundle of notes, assuring him that only when his wife had recovered would I expect it back. I got the odd health report. "Coming on nicely," he said, and we continued with the play. One Saturday night, I was going out to dinner after the show and, as my salary always went direct to my agent, I inquired, rather timorously, if I could have a small advance.

Our young female manager gave a laugh. "Well, of course. How much would you like?" Counting out the money, she gave another little laugh. "Now, if you'd been…!" She saw my reaction and said, "How much has he had off you?"

Well, it wasn't the £100 that mattered but the wicked story that had gone with the confidence trick. No car had ever hit his wife, the children were fit and well and it seems that money had been conned from most of the stage staff and cast and spent in the local pubs. They were all resigned to not getting the money back, as dud cheques had bounced with monotonous regularity. It was then that inspiration came to me. "I'll see him in my dressing room right away," I said.

Before the torrent of excuses could start, I carefully explained to him my relationship with the stuntmen and how they felt deeply indebted and desperately wished to pay off that debt. I also explained that I originally felt no desire to take them up on their offer of violence, but now I was having second thoughts. I expected to be handed, in cash, £100 *before* the show on Monday night but, should this not happen, my two friends would be waiting outside the stage door *after* the show on Monday night. Naturally, I was not to know just how much damage they might inflict, but they were both very large and very fit. I hadn't the slightest intention of actually speaking to my stuntmen friends, but the money was in my hands on Monday.

In this bizarre and very funny show, I wore a natty desert rats officer's uniform, and a highlight of the second act was my onstage marriage to a glamorous lady, Margie Lawrence. As we neared the culmination of the ceremony, the bride and I started to undress and, as we both said, "I do," the vicar fired a starting pistol and Margie and I dived towards a double bed. To add glamour, Margie stripped down to a black corset – still keeping her bridal veil on – while we had a brief tango together. During the run of the play, she confided that she was pregnant, and one Thursday matinée I clasped her in my arms, we made several gliding movements...and I got a big kick in the stomach. It was obvious that the baby had got carried away with the music and joined in.

On 8 August 1963, the arrival of my first baby shot me up to the second floor of the London Clinic, where inquiries about the birth were met with tact and diplomacy. The matron glared at some hovering nurse. "Has *it* been born yet?" Audrey, looking beautiful but a trifle dishevelled, was fine. A small and petite Chinese nurse asked me if I would like to see my son, then led me to a room with a cot. She quickly whipped the blanket off, presumably to let me see everything was in its proper place, then covered him up again. A cleaning lady, gently moving a mop in circles, gave me a nod and a knowing look. "Proved yourself now," she said.

As children, my brothers and I were rather toffee-nosed about the Cunard shipping line. Upstart rivals to my father's ships we thought. However, having sailed on one of the Queen's to America – a wonderful, majestic ship and a floating gourmet's paradise – my loyalty wavered. I had even more reason to like Cunard, as Peter Sellers, fresh from the triumph of *The Pink Panther*, sailed back to England with its director, Blake Edwards, and on board it was decided that I should play Clouseau's assistant, Hercule, in the sequel. In November 1963, on the stages of MGM Studio at Elstree, we began shooting *A Shot In The Dark*, and twelve weeks later one of the most successful comedies made in England was finished. Blake had an extraordinary ability to run a very smooth film, and he never showed any strain, despite the problems he had with Peter, particularly later. It was the start of what would become the most famous (and financially successful) series of film comedies ever made.

It was the first film for me with Blake (I made nine with him eventually), and also the first film in which we had to deal with the Sellers disease, which took the form of the giggles. Well, it was more than that really – it got to the stage of having to lean on the scenery for strength while you recovered from the ache of laughing. Peter had always laughed a lot with Spike and Harry on *The Goon Shows*, but this was something that grew and grew gradually until, later in the Panther series, the laughs during scenes became legendary and the most sedate actors became infected. George Sanders could never be thought of as light-hearted, as by nature he had a gloomy Slavic personality, but even he joined the hysterics. Only the threat of large fines – given to the crew, of course – managed to stop him.

I always remember the casual, off-hand way Peter Sellers phoned me on 19 February 1964. "Doing anything special tomorrow?" he said. "Wonder if you'd like to come down to Elstead for the day?" There was a slightly embarrassing pause. Much as I would have liked to have gone to the house, it was a fair drive beyond Guildford to where Pete lived, and as my house was in North London, it was at least two hours in the car.

"Yeeees," I said. "That would be, er…"

Fortunately, Peter didn't pick up on the long, agonised "Yeeees". "Right," he said. "By the way, the Swedes always have two best men, so you and Dave Lodge will be doing the honours. Her name's Britt Ekland. You'll love her!"

And so it was that Peter told me he was getting married for the second time (there were two more marriages to come) and Dave Lodge and I would be his best men. We fought our way through a million press men at the registry office and, by coincidence, only a few days after the wedding I started work at Pinewood on a film called *Guns At Batasi*, in which Britt played the female lead. Dramatically, after only a few days, she vanished to Los Angeles to join Peter, and 1,000 headlines worldwide told of her leaving the film to get back to her newly married husband. The story of the beautiful Swedish actress flying back to her honeymoon bed made newspaper editors talk seriously of taking up religion again. The great press lord in the sky had not only given them a story to make a shortage of printers' ink a certainty, but guaranteed that several paper-making forests were cut down as well.

Over time I got to know Britt very well, and she was great fun. Some years later there was a nasty afternoon in Paris when, heavily pregnant with her daughter Victoria, she decided to do the shops on the smarter streets of the city. As my wife, Audrey, and I were there at the time, visiting her and Peter while he was making *What's New, Pussycat?*, she naturally invited Audrey to accompany her. Weeks later, checking my Diners' Club statement, I found I had developed a slight anti-Swedish bias.

However, Britt was a very kind and thoughtful girl, especially to Peter's two children by his first wife. In retrospect, I always thought that she had a bad press. Wear a slit skirt and be a *femme fatale* and you're a marked woman. She did possess extremely good manners. Casting her in a film comedy in the early '70s, I received a phone call from her telling me that she was not available owing to another film, but she was just calling to thank me personally for thinking of her.

I always remember Peter Cook and Dudley Moore when I look at the picture I took of her as, in one of their funniest sketches, Peter proclaimed that it was only really great art when the eyes followed you around the room. In that case, he would have definitely decided that this photograph was grade A, 100 per cent great art.

After Britt's departure from the set of *Guns At Batasi*, she was replaced by the very young, very shy, very pretty Mia Farrow, who dealt with it very well. On her first day on the set, she smiled when I told her I was in love with her mother (Maureen O'Sullivan, the first Jane in *Tarzan*), and then went on to give a very good performance in the picture and captivated us all. It was her first film, and she'd been thrust into the centre of a distinguished cast consisting of Richard Attenborough, Dame Flora Robson and Jack Hawkins. She often came out to our house at weekends and walked on the lawn reciting poetry. Then overnight she made the move into television and the first of the great soap operas, *Peyton Place,* which ruled supreme on every channel it played on. And with it came the haircut. Or was it Frank Sinatra?

Like many events of world-shattering importance, people always seem to remember where they were when it happened. I don't suppose there are many ladies of my generation who wouldn't remember where they were when they first heard Mia Farrow had had all her hair cut off. Well, nearly all. Hairdressers had to call in extra staff while sackfuls of tresses were carted off to wherever hair cut off in hairdressers' gets carted off to. Millions of men returned home to find they were now the husbands of elfin, androgynous wives. I think it was even more of a shock to me, as I'd photographed Mia leaning on a stone pillar at Pinewood Studios, her long and lustrous hair flowing down either side of that beautiful face. Then came the opportunity to get the new haircut on film.

Invited to a lunch at the *Sunday Telegraph,* one of our more august newspapers, I was cornered by the editor, John Anstey. With phraseology that PG Wodehouse would have been proud of, he gave me a look: "Hear you're a bit of a dab hand with the old camera, what? Do something for us, eh?"

Inspiration struck me. "How about my favourite leading ladies?" I inquired.

Delight spread across his face and, still in the parlance of the great PG, cried, "Love piccies of the gals!" His picture editor, Tom Hawkyard, was summoned and it was all systems go.

Mia was no problem. Married now to André Previn, she agreed at once, and I arranged to take the pictures at her home. As I climbed out of the car, crashing chords of music were reverberating down the hall. Mia opened the front door and vaguely gestured to the lounge, where Previn was giving a serious workout to one of the louder Rachmaninoff pieces. "Concert next week," she explained. Five children were swirling round her feet as she led me to the conservatory and quite calmly seated herself on a wicker chair. "Would this be all right?" The pose was perfect and, making sure the children didn't knock over any of the lamps, we set to work.

With cheekbones to die for and a hairstyle made for backlighting, it was quick and easy. With her film experience, Mia knew just how to pose and then it was inside to meet Previn, by now busy playing duets with one of the boys. It was my chance to pose the million-dollar question. "Did you," I said, "actually say, 'Do you want it good, or do you want it Thursday?'"

Previn, his hands idly running up and down the keyboard, faced the question bravely, having been reminded of a phrase that had passed into mythology, a phrase that summed up all the idiocy of Hollywood. He gave a nod. "It was MGM," he explained. "They wanted it quickly, I wanted it right. I didn't know how to get it through to them." I felt a satisfaction akin to finding the source of the Nile.

Within two days, the transparencies of Mia were ready to be viewed, but she explained that the only time she could see them was at the Royal Festival Hall, as Previn was conducting a concert there the next evening. Viewing the glorious colour emulsions of Messrs Kodak by the lamps of the Royal Festival Hall bar was not quite what I had in mind. However, my agreement with Mia was that she could see and vet the pictures. The light from the lamps was worse than I could imagine, as the tiny candle bulbs were made duller by the shades that covered each one, but Mia was too engrossed with the question of the smile, and picture after picture was rejected if there was a glimmer of humour on any of them.

"Nasty wrinkle either side of the mouth every time I smile," Mia explained. Not easy to argue with such logic, but even with a magnifying glass I couldn't detect the slightest sign of a wrinkle. Suddenly Mia looked at me. "I owe you such an apology. When you came to the house, I expected a few snapshots, but these…" The pause was eloquent. "These are just so…"

Anstey was over the moon. "Stunning piccies of a stunning gal," he said, and they were duly published.

Now that Stanley Kubrick has passed on, the hacks who exist by destroying past reputations have had a field day, describing him as the Howard Hughes of Hertfordshire, the deranged director behind the camera who reduced actors to fear-ridden robots, someone whose eccentricities apparently classified him almost into the mentally deranged class. All a load of rubbish.

Meeting him many years ago with Peter Sellers, while they were making *Lolita* in 1962, Audrey and I became friends with both Stanley and his wife, Christiana, who in turn became godmother to our youngest son, Timothy. We were frequent guests at the Chancery, the huge Edwardian house he rented near Elstree Studios, which he rapidly tailored to his own use, installing offices for his studio staff and a private cinema to view sections of his current film. The supposed eccentricity of having so much of his work at home was, in fact, typically Stanley, as it was highly efficient and enabled him to take infinite pains with the editing and all the other hundreds of details that make up a movie.

Stanley and I had a common interest that was photography. I had a studio and colour darkroom at my house, while Stanley had been a *Look* photographer for many years and had never lost his passion for cameras. Chromatic spherical aberrations, nodal points, depth of field – all part of our normal conversation. While making *2001: A Space Odyssey,* he had personally tested every known make of camera lens just to check the definition and quality, as it could come in useful when making the film.

One afternoon, his three young daughters were clustered around an armchair while I took it upon myself to play storyteller. Christiana, already an accomplished artist, supplied me with crayons and art boards and I launched into a modern version of *Cinderella* (always a sure-fire hit with little girls) and I guaranteed success by making Buttons one of The Beatles. With squeals of delight, they heard me in my broad Liverpool accent declaim, "Cinders, you *will* go to the ball tonight," while sketching Buttons with a Beatle haircut. Later, Stanley handed me a set of photographs he'd quietly taken while I was in the middle of the story. The quality was amazing. Shooting with his almost silent Leica, at the unbelievably slow speed of a tenth of a second, every print was pin-sharp. He explained that all *Look* photographers were trained to shoot that way.

Stanley's partner and producer, Jimmy Harris, became an even closer friend. We both shared an addiction to Lenny Bruce, Mort Sahl, Woody Allen and any other stand-up comic brave enough to risk the dreaded hecklers. (Jimmy would have liked to take that risk himself but finally, following in his partner's footsteps, turned director himself, making *The Bedford Incident*, a classic movie of the '60s.) Stanley's children laughed and screamed in the huge garden but video cameras were a thing of the future so, typically Kubrick, the very best 16mm camera was procured, plus full sound equipment, so that he could record his children. A heavy-duty tripod was set up, fill-in lamps were arranged, and finally Jimmy and I sat in the private cinema watching one of the most terrible home movies we had ever seen. Locked stationary on top of the tripod, the camera stolidly filmed while Stanley's three daughters swung across, one at a time, in front of it. This tedious action, mostly out of focus, was accompanied by Stanley's voice on the soundtrack pleading with the children to swing just a little bit higher, and could they please take that look of fear off their faces.

The great delight of the Chancery was the huge, ornate, billiard room in which Jimmy and I played constantly. Typical of the Edwardian era, raised leather-covered seats ran round each wall, while massive mahogany legs supported the full-sized table, the green baize smoothed by many years of patient brushing and ironing. An enormous, chain-suspended lamp-cover hung from the ceiling. Occasionally, Stanley would appear. As a born observer, he seemed happy just to amble into the room, sprawl on one of the seats and calculate the various angles and necessary impact for the balls to go into the pockets – that is, until one day when Tony Curtis arrived. Friendly with Stanley since working together on *Spartacus*, he erupted into the room like a minor explosion. Bursting in on us, he poured out all the latest Hollywood gossip and then, hardly taking breath, assured me that, if only I would follow this latest diet, which he absolutely swore by, it would change my life for the better and (lowering his voice to a confidential tone) also improve my bathroom habits. This joyous gentleman endeared himself even more to Jimmy and me by suggesting that we must not only play a team game of snooker (he and Stanley versus Jimmy and I) but that, to make matters just that little more *interesting*, there should be a small side-bet on the result.

To say that Stanley was careful in money matters was a bit of an understatement. Getting things right on one of his films could mean hours of overtime and hang the expense, but in his private life much more care was taken. Shuffling about in his (to him) comfortable dressing gown, his hand invariably hovered near one of the light switches in the big house. Lights were not to be left burning unnecessarily. Paradoxically, his methodical way of life made him a serious bulk-buyer and large cardboard boxes of washing powder, toilet rolls and anything that Stanley thought they might conceivably run out of were dotted around the house.

Considering that pool was their usual game, both Stanley and Tony Curtis played rather well – Curtis especially, displaying the same dash as he did in his screen performances. He was all fire and bravura, taking on daredevil long pots, while Stanley carefully summed up the chances, steadying the cue, then delivered the deliberate shot. Being blessed with a partner like Jimmy, who was a natural sportsman with the eye of an eagle, we soon moved into the lead. While I was steadying myself for what I hoped would be an easy red into the middle pocket, I became aware that gamesmanship was afoot. Stanley was not cheating, strictly speaking, but he was making certain that he was standing directly in my eye line, peering closely at his cue and rapidly chalking it.

The rules of etiquette are simple. When you are a guest in someone else's house you never, under any circumstances, accuse them of questionable behaviour, but Jimmy, a sportsman to his fingertips, made the first accusation. "Come on, Stanley. Let's play by the rules. No distractions while play is in progress."

Curtis nodded agreement. "Especially while money is on the game."

Well, it was a foregone conclusion we would win. Jimmy took the final black and Tony Curtis reached for his wallet. "Surely just a friendly game?" Stanley said.

Curtis leaned close. "A bet," he said, "is a bet. Pay up, Stanley."

Lodged in the files of the ACTT (Association of Cinematograph and Television Technicians) is a sacred document. It is my full membership as a producer/director of the ACTT and is one of the most highly prized pieces of paper in the cinema business. You spend some time as a temporary member, then (providing you get three fully paid up film directors to sign your application form) you'll be accepted, but not until then can you direct. I had a feature film signed, so it was favour time. The first was easy: Ken Hughes had directed my favourite fantasy movie of all time, *Chitty Chitty Bang Bang*, and was an old friend. He signed at once. Peter Sellers, who of course had his own director's ticket, signed as number two. Letting the whole thing go to my head, I decided that Stanley should be number three.

He was on location near my house, doing some night shooting on *A Clockwork Orange*, so I drove up there. Derek Cracknell, first assistant on the picture, nearly had a fit. "You can't see Stanley now, Gra. He's rehearsing Malcolm McDowell. Just the two of them. I daren't let you through." God knows how I managed to get past him, but I did. At one end of a small, bare room was Malcolm wearing his bizarre costume and the terrifying boots which, in the film, he used to kick a victim to death while he sang 'Singin' In The Rain'. At the other end of the room, Stanley sat on the floor, watching him through the eyepiece of a 16mm Arriflex camera. Without pause, I sat down beside him, took out my application form and asked him to sign. "I'll hold the camera," I said.

Stanley was too bewildered to do anything but sign, and the next day I presented the form, with the three signatures on it, to Les Wiles of the ACTT. He took one look at it and said, "Why didn't you get Carol Reed and David Lean while you were at it?"

Stanley was undoubtedly eccentric, but that had its comical side. In the early '60s, at the height of the Cuban missile crisis, he quite seriously started to research where the safest place in the world would be just in case idiots started turning keys and pressing buttons in those concrete silos. As I understood it, some part of central Australia came closest to filling the bill. Then, I'm afraid, I rather put paid to his plans. "It just occurs to me," I said, "that that could well be the place where some brilliant scientist might suggest they drop one of the bombs just to prove they weren't joking."

I shall always remember the look on Stanley's face as he mentally digested this information. Then he nodded his head sagely. "Graham, you know, you could be right." His search for a safe retreat ended there and then.

He was never a bully. He was a very modest man, with a relentless, inquiring mind. Mind you, he didn't quite play the game at snooker and was hopeless at home movies, but there are not many of his kind around.

10 Serving Spaghetti On A Plate –
Where's The Romance In That?

The television show I did with Peter Cushing spawned a disaster. Peter's show was very good, and I had one of those you've-got-to-get-laughs-with-these-lines parts. The head of Light Entertainment at BBC TV thought he had star material on his hands and duly negotiated with Dennis for me to have my own television series. Johnny Speight, who had written some of the best sketches in the *Art Of Living*, was commissioned to write the scripts, and everything in the garden looked wonderful. Sadly, weed killer was raked into the soil and it was a total failure. An audience sat in the studio for the first show as we actors valiantly strove to get laughs, but it wouldn't have mattered what we did, as nobody could see us. Nor, for that matter, could they hear us; for some mysterious reason, the sets were built with their backs to the audience, none of the television monitors were working and the sound system was switched off. A few hundred people sat and looked at a lot of blank canvas walls and wondered what was going on behind them. In the rest of the series, we tried to repair the damage, but the critics quite rightly condemned our opening show and phrases such as "Stark tragedy" were bandied about. You can't recover from that sort of press. Fortunately, I was in good company as several other new shows foundered that year, but I did retire hurt.

I had another run in the theatre in Marcel Archard's play *Voulez Vous Jouer Avec Moi?* The literal English translation, *Will You Play With Me?*, was quickly rejected as the thoughts of what graffiti artists would do to the posters was a bit mind-boggling, so they called it *The Love Game* – a wonderfully nondescript and anaemic title. It was put on at the Arts Theatre, and it was not a success. Our leading lady was the brilliant actress and world-class neurotic Jill Bennett, who played a circus girl, while I played a sad clown. Frustrated in my desire for her, I took refuge in manic displays of magic, frantically performing tricks whenever we met. Her husband, the writer Willis Hall, who had adapted the play from the French, was an amateur magician of some repute, and he taught me all the tricks of the trade. With a flesh-coloured card dispenser clamped on my middle finger, I could produce cards apparently from midair; I turned my hand and a cane appeared; and the top hat I carried produced everything from rabbits to endless coloured scarves. Unfortunately, just before rehearsals started, Jill's letters to a boyfriend were discovered, divorce proceedings began and, while I was on stage rehearsing with Jill, the cuckolded author and injured husband, Willis, sat in the stalls watching. The opening night was a disaster as the director insisted that Jill sang some songs and, shaking with nerves and totally off-key, she wasn't much help. But once the songs were cut, she was a delight to work with.

The meal after the opening night was just as bad as the play. The cast ate at the Pickwick Club, opposite the theatre, and after dinner Audrey and I went to say goodnight to Jill. John Fraser, who was also in the play, was with her. Six feet from their table I knew we had trouble as, with a large amount of drink inside her, Jill's neurosis was in full cry. "What the fuck do you know about marriage problems?" she shouted, glaring at John. "You're fucking queer!"

Like all actors under siege, it was instant combined-forces time. John, ignoring Jill's tirade, took her by one arm and said, "Shall we get a taxi?"

I took the other arm and said, "What a good idea!" And then, like tied-together contestants in the three-legged race, we set off in a crab-like walk to the door. Jill was now in a fighting mood, but we got her outside and pulled her into a shop doorway, which was, unfortunately, right opposite the London Hippodrome, the busiest stretch of pavement in the West End of London. John vainly called for a taxi while the great British public – sensing a scandal and not wishing to miss one iota of what could be a public punch-up – gathered round.

Within moments, a young policeman, fearing public disorder, confronted me as I stood, my arms tightly wrapped about Jill, who was trying to lash out at all and sundry. "It might be advisable, sir," said the policeman, "to get this young lady off the street."

Jill seized on these words as some threat to her freedom, shouting, "Arrest me. Go on, fucking arrest me!" At that very moment, a publicist, who we all knew, and who had been to the show, opened the door of a taxi he'd hailed and he and his girlfriend climbed in. I seized the chance and shoved Jill in after them.

Two weeks later, the publicist and I met on the street. "Thought you'd like to know," he said. "The lady who shared our taxi the other night was very courteous. She climbed off the floor, shook hands and said, "We haven't been introduced. My name is Jill Bennett.""

Many years later, Jill tragically ended what was tormenting her by committing suicide. Even more tragically, her (then-)husband, John Osborne, declared that he wished he'd spat in her grave.

Luckily, there was something around the corner that made up for it all. I'd made a brief appearance in two early films, *Emergency Call* and *Sink The Bismarck*, both directed by Lewis Gilbert, who was always very workmanlike but had never had the chance to sink his professional teeth into anything with originality. Then I was sent the script of *Alfie* and it was suggested I play the husband of a lady who is made pregnant by a brief affair and then has an abortion. I have to confess – and I'm not the only guilty one in this – that actors check their scenes first, ignoring the rest of the plot. But this script I read right through at one sitting, as you couldn't put it down. Perfection of a screenplay. I gathered that six well-known actors, suitable to play the lead, had turned it down, as the abortion scene was the deciding factor. Film actors, sensitive to their audiences, couldn't imagine recovering from the callous lothario image of *Alfie*, but Michael Caine, to his eternal credit, thought differently and took the part.

All set to film at Twickenham, Dennis had a call from Lewis Gilbert, who, always a gentleman, was deeply apologetic. "Since casting Graham," he explained, "we have cast Vivien Merchant to play his errant wife and, frankly, Graham looks too young." Naturally, Dennis and I accepted the situation, and they recast with Alfie Bass. Three days later, Lewis spoke to Dennis again. "Both you and Graham behaved so well about the recasting that we have had another and, I think, better thought. We would now like Graham to play the part of Humphrey the bus conductor, who finally marries Alfie's girlfriend and becomes stepfather to Alfie's son." Two weeks later, we started shooting.

It was on my third day of filming that the large, black limousine brought Shelley Winters onto the set. Well, strictly speaking, it brought Shelley Winters to a small, delightful churchyard on the banks of the Thames where we were filming the sequence in which Michael Caine discovers that I, the timid little bus conductor, has become the stepfather to his son. We'd already shot the dramatic scene in which Alfie, looking through the churchyard gates, sees me catch hold of his little son, saying, "Come to Daddy." Then it was lunchtime and Michael, myself, Julia Foster (playing the mother of the little boy) and director Lewis Gilbert sat around the table out of doors, overlooking the river, while the film caterers set out to make sure we all gained a lot of weight while we were filming.

Trying to summon up resistance to the delicious food, we watched as the large car disgorged the equally delicious Shelley Winters. Florid, oozing with sex and with a non-stop stream of Hollywood anecdotes, the lady proved an incredible lunchtime companion. What *Marlon Brando* had said… What *Burt Lancaster* had said…and done! The magical gossip poured out in an apparently endless stream. The food lay untouched as we all sat, open-mouthed, while the nothing-sacred scandal erupted. Then it all switched. Marriage, that all-important part of woman's life, took over. "I married Vittorio and I made the best spaghetti in Italy, and what good did it do me?" she appealed to all of us. The reference to her husband, Vittorio Gassman, one of Italy's biggest film stars, was sobering. During the delights of the Hollywood scandals, the words "Really?" and "What happened next?" came easily from us, but now marital discord was a damper. The more sympathetic "Ooh!" was in the forefront. There was a lot of dramatic arm-waving and curl-tossing, and her glossy lips parted as she went on dramatically. "Ladling spaghetti onto dining-room plates. I mean, *where's the romance in that?!*" Michael got a fit of coughing and suddenly became intently interested in a passing barge and Lewis busily started to make notes on his paper napkin while Julia made small whimpering noises. I carefully avoided her eyes, as I well knew what a terrible giggler she was.

Lewis finalised his notes on the napkin, then looked at Shelley. "The car," he indicated, "is ready to take you to the studio for your clothes fitting. We start shooting you tomorrow." She waved regally from the car window as it glided away. Lewis watched as it disappeared, then turned to Michael. "You do realise that there is a *very* unhappy lady. Unloved, apparently unwanted and *deeply* frustrated. This is not the state I wish her to be in. Therefore, Michael, it will be up to you. After all, the film comes first." His face had taken on a suitable solemn mien. "Naturally, Shelley, as befits a star, will be given a luxurious caravan on the set. Each day, I hope to see that caravan rocking on its springs." He paused for effect. "Quite vigorously!"

Michael took the bait and leaned close to Lewis, his finger stabbing at the director's chest. "Just you show me," he said, "just you show me where in my contract it says I have to keep my fellow female artistes happy and—" his pause for effect was just as telling as Lewis' "—satisfied!"

Julia wasn't whimpering any more. Now it was a full-blown cackle. I buried my head into the table with a lot of shoulder heaving while Lewis had a severe attack of coughing behind the paper napkin. Suddenly, Michael twigged and threw his head back, the sunlight catching the heavy horn-rimmed glasses. He looked at Lewis. "You rotten, horrible bastard, you! Had me going there, didn't you? Mind you, if I catch you havin' a bit of a smirk while Shelley and me are doing that scene in the bedroom with those mirrors on the ceiling, I'm walking off."

Well, he didn't walk off, and the film was an absolute smash. All the *Alfie* girls, including Shelley, were delightful. Strangely enough, some years later, Michael gave a very funny performance as a film star in the picture *Sweet Liberty*, and during one sequence the director had him disappear into a caravan with a pretty girl. The caravan then rocked steadily during the rest of the scene.

I took a picture of Michael sitting on the steps of the lovely little church we used. It's slightly wistful and, I think, the perfect picture of him as Alfie. Sadly, the architectural gem that he's sitting in front of now has the largest and most bizarre building in London stuck up behind it. God rot the planners, I say.

As a bus conductor, I had a long scene in the picture with Julia on my bus and, with the movie-maker's attention to detail, we used a real bus, with several rows of seats downstairs taken out to give room for the lights and camera. We started off on the Embankment, then up and down the King's Road, Chelsea, while I was acting away, conducting the bus at the same time. I'd had an expert to give me all the correct procedures. Apparently, there are certain rings you can give which make the driver keep going no matter what, and I should have used a few of them along the King's Road. Every time we pulled up, people tried to get on the bus, no matter that there was a huge camera, lots of lights and a film crew on board. One man kept saying, "I want to go to Highgate," and threatened to stay on the bus until we took him there.

There was a sad, and nostalgic, sequel to the film. The première was held at the Plaza, at the top of the Lower Regent Street, and as soon as Michael Caine looked at the camera, saying, "I suppose you think you're going to see the bleedin' titles now," getting a huge laugh, we knew we had a big hit. It was a tremendous success and the film company had laid on a party across the road. Apart from Michael, it had been an episodic film, none of us meeting each other until the première. Vivien Merchant, with her (then-)husband, Harold Pinter, raised a glass to me and said, "I always wanted to meet you again." I looked blank because as far as I knew we had never met. She gave a smile and said, "We were both pupils at Shelagh Elliott Clarke's dancing school in Liverpool. You were a bit of a star, won a few medals. I was a lot younger – I was only twelve and got bullied by the other girls, and you always used to stop them. So now I can say thank you." She got an Academy Award nomination for her performance in the film. Sadly, and very tragically, she later committed suicide.

Alfie was shot at Twickenham, one of the smaller studios. I've managed to film at most of the others, but I do have a particular love for Pinewood – the English countryside at its best location, with gardens to take your breath away, a magnificent dining room (very high on an actor's priorities) and the studios themselves were second to none. It was there that my fateful lunch with Sean Connery took place. The unbelievably publicised film sequence from *Goldfinger* was being shot there, in which a nude Shirley Eaton was to be painted with gold. Even today, it's still a great news story, and I remember how Sean invited me onto the James Bond set, where he and I very solemnly discussed with Shirley which part of the body they would not paint, as naturally we all knew that a small area of skin should be left ungilded. Wearing an all-white tropical uniform for my part in *Guns At Batasi* (which was being filmed at the same time), I asked Shirley to give me a big hug so the rest of the studio would know, by the circles of gold on my uniform, that Miss Eaton and I had been romantically involved.

The real success of Pinewood was that magnificent oak-panelled dining room, which gave the studio such a country-club atmosphere, with its complete wall of huge windows looking out onto the beautiful gardens. It was in that dining room that I first met Sidney Poitier and, if ever an actor was an ambassador for his race, Sidney has got to head the list of candidates. The troubled history of films regarding black actors goes back many years. We shudder nowadays when we watch Tarzan films flickering across our TV screens and see the resident black actors of Hollywood rushing out of grass huts to threaten the oh-so-beautifully dressed and coiffeured heroines who accompanied the great white hunters into the African bush. Carefully chosen, with their long blonde hair, they acted as a suitable contrast to the black, evil tribesmen. And the gleaming silver trains that ran across America throughout the '30s – glamorous and pristine, they were all, without exception, staffed with jovial, comical, not-too-bright intellectually, black actors who busied themselves getting the sleepers ready, serving trays of food or telling everybody, "This here is Pennsylvania Station." A few achieved near-stardom with their comical ineptitude. Stephan Fetchit, rolling his eyes in mock horror, almost stole the picture from Bob Hope and Paulette Goddard in *The Ghost Breakers*, but seeing his performance today is to flinch with embarrassment.

Then came the film *The Blackboard Jungle*. This worldwide smash made audiences itch to jump up and jitterbug in the aisles as, behind the credits, 'Rock Around The Clock' blasted from the soundtrack. Film distributors knew they had a winner, so they carefully notched up the volume at every screening. Bill Haley's records sold in their millions, but the greatest impact was Poitier, as one could feel audiences almost cheer as his character, seemingly villainous, looked at Vic Morrow and said, "Don't call me boy." Those few words sounded the death knell of the coloured man's subservience in the cinema, and it came at precisely the right time. From then on, black actors came into their own, and leading the movement was Sidney. In the dining room, I took courage and asked for a picture, and without a demur he flashed a smile and off we went for a tour round the lot. He gave up the rest of his lunch hour and, mainly because of that, the results were very good. Following my standard routine, I presented him with a set of twelve-by-ten prints and, three years later, at the very same studio, a hand descended on my shoulder. Sidney gave a smile and told me the pictures were permanently displayed on his mother's piano, and woe betide anyone who tried to move them.

The Tartar blood, or whatever, gave Yul Brynner a fearsome appearance, and rumours that he was difficult were rife. Mind you, the film world has only been too happy to spread the bad word about any actor, but the studios in the late '60s were full of gossip concerning the small – one would have thought insignificant – matter of the film seat that Yul Brynner had designed for himself. The really important status symbol for the film actor has always been the canvas-backed folding chair that is placed on the film set on the first day of shooting with his or her name boldly stencilled in black across the canvas. The stencilled name was the recognition that the actor in question had reached a certain status. Needless to say, in the bizarre world of the cinema it was then necessary for the actor to make quite sure that he or she was never seen actually *to sit in* that chair – such behaviour is far too subtle to inquire into, but it existed; it was considered sufficient that the chair was on view for the world to see. Absolutely in tune with the flamboyant image that Brynner displayed (in the large dining room at the studio, you could spot the shaven head at 100 yards), he apparently did not accept the film seat cliché. Going from the sublime to the extremely ridiculous, he had one made with very long legs, with leather replacing the grey canvas, and the lettering on the leather was gold. Seated on top of this chair, Brynner was able to view the world from on high.

Working at the studio myself on *Finders Keepers*, I wandered onto the set of *The Double Man* (the film Brynner was making at the time) and, with a photograph of him in mind, I was prepared to dare all. Fortunately, Britt Ekland was only too happy to introduce us (our friendship dated back to the time when I was best man at her marriage to Peter Sellers). Co-starring in the film with Brynner, she gazed up at him (he really was that high up) and spoke in her delightful Swedish accent: "Graham has shot some *beautiful* pictures of me, Yul. You really must let him expose himself!"

He made the descent, gave a smile and assured me that now was the time. "They don't need me for half an hour," he said. "We'll go out on the back lot and give you a chance to expose yourself!"

When it came to my shooting him, it was really very easy, mainly due to our shared passion for photography. The camera I was using at the time, a Linhof Technica Mk IV, was a glorious riot of levers, cams, chromium plate, a matching set of three lenses plus a magnificent roll-film holder, all made to a standard that was awesome. To add to this, it was housed in a very large hammered-metal case lined with red plush which was enough to make a camera fanatic go weak at the knees – which is exactly what happened to Yul. I told him of the history of this extraordinary camera. Peter Sellers had presented it to me as I had made an LP some months earlier with him and, not wishing to discuss the sordid matter of a fee, he had seen the outfit in the window of a celebrated camera shop in Baker Street and reasoned that it was the perfect fee. The sight of the camera alone was enough to satisfy Yul that I knew what I was doing, and he gave the exact look I wanted. Some years later, Kodak showed an exhibition of my photographs, and the head printer (in charge of all the enlargements) made a point of asking about this picture, as it had such amazing definition. Regarding Brynner's fearsome reputation, I can only say that he was – to quote Mel Brooks' description of Shakespeare on one of his comedy records – a little pussy cat. The picture is a nice memory of a very patient sitter. Well, actually he was standing up.

The film I was working on at the end of the '60s was filmed on the back lot at Pinewood. This area of land at the rear of the studio was not built on, in the permanent sense, but rearing up were many exotic constructions, ranging from World War I villages, castles in Bavaria, chateaux on the Loire and an odd section of some Balkan railway station complete with half a train. Eventually, the huge 007 building was constructed there to house an enormous submarine set for a Bond film. The set I worked on was a reconstruction of a Spanish village, and it was in this village that I made a film with Peter Pan. Well, I am exaggerating – in fact, it was with Cliff Richard.

Everyone wants it. Glossy adverts in every woman's magazine promise it, if you're willing to spend large amounts of money to buy minuscule tubes of cream. Various white-coated gentlemen found in obscure clinics in Switzerland flourish hypodermic needles telling you that this is the panacea. Videos by their hundreds of thousands, starring leotard-clad film stars putting octopuses to shame with their gyrations, are avidly watched by devotees prepared to give their all in pursuit of it.

Eternal youth! Marlowe knew that he was on a winner when he wrote *Faust,* and the thought of beating the ravages of time has always been on the human mind. Agelessness fascinates, and who better to illustrate this phenomenon than Sir Cliff, as he has now become? One can only imagine that, at the moment of this accolade, as Her Majesty tapped both of his shoulders, she might well have been tempted to lean a little closer and ask, "How do you do it?" – referring, of course, to the secret of Cliff's eternal youth. Place any recent shot of Cliff next to a picture of him I took some 35 years ago on the set of the film *Finders Keepers* and you won't really see that much difference.

The plot of the film was something preposterous about losing an atom bomb. Robert Morley and I were cast as the two comedy villains, as we were facsimiles of Laurel and Hardy, certainly when it came to size. I darted about like an animated doll while Robert serenely sailed through the film like a galleon in full sail. There was a slight tetchiness, however, as we were both hoisted, separately, high in the air for some comedy effect. Both wearing our Kirby harnesses (onto which the cable to hoist you is attached) and dressed as angels, we circled slowly some 20 feet above the studio floor and, as we gracefully glided past each other, Robert gave me a look. "Can somebody tell me," he said, "why there are *three* men holding my rope, but only *one* holding yours?" A very witty man, he looked at me one day and idly said, "Laurence Olivier doesn't like me very much. Unfortunately, what I said about his Othello got back to him. I merely remarked that all his performance needed was the white gloves."

Beneath this veneer of apparent cynicism, there was a very feeling and generous personality. At the end of the film, quite by chance, I had to talk to the accountant on some matter and he told me that the wife of one of the crew members had been very ill. Robert had given a considerable sum of money anonymously to the accountant, merely asking that it should reach her safely and that Robert's name was never to be mentioned.

During the filming I had idly mentioned that, before the war, I had once made a fleeing appearance as a bellboy in a production of *Dodsworth* at the Palace Theatre in London which starred his mother-in-law, the glamorous Gladys Cooper. Robert smiled benignly, recounting how, even at this late age, she was partial to diving off yachts in the Mediterranean and swimming to the shore. A few nights later, after shooting had finished, he appeared at my dressing-room door attired in black tie and dinner jacket. "Got to fill in time waiting for my dinner date. Join me in the bar?"

The bar at Pinewood, also wood-panelled (like the dining room), had the same gentlemen's club aura, and as we sipped our drinks Robert and I saw the room full of cameramen, technicians and actors all slowly swivel their heads, looking to the door. There, framed as in a film shot, stood Gladys Cooper, done up to the nines. Still incredibly glamorous, she moved slowly towards us, and I swear I saw most of the men in the room get to their feet in tribute. Duly kissing her affectionately on the cheek, Robert turned to introduce us and then paused. "But you two already know each other." To the bewildered lady, I explained that I had been a non-speaking pageboy in a play with her many years ago, and that her son-in-law was being beastly.

11 That Comes Direct From Buckingham Palace

Meanwhile, at another studio (Shepperton), the monster picture of 1966 was being made. It didn't have Baron Frankenstein or the Wolfman, and there certainly wasn't a stake being driven into the heart of Count Dracula, but what it did have were five directors, an enormous budget, dozens of stars and a script that was, literally, concocted on the set. *Casino Royale* was the epitome of all that was wrong with the film industry, and yet the talent was there; there was just too much of it and seemingly there was no control. Peter Sellers was playing one of the Bonds (I think there were five of them) and, knowing my love of photography, he suggested that I not only appear in the film but also bring a camera to the set with me. There were, he assured me, many delightful and voluptuous creatures that I might care to photograph. He was absolutely right, of course, as in the casino sequence Orson Welles wafted about, surrounded by 50 beautiful girls. However, none of these distracted me from the vision of one of the most photogenic creatures I had ever set my eyes on.

In a long grey dress trimmed with white arctic fox was Ursula Andress. To make matters even more delightful, the brief scene I had in the film also included her. A tentative cough, and then I launched into my standard "May I take your photograph?" appeal.

Delightful lady though she was, her reaction was not quite what I had hoped for: "Yais." the voice was as seductive as the face… "Yais. That would be vairy nice." The mood was of cold porridge.

Realising that this was not to be my moment, I had half turned away when Peter came to my aid. "Urst," he exclaimed (the familiarity of the greeting was enough to soften the heart of any reluctant poser), "my friend Graham is extremely adept with a camera. He is, in fact, a bit of a whizz when it comes to picture-taking."

I can only presume that these delightfully old-fashioned compliments did the trick, as she duly posed for me. Two days later, after an evening in the darkroom, I gave her a set of twelve-by-ten prints and she was delighted. "I shall geev thees to my mozzair!" What higher compliment can you get? Your subject tells you that your pictures will be displayed in your parent's home. I could only hope they got a reaction similar to that of Sidney Poitier's mother.

Looking slightly shamefaced, she felt that Peter and I deserved an explanation for her reluctance to pose. "The trouble iz wiz my teets!" The statement was firm and not to be argued with. Peter and I immediately assured her that, if there was a department she need have no troubles with, that was it, but she persisted. "The trouble ees definitely weez my teets. You notice I am wearing the low-cut dress, yais?" We told her we had not been looking in that direction but, now that she'd come to mention it, possibly we had become aware of it. "I bend over to put out my cigarette like so," she demonstrated, "and you see 'ow my dress falls away from my body, yais?"

Peter nodded gravely. "Gra and I see just what you mean, Urst." Now Ursula dramatically acted out the whole story.

"Over zair", her finger pointed into the middle distance, "eez a naughty photographer, hiding behind the scenery. Thees naughty photographer, 'e 'as the lonk lens."

Peter looked baffled. "Long lens," I translated.

"Thees feelthy swine," Ursula went on. "'E wait until I bend forward, then, cleek!, 'e takes the snap. A week later, I open a magazine and there, in ze middle pages, are my teets." The perfect description of the way in which the paparazzi get their intrusive pictures. Well, I didn't have a lonk lens, nor was I hiding behind any scenery, but if there is a more elegantly seductive and delicious picture of Ursula Andress anywhere about, I'd like to see it.

During filming, I sat for a while at a table with Tracy Reed, daughter of Sir Carol, when Orson Welles joined us, and for once I lost my nerve. There was just not enough iron in the backbone to make me ask if I could take a photograph of him, a lack of fortitude I have regretted ever since. He talked to Tracy about her father, who had directed him in *The Third Man*, and then looked at the hysteria on the set and said, "I could make a whole film for what this scene is costing." He sat playing patience, neatly arranging the cards in rows, occasionally exhibiting a little sleight of hand and a few magic tricks to delight the extras. An excitable young man kept passing flimsy pages of script out of the door of a caravan parked on the set. I got one of them. "You and Peter Sellers will be *so* wonderful in this scene." Politely, it was given back.

Welles' answer was more direct. Passed some of the sheets of script, he rolled them into balls, made a few quick passes with his hands, said, "Hey presto," and they vanished.

One of the great perks or bonuses, call them what you will, about the acting profession are the foreign climes you get taken to while filming. The cinema industry went location-mad in the mid '60s and yet, of all the exotic places that I've been lucky enough to get to, Dublin has to be one of my favourites. I have bathed off the shores of Mauritius, been scuba-diving in Florida and waterskied in the south of France, but I have to say that, for sheer unadulterated enjoyment, filming in Ireland is very hard to beat.

The reason is simple. It isn't the weather, as whatever rain doesn't fall on Britain soon drifts across the Irish Sea and dumps itself on Dublin; it's the people. They are, of course, all pixies and, having been brought up on Merseyside, I naturally have an affinity with them. My very first day in Dublin took me to a large store purely to buy an old-fashioned tin of boot polish, and the lady behind the counter, all four foot ten of her, was immediately concerned. "Oh, God help us," she said. "A fine-lookin' gentleman like yourself havin' to black his own shoes! Never mind, this is the best tin we have in the place. Now," she gave a glance to my feet, "you'll be wantin' some brushes to put it on with." Without pause, I was pulled down several aisles to another midget assistant. "Lovely young fella here," my mentor said. "Get him the best brushes you have there." They were put on the counter and once more I was pulled to yet another counter. Just as I thought I had entered the land of the Munchkins, I found that the next lady was of normal height. She was given her instructions. "The finest yellow duster you have, if you please. I want his shoes like a mirror." No matter that it should have been dealt with at one counter; this was Ireland. And matters got more joyous as the days went by.

The film was a very comic script (by Dave Freeman) of Jules Verne's *Rocket To The Moon* and was set in Victorian days. The streets and surrounding countryside were a perfect setting for the picture, and we soon settled into that delightful routine of filming all day and eating most of the evening. At my hotel – the Gresham, an ornate building on O'Connell Street – another pixie, this time a male waiter, peered around a pillar at me: "Is it one of the golfin' tycoons you are, from the Americas?"

I gathered that he was referring to the Bing Crosby golf tournament that was being played that week in the city, and I was about to assure him that I was no sportsman when another leprechaun waiter popped out from the other side of the pillar. He pointed at me firmly. "He's a fillum star, that's what he is. A fillum star!"

The first leprechaun gave me an X-ray eye. "I've been goin' to the pitchers every week for the past 30 years and I've never seen him."

It was open war. The voices were loud and very clear. The second waiter prodded me in the arm. "Go on," he said. "Tell him all the fillums you've been in, go on."

I rose from the table, looked at them both and said, "I do not intend giving an audition during dinner." Trying to keep my dignity, I went up to my room.

The reference to Bing Crosby was very apt, as the next morning I found myself sitting next to him. Having a day off, and reading his newspaper in the lobby, I heard him say, "Naturally, Father, I would like to help but I am committed in so many other areas." The deep voice was unmistakable and he sat in the next armchair, being very charming and evasive to a priest in his robes who was (to use the modern parlance) putting the bite on him. However sophisticated, however long the list of showbusiness people you may have met, sitting next to the dean of 20th-century popular music made one pause. How many times had I sung (still changing key, of course) 'Love In Bloom' and 'Moonlight Becomes You' in the bath?

Then lightning struck twice. The Irish publicity man on our film bore down on me and frantically whispered in my ear. "Up you get," he said. "Up you get and shake the hand of the greatest." With that I was taken across the lobby to meet the champion of champions, Joe Louis, who was over in Ireland for some publicity, and our publicist made sure everyone on the film met him. A big, shambling man, he good-naturedly took my hand in his huge fist, gave it a gentle shake, dutifully said, "Hi," and then retreated back into his placid shell. Crosby and Joe Louis in one morning was really too much.

It is a tradition that, at the end of every film, you always handsomely reward your stand-in, because this is the gentleman who stoically deputises for you while the lights are adjusted and fetches your tea to save you having to queue. And of course it could only happen in Ireland – at the end of filming, my stand-in gave *me* a present, a £1 Irish Sweepstake ticket with a note of thanks for our time together. It didn't win, of course, but I kept the note.

While we were filming in Dublin, the tragedy of Aberfan took place and worldwide headlines told of over 100 children being buried alive in cascading mud from a slagheap in Wales. Every actor, technician and member of the stage staff in Dublin instantly gave their services free for a charity show at the Gaiety Theatre in aid of an Aberfan fund and raised a great deal of money.

Perhaps because they, too, live in a totally artificial world, the royal family has always been fascinated by showbusiness. It was once called "the theatre", but the moment the industry escalated in the post-war world the word "business" was tacked onto it, and even that has now been abbreviated to "showbiz", while royals have been abbreviated to "the Windsors". Once a year, the prestige of the Royal Command Performance brought every famous theatrical onto a stage in London in aid of charity and at the end they all joined together to give hurrahs for the King and Queen sitting in the royal box.

Nowadays, a few too many scandals have dampened down the awe and respect, but in the '60s Princess Margaret still excited a lot of interest. I met her a few times and realised, quite early on, that she was in the wrong job. Forget the parading on the balcony at Buckingham Palace, for she really should have been playing comedy sketches in a West End theatre, and I told her so. "Darling," I said. "You should be in the business." In case there are people who think this story might be an exaggeration, I can assure you that the next morning she reported it over the telephone to Peter Sellers, adding that she was delighted at the compliment, as well as at being called "darling". And, of course, you couldn't keep her off a film set.

If ever there was a bizarre film, with almost certain box-office failure at the end of the day, it was *The Magic Christian*, which Peter Sellers set up at the end of the '60s. To cast every part with a famous face, as with *Casino Royale*, would almost certainly mean disaster. The film started shooting. Raquel Welch twirled about in a fantasy sequence, lashing a long whip at topless ladies acting as galley slaves; Ringo Starr ambled amiably through his part; Yul Brynner sang 'Mad About The Boy' dressed as a woman; I played an unctuous waiter; while Princess Margaret watched from behind camera. (Well, actually she was in front of the camera, just below the lens.) In a restaurant scene, director Joe McGrath decided that I should back towards camera in a suitably servile crouch. "But who," said Joe, "will see that he doesn't bang into the camera?"

The voice was high, shrill and very excited. "I'll do it," said Princess Margaret. "I'll stop him. Honest, I will!"

The clapperboard marked the start of the scene, Joe said action and I backed straight into Princess Margaret, sitting well and truly on her lap. She looked quite smug as I said, "I told you you should be in the business." I felt it would be a bit to much to add "darling".

I don't know if I can put a cap on the rumours – which are still being peddled to the press – about Princess Margaret and Peter. It's got to the stage where we are now being given details of where the alleged coupling actually took place, and the settee in the lounge of Kensington Palace seems to be favourite. Why they never bothered with the bed hasn't been mentioned. The simple truth is that Peter was an extraordinary sexual fantasist and was very partial to naming ladies with whom, according to him, he had had sexual relations. There are only two people in the world (we presume there were no spectators) who can say whether Peter and Margaret had an affair. Sadly, both of them are no longer alive and able to enlighten us.

Then it was time to roll up the sleeves in earnest, as I was busy buying a new home to give space to the two children joining Christopher. Julia was born in early 1969 and Timothy followed in late 1970. Before moving house, strict instructions were given to our current au pair – a sweet and charming Brazilian lady who delighted me by bringing with her an LP of genuine sambas – that, on every shopping trip, cardboard boxes must be collected. Gradually, our double garage filled with boxes of all sizes and finally, giving her a large felt pen, she was told to start packing all the small items in the house and to label the box they went into. I explained that this would save hours of time when we unpacked. Only days after our move, the Brazilian girl, her mother ill, had to return home, and I was then faced with a mountain of boxes – all carefully labelled in Portuguese.

Flying back from Copenhagen in 1970, after filming *A Day On The Beach* with Peter Sellers (produced by Roman Polanski), I bought a model fire engine at the airport for my son Christopher that gave me an idea for a half-hour film. The production company Hemdale backed it, and it turned out to be more successful than we had ever hoped. The film was called *Simon Simon*, and the real star was a Simon Snorkel hoist, nicknamed "the cherry-picker" by all the television crews who use it. It can be seen at every television golf tournament, towering above the crowds like a spindly giraffe, a camera in its top basket. It lent itself to lots of film jokes. But also, the reason for the film's success was a lot to do with all of the actor friends who appeared in the film as a favour to me. Going to dinner with Michael Caine, I had an idea for a joke for him, and without a second's pause he said, "I'll do it." Then came Peter Sellers, Morecambe and Wise, Bob Monkhouse, David Hemmings and, of course, the lady I had played opposite in *Alfie*, Julia Foster.

Suddenly, I was told I was flying to the San Sebastian Film Festival at the invitation of the British Film Institute, as *Simon Simon* had been selected as the British entry in the short film competition. San Sebastian, the jewel of the north coast of Spain, was a demi-paradise, as far as I was concerned, as the hotel, the Maria Cristina, was five-star and located a mere 100 yards from the Palicio del Festival, the cinema where all the films in the competition were to be screened. A few languorous days at the swimming club, and a new film screened every night – paradise! Then came the day when, for the first time, my film would be flickering across the giant screen. It would be screened as a support to a major film, and tradition demanded that I had to sit alongside the other director in the royal box at the theatre. Until this moment the film had never been publicly shown, and I had nightmares of fiery Spaniards, unafraid of showing their emotions, hurling abuse at the screen. However, I was a Britisher in a foreign clime, so nobly I prepared to face what could be hostile natives by doing what all Englishmen do in moments of crisis. I laid out my dinner jacket on the bed.

At the time, I had a rather annoying physical complaint called athlete's foot and was using an extremely powerful fungicide powder to deal with it effectively. Having carefully shaved and showered, I liberally dusted myself with some incredible woman-alluring talc (so the adverts told me), applied the fungicide to the feet, slipped into my little black number and left for the cinema. As I said, it was only 100 yards from the hotel and, in San Sebastian Festival tradition, an escort of Basque men stood on the entrance steps, holding an archway of curved swords for you to walk under as you climbed to the foyer. It was precisely as I was passing under this span of steel that I realised that, owing to the emotional stress of the first screening of my film, I had made a simple but, as it turned out, extremely serious error. The so-called sexually alluring talc had gone onto the feet, while the fungicide had been well and truly sprinkled onto the body, including the genital area.

I presume the swordsmen thought my sudden, strange, crouching movements were something to do with my being scared of their unsheathed swords. As the hot, burning pain began to really strike I hobbled, crab-like, across the foyer. The royal box was framed with florid gilt, set in the very middle of the horseshoe-shaped dress circle, and to make completely sure it was the centre of attention two spotlights shone down into it, thus highlighting my impression of Charles Laughton as the Hunchback of Notre Dame. Glauber Rocha, the distinguished Spanish director, whose film *Cabezas Cortadas* was the main feature that night, was too much of a gentleman to query my peculiar entrance. Too much of a gentleman, also, to question why, having acknowledged the applause, I sat in my gilt chair and kept continually crossing my legs.

I somehow managed to sit through the 31 minutes of *Simon Simon* (thank God I hadn't made *Gone With The Wind*) and eventually the lights went up. Señor Rocha applauded and so, fortunately, did the large audience. Nodding my thanks, I stumbled to my feet, muttering, "Lavabos" to all and sundry. I'm sure Señor Rocha thought I was uncivil and rude to leave the moment my film was over, but that's life. Thank God the arch of swords was gone, and I made some sort of record 100-yard dash back to the hotel and the sanctuary of my bathroom. Fortunately, a Spanish plumber had installed a very efficient flexible shower unit at the end of the bath and the cool spray made life bearable again. Should Señor Rocha ever read this confession, he will realise that the mad Englishman meant no insult.

Following the selection of my film for San Sebastian, I got a call to Wardour Street, home of the major British film companies. Had I an idea for a film – not too expensive, of course – with lots of comedians and saucy girls? The phrase "saucy girls" was actually used, but brushing this aside I assured the gentleman I would come up with something. "I've got the rights to *The Seven Deadly Sins*," he said.

Dave Freeman, my staunch scriptwriter friend, told me to go back in and tell him, "I'd like to make *The Magnificent Seven Deadly Sins*."

I did, and he said, "Here's the contract."

The most important person on a film is the one with the least romantic title – production manager. In the early '70s, back at Pinewood Studios and making my first feature film, I met the gentleman who was to be production manager, Jack Causey, who had a habit that became very endearing to me. A dyed-in-the-wool professional, he thought only of films. Dedication to the industry was his whole life and his language mirrored it. Everything as far as Jack was concerned was in film parlance. A waiter only had to hover somewhere to the left and he was referred to as being "edge-of-frame governor" ("governor" was the title he bestowed upon you the moment you were appointed director of the film). He was a walking lexicon on any subject you could think of and possessed a placidity that was never disturbed or ruffled. At times you were tempted to ask the impossible just to see if the mask could ever be disturbed, but there was really no need, as the impossible was always being asked of Jack.

Then came the day that was surely sent to test him. The script section of "Avarice" starred Bruce Forsyth as a chauffeur hunting through the sewers of London for his Scrooge-like employer who had inadvertently dropped a 50-pence piece through a grating in the gutter. Jack glanced through this piece of script, then faced me with the immutable face of a never-to-be-surprised jack of all trades. The merest lift of an eyebrow as he spoke. "May I know what your wishes are regarding this sequence?"

I gave him the answer in language I knew he would understand. "*The Third Man*," I informed him.

Jack acknowledged the shorthand film parlance by the briefest incline of his head. "Just south of Vauxhall Bridge," he said. "I'll talk to Mr Peabody in the morning." By this time, the fact that Jack was quite capable of walking on water, procuring 25 elephants within the hour and making quite certain that a blanket of fog six feet thick could smother Hampstead Heath overnight was becoming the norm, so without further inquiry I was "just south of Vauxhall Bridge" the next morning, waiting for Jack.

Large wooden doors with a smaller door inset faced us, and on them in large but faded letters were the words "London Water Board". The bell was pressed, the small door opened, and we were in the company of Mr Peabody, a slight and courteous gentleman who listened politely as Jack introduced us, explained I was the director, and that we needed to reproduce, if that was possible, the cavernous underground sewers depicted in *The Third Man*. At once regarding me as a simpleton of limited intelligence, an attitude that most people adopt when meeting people in showbusiness, he ushered us into a small room, where hung many pairs of gigantic rubber waders. "If you would be so kind," he indicated and, after a certain amount of struggling, Jack and I were clumping about like deep-sea divers while safety helmets were given to us. Finally, a very broad, thick, webbing belt was pulled tight around our waists. Three large steel hoops were spaced round the belts and Mr Peabody carefully pulled at each one obviously, checking their strength. A questioning flicker passed across Jack's face, so Mr Peabody felt he should reassure us.

"Down there," he pointed at the floor beneath us, "you will be accompanied by myself and one of my staff and he will be carrying this." Realising he had a totally captive audience, there was just a touch of theatricality as he produced a long, thick pole, at the end of which was a large steel hook. "Should, and I repeat only should you be unfortunate enough to fall in, the gentleman accompanying you will be able to place this hook into one of these rings, thereby enabling him to pull you out!" A momentary thought of Orson Welles being put into one of these flashed through my mind as we were led to a metal ladder that disappeared into the damp, warm, misty darkness below.

The curved roof of the sewer was gargantuan. Like a gigantic brickwork worm, it curved away in the darkness on either side of us. The wide, sloping concrete floor had a trough in its centre through which a rivulet of murky, brown water slowed moved, and a few lights gave us the chance to see what was necessary. At a conservative estimate, it would have required about 50 giant arc lights to enable us to film down there, but any doubts we might have had about its suitability were settled for us by Mr Peabody.

Still in his best guide mode, he proudly stood in the centre of his glorious sewer, and gave a cautionary wag of a finger. "If you *were* to film down here, my assistant would be with you at all times, and," his pauses really were of the highest standard, "should he tell you to get out, get out! Do not try to move any lights or equipment, do not worry about the cameras. *Get up that ladder straight away!*" His figure stiffened and his diction became more precise. "Should there be a cloudburst in north London, it comes through here as a solid wall at 80 miles an hour."

It really didn't need Jack and I to dwell on what was going to come through that huge sewer at 80 miles an hour, and a terrifying picture of our lamps, equipment and (God forbid) a few members of the cast being swept under London faster than the speed limit settled matters. It would have to be shot in a set at the studios. Politely we thanked Mr Peabody for all his

Sammy Davis. *Salt And Pepper*. Shepperton Studios, 1968

"Are you sure Howard Hughes isn't paying for this?" Albert Finney, St Tropez, 1969

HRH Princess Margaret on the set of *The Magic Christian*, 1969

Tom Jones. ATV, 1970

Ringo Starr and the first Mrs Starr. *The Magic Christian*. Twickenham Studios, 1970

"Now, Michael, if you want to be a film actor, this is what you've got to do!" Directing Michael Caine in *Simon Simon* while being watched by Norman Rossington and Dennis Selinger. London, 1970

Roger Moore, the original naughty boy of British films, helped the atmosphere of *The Magnificent Seven Deadly Sins* by dressing up as a silent-film director and coming onto the set on the first day to show me exactly where to put the camera. Pinewood Studios, 1971

"Beautiful baby!" Teaching Bob Guccione how to take a photograph. *The Magnificent Seven Deadly Sins*. Pinewood Studios, 1971

"I'm playing the right notes. Not necessarily in the right order!" Eric Morcambe, Ernie Wise and André Previn. BBC TV, 1971

Bruce Forsyth and Frankie Howerd. *The Generation Game*. BBC TV, 1972

The Very Sound Jonathan Miller, London, 2003

Michael Caine at home, 1973

Pepe. *The Return Of The Pink Panther*. Morocco, 1974

Christopher Plummer doing more damage to my fingers. *The Return Of The Pink Panther*. Morocco, 1974

Christopher Plummer and Blake Edwards. Morocco, 1974

Julie Andrews. Casablanca. Morocco, 1974

"Tell me, Franco, what happens eef ee gives a signal?" Director Franco Rossi and actor Vittorio Gassman. *Virginity*. Rome, 1974

Spike Milligan. WH Smith advert, 1975

Charlton Heston as Henry VIII. *The Prince And The Pauper*. Pinewood
Studios, 1976

"Has he spoken to you yet?" Rex Harrison, *The Prince And The Pauper*.
Pinewood Studios, 1976

The inspector views the case. *The Pink Panther Strikes Again*. Munich, 1976

The trusty Hasselblad about to capture the beauty of Ludwig's fairytale castle.
Hohenschwangau, Bavaria, 1976

Denholm Elliot. London, 1977

Tony Hagarth and myself in full post-mortem mood with mortuary assistant in *Let's Get Laid*, 1978

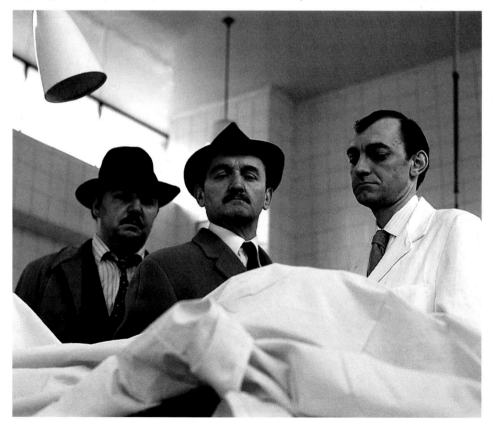

patience, but moving back to the ladder, and the fresher air above, Mr Peabody had his final moment of glory. We had passed several small tunnels that led into the main sewer when he paused by one. I don't think it was my imagination, but he seemed to be standing slightly at attention. "You do know where that comes from, don't you?" he said. My face was as mask-like as Jack's as we both shook our heads. Mr Peabody's voice had a note of pride. "Buckingham Palace!" he said.

12 Make Certain Your Cohorts Are Available

The sewers, with the expertise of Pinewood's set builders, were constructed at the studio, and in the "Avarice" sequence Bruce Forsyth gingerly walked down a large, brick-faced, hollow tube which gave the perfect illusion of subterranean London. *The Magnificent Seven Deadly Sins* had been scripted by seven different sets of writers, all of whom had done me proud. The proudest of all were Ray Galton and Alan Simpson, who years earlier, lying on their backs on the floor of their office in despair and bereft of inspiration for a Comedy Playhouse script, perked up when I gave them an idea. It was a true story of two motorists whose cars were locked, bonnet to bonnet, in a very narrow country lane. Neither would give way and eight hours later the police had to have them towed apart, and that very morning *The Times*, sensing a magnificent, eccentric, typically British story, featured it on their front page. Both Alan and Ray at once wrote it as a half-hour comedy and offered it to me as a gesture of thanks, but as I was already working I couldn't play it. Asked to contribute to the film, they gave me the script, free and gratis, and under the title "Pride", with Ian Carmichael and Alfie Bass playing the leads, it was one of the most successful episodes in the film.

But the tempo of shooting was horrendous. The powers that be, crouched permanently over the accounts books, constantly muttered dire threats about the cost of the film. This governed us all and, as we peered daily at the sky dreading dark clouds, or heard actors stumble on lines, our hearts sank. The first assistant director, a genius called Derek Cracknell, willed the crew to shoot at an incredible speed, and somehow we kept to schedule. Each sin had to be shot in a week and certain members of the crew suspected that satanic deals had been made, as the sun never stopped shining. Orson Welles' famous quote about directing a film, "the biggest toy train set a boy ever had", is basically true, as every decision, however minor, has to be made by the director, and were it not for the humbling experience of watching the so-called rushes (the film you shot the day before) every night, megalomania could easily set in. But those rushes soon brought you back down to earth. "Christ, why did we do that?" is the most-used phrase.

The most difficult aspect was switching myself from actor to director, and the casting sessions prior to the film weren't a lot of fun. Actors and actresses that I admired, some of them friends, would come into the office so I could give them what was basically an audition. But there was really no need to worry. As I was about to start this book, the *Independent* newspaper asked me to write an obituary for one of my oldest friends, Sir Harry Secombe. Then plain Harry, he was one of the first to be cast in the sequence "Envy", written by Dave Freeman, and what an example he was on the set! The last film he performed in before mine was *Oliver!*, directed by Sir Carol Reed, and Harry gave me just as much respect, just as much endeavour, as he did on that musical.

There was a technical problem on "Envy" which took some delicacy to overcome. I had cast June Whitfield, who had to spend some time in a bubble bath. The film company was hoping for a young curvaceous *femme fatale* to stretch herself provocatively through the foam, but it was June I wanted. Sadly, she wasn't too pleased about the small amount of bubbles, even though we'd provided her with a flesh-coloured bathing costume. The crew worked like mad in the small bathroom to protect her modesty. Finally, a tube connected to a cylinder of compressed air was used to blow a wall of foam around June. Obviously, the air pipe had to be in the bath, and because there was so little room (there was only the camera and myself) I was forced to kneel, my arm elbow-deep in hot water, holding the pipe between June's legs. Knowing the complaints she'd made about the foam, I dreaded to think what would happen if the pipe got away from me! It took a lot of extra time, but at least she couldn't say we hadn't tried.

Then we had another problem with a female body. *Penthouse* magazine – approximate circulation, 5,000,000; chief editor and founder, Bob Guccione; various staff, including a set of contributing editors, namely Kingsley Amis (drinks), Clement Freud (food), Stirling Moss (cars) and Graham Stark (cameras). This list gives you an idea of the quality that Bob Guccione poured into his brainchild. Naked ladies were spread across double pages (the staple always seemed to be in the navel area) and the magazine was dedicated to female flesh. Ladies viewed themselves in bathrooms and mirrors and lay provocatively across four-poster beds. Sometimes a finger would be placed sensuously on her lips while giving an innocent gaze at camera. The gentlemen readers were delighted, but Bob knew that there would have to be some editorial content as well, so the contributing editors were appointed.

Camera editor gave the most trouble. Kingsley Amis had no bother about the drinks, Stirling Moss could be taken seriously as motoring expert and Clement Freud did very well running up expenses in West End restaurants checking the menus. But *camera editor*! The appendage caused consternation wherever I went. Rib-nudging, pursed lips, "Oh, I say!" expressions. Vainly, I explained that I never got within a mile of those naked ladies – photographed in some secret studio, away from prying eyes, the nudes remained a secret available only to view by purchase of the magazine. My province remained the hardware of the photographic world. But it had its compensations. Leicas, Hasselblads, Minoltas, Canons, Pentaxes, Nikons – every day was Christmas Day as these exquisite pieces of machinery were delivered to my door for me to appraise and report on.

My children grew up with the noise of the clicking of shutters and my darkroom was continually in use, as film after film was developed there. I took it all very seriously and I'm glad to say Bob did seem to appreciate all my efforts. Finally, casting for the film arrived. The "Greed" sequence required a nude lady to be seen being photographed in a studio, and for once I was able to beat Jack Causey to it by telling him to contact Bob Guccione. I carelessly let drop the bait to Bob that I was making an epic comedy at Pinewood Studios, and could he arrange to have a nude lady available? Then I added, "We will also need a photographer to be seen photographing the lady, and he *has* got a line to speak."

The silence was quite telling. Bob then said, "You mean you want *me* to?"

My reply was very truthful – "Can't have someone taking a picture who doesn't know how to take a picture" – and a script was duly sent to him. He had to plough through all of it to get to his one line, but he seemed satisfied.

It is a truth, universally acknowledged, that every person would like to appear in a movie. There's no better way to get your 15 minutes of Andy Warhol fame, so promptly at eight o'clock the next morning a limousine arrived at Pinewood, with Bob seated in the back, plus one of his most beautiful models, Tina McDowell. To the delighted twittering of the make-up ladies, she was dispatched to the make-up department while I explained to Bob the scene where he would be photographing the lady, using a Hasselblad camera and tripod. On the line "Ready, Bob," we would cut to Guccione behind the tripod, cable release in hand. He would then say, "Beautiful, baby," press the camera release, the lens would zoom tight into the lens of the Hasselblad and the shot would be over.

Simple scene, nicely lit by cameraman Harvey Harrison, who busily checked the lights while we waited for our lady model. It was then that I noted Bob. His moment had come and he wasn't going to let anyone down. To and fro across the back of the set he went. "*Beautiful*, baby!" Then we got "Beautiful, *baby*!", and an interesting third version, "*Beautiful, baby*!"

I realised that the judgment of Paris was on me. "I'll shoot it all three ways," I said. Elegant and beautiful, Tina arrived on the set and was placed in position, and on "Action!" Leslie Philips, starring in this episode, gave a nod, and there was Bob Guccione in his moment of glory. He spoke the line perfectly, all three versions, and that was that. Several weeks later, in the editing room, I chose the version I felt was best and was rewarded for my efforts by my editor. "I'm sure it's been said before," he said, "but you are a cheeky bugger."

Penthouse, and the articles I wrote for it, did have a drawback. I had a telephone call in the early '70s from my accountant. "I must read you a letter I have just received from the income tax authorities," he said, and did. "Dear Sir. The information you have supplied re Mr Stark's income does not tally with the information we hold. I would suggest a meeting." I suddenly realised his voice was sounding slightly muffled due to the buzz in my eardrums. "I have arranged the meeting," he continued. "Next Tuesday at 10am." The letter, following the cunning procedure, invariably adopted by the Inland Revenue, of posting the letter on a Thursday so you got it on Friday, gave us several days of worried nights over the weekend. The following Tuesday, a thick file regarding my income clutched to my chest, we entered an office to meet a tall, broad-shouldered Scotsman, who gave me a beaming smile. "I'm a great fan of yours, Mr Stark. Love your work!"

I felt frontal attack was the only answer. "Never mind that," I said. "What about this 'not tallying with'?"

His hands folded across his stomach and the smile was still there but just a trifle more secretive. "If I told you that," he said, "you could easily correct it."

It was stand-off time. In desperation, I put the folder on the desk. "There," I pointed dramatically. "Every penny I earned carefully listed. Right through the year!"

He pulled the folder closer, peered at it, then compared it to a document in front of him. "Quite right. Very carefully listed. Thank you for coming in and clearing matters up."

I closed the folder and stood up. "I have spent several days of worry. Please explain." And he did. It seems that a prudish person in my accountant's office had carefully changed the name of *Penthouse*, whenever it appeared, to something completely different, so as not to connect me with anything that might be considered naughty.

Al Jolson, Judy Garland, Ethel Merman – all American entertainers brought up in the hard and tough school of Broadway, where bad notices can close a show overnight. They were performers trained to beat audiences into submission. It was not by chance that the runway, jutting out like a pier into the audience, was loved by Jolson. Unashamedly, he would kneel at the end of it, a few feet from adoring fans, pleading with a child called Sonny Boy to climb upon his knee, despite the fact that friends were forsaking him.

You imagined that that era had ended until, in the late '50s, rumours crossed the Atlantic that a man named Sammy Davis Jr, starring in the New York show *Mr Wonderful*, was carrying on the tradition. There was talk of a phenomenal entertainer, but the label "Jr" made one have reservations – until he played the Pigalle, a new cabaret restaurant in Piccadilly. In his opening-night performance, he set a new standard in singing, in dancing and in dazzling impressions that set London back on its feet. As I was one of that audience, I can speak with first-hand knowledge.

The PR people had their celebs-available-to-go-to-opening-night lists ready, which explains why Alma Cogan, Alfred Marks, Paddy O'Neill and I sat at a small table at the opening night along with a fair representation of the best of British showbiz. The band played the brassy opening music and a small, very slim black man came onto the cabaret floor and destroyed all the existing standards of entertainers as we knew them. He sang better than Sinatra, he joked on the level of the very best nightclub comics and he danced! Oh, God, how he danced! I was a dancer myself and, knowing the technical aspects, just sat there open-mouthed at what was going on in front of my eyes. At the end, storms of applause, a triumph in every sense of the word. At our table, heads drooped, then slowly Alfie raised his. "I don't know about you lot," he said, "but I shall never go onstage again."

Years later, I was cast in the film, *Salt And Pepper*, starring Sammy and Peter Lawford. Michael Bates and I played an incompetent pair of Scotland Yard detectives, and we made the film on a huge set, depicting Soho, built at Shepperton Studios. Throughout several weeks, Sammy was his usual ball of fire while Peter Lawford wandered about wearing a lazy smile with a cloud of some exotic weed floating about his head. Lacking any charm (except to the ladies, of course), he was able to dictate on the film as it was his money behind the picture apparently. A young director named Richard Donner did his best and was very inventive, but against a backer you haven't a chance.

Sammy used to call himself the one-eyed Jewish nigger. Most people knew of the car crash that cost him the sight of one eye, but oddly enough you were never really sure which one was missing, as his reflexes were so perfect. And then there were the cameras. I thought I was keen, but Sammy put every camera buff I knew to shame – it seemed that every other day a new piece of gleaming chrome equipment was produced. He soon realised that he and I shared a mutual passion, and Michael Bates, a very comic actor, would sit bored out of his mind as Sammy and I swapped photographic knowhow – "When it comes to portraiture, you can't beat the 9.5mm Elmar on a Leica," Sammy would say.

"Yes, but what about the quality Ansel Adams got on those old Speed Graphics?" I would say. The glaze would slowly descend on Michael's eyes.

Halfway through the film, Sammy gave an extravagant party in the Maharajah suite at the Mayfair Hotel, where he was living, and most of the cast and technicians, plus a few extra guests, were there. A dark-haired, attractive girl with a pronounced Cockney accent sat by me on a settee and viewed me with some interest. "Sam tells me—" the name abbreviation made it clear she and our host were on close terms "—that yew knows a lot abaht cameras." I gave a modest knowing acknowledgement. "Well, you see," she went on, "I've got this 'ere Polaroid camera, and wot I want to know is, is it werf anyfink?"

Any woman asking any man his advice based on his technical superiority will always get his full attention. "If you could describe the camera in detail," I said, "I could possibly let you know what it's worth." She went blank, then I realised question and answer was the only way to get results. "Does it have a rangefinder?" Still blank. "Two little people in the viewfinder merging together?" The head nodded. Gradually, through the inquisition, I was able to establish the camera model. "You're all right there," I said, giving a sage and knowing nod. "An S1A – worth quite a bit of money. Definitely top of the range."

I got a smile of thanks then she waved at Sammy. "Found out what I wanted. I'm leaving now."

He gave her a farewell wave. "Bye, Christine, baby!" And that was how I helped Christine Keeler – the young lady whose affair with the War Minister brought down the British government – to value her camera. She never asked me the value of any of the pictures she may have taken with it.

The film progressed for a few more days, then Sammy, expensive leather case in hand, confronted me. "Wanna buy a Hasselblad?" he said.

"I already have one," I replied.

"In that case, you'd better have two." He put the heavy case into my hand. "Get used to carrying it about. You're going to buy it!" With that he walked away.

It was a *fait accompli*, brilliantly executed, and when I opened the case the heaviness was explained. It was another Hasselblad, nestling in the padded sections of the case, but an outfit that put mine in the shade. Camera body, removable back, three lenses, a set of Proxar close-up lenses, plus the rare (and very expensive) eye-level finder. Sammy was soon tracked down. "No," I said. "Sorry, I just can't afford it. Very beautiful, but just can't afford it."

He gave a little pause. "You got £200 to spare?" He might as well have given it to me for nothing, as the outfit was worth a minimum of £2,000.

The film ended and we had our final picture party (the undying film tradition) in a large marquee on the lot, the music provided by a small group of local boys booked to play for dancing. The three musicians sat on a tiny stage in the corner – pianist, bass player and a boy of 16 with a snare drum wedged between his knees. Everyone hoped Sammy would do a song and, as he was the original performer that opened the fridge door and did six numbers, as the light went on he wasn't difficult to persuade. Someone called out, "'Night And Day'," one of Sam's great party pieces, and the boy drummer suddenly had a look of terror straight out of *The Blair Witch Project*. Sammy always performed 'Night And Day' totally unaccompanied, except for the drummer. Sammy flashed several thousand pounds' worth of dentistry (of which he was very proud) at him. "Just give me a nice easy beat and keep going as long as I do." The terror subsided, the brushes started to move across the drum and Sammy was away – "Like the drip, drip, drip of the raindrops..." Entranced, we watched and heard one of the greatest performing artists of the 20th century. He was also a very nice man.

There's a follow-up to the story of the purchase of Sammy's camera. Realising there was no customs certificate, I called their office and explained that I was in possession of the camera and felt I should declare it. Invited to their office, next door to the Mermaid Theatre, the customs official peered at the mass of chrome in its beautiful fitted case, then said, "It's had a lot of wear."

Outraged I looked at him. "There's not a mark on it," I said. "It's in mint condition!"

Slowly and patiently he said again, "It's had a *lot* of wear, and I suggest you pay £49 customs duty." I still have the receipt, which should have been for at least £1,000. As I was leaving, he gave a smile: "After all, you didn't *have* to ring us up, did you?"

Peter Sellers was having a very bad time. Self-exiled in Ireland, financially insecure and not happy in his marriage, things could have been better. Fortunately, the self-satisfied, tail-waving creature was all set to save him. Inspector Clouseau, created by Peter and Blake Edwards, had never died in the public's affection. Peter had tried hard to break away, but the image clung like a limpet. An obituary for the King of Nepal, who tragically died in a dreadful massacre at his palace, revealed that the Pink Panther films were banned in Nepal, as unfortunately His Majesty's subjects found the resemblance between Clouseau and their monarch, King Birendra, so extraordinary that they laughed openly when the films were shown. It was strange to think that Peter and Blake had made only two films starring Sellers as Clouseau (*The Pink Panther* and *A Shot In The Dark*) and then he was discarded. A brave attempt to revive him with Alan Arkin was made, but the public would have none of him; Sellers' bumbling, accident-prone, proud but idiotic inspector was what was they wanted. After his spell in the doldrums, Peter and Blake got back together again, and off on the road to Morocco they went.

The (then-)King of Morocco was in every sense master of all he surveyed. He ruled his North African kingdom in an autocratic manner and Allah help anyone who opposed his wishes. What the King wanted, the King got – that is, until he met up with Mary Poppins, in the person of Julie Andrews.

In Marrakech, one of the major cities of Morocco, a hotel was built in the late '20s. North Africa had become the new playground of the affluent, and this hotel was to be the biggest and best. The scale of the Mamounia was vast. Each bedroom had twin king-size double beds. Their balconies were big enough to hold a small dance, and they all overlooked a gigantic, opulent swimming pool. The gardens seemed limitless. The main dining room, apparently built in case the Graf Zeppelin needed a spare hangar, boasted a string quartet, and while guests had their meal breaks an urbane, dinner-jacketed pianist played on a white grand piano. A time-warp to the '30s surrounded him. His collection of Billy Mayerl 78rpm records was his most treasured possession, and we were regaled with Noël Coward's 'A Room With A View' on every possible occasion.

With the largesse that only a major film company can afford, early in 1975 United Artists booked most of this exotic Xanadu to provide accommodation for the cast and crew of *The Return Of The Pink Panther*. The Mamounia gave Peter the Churchill suite, so called because Winston Churchill used to indulge his hobby of painting there. From the balcony there you could see why the part-time bricklayer, full-time prime minister came here to paint, as the light was so clear you felt you could put your hand out and pat the snow on top of the mountains miles away.

Working hard under the hot Moroccan sun, we were glad of our free weekends. The pool naturally became the centre of social life. Peter stood on his head for half an hour at a time (he was very into yoga at this time) while his current lady friend, Titti Watchmeister, more sensibly lay back relaxing on her towel. Bikinis were all the rage and the male members of the crew duly admired what the female members intended them to admire, and everything was under control – that is, until the Italian model arrived for a week's stay. Dark-haired, elegant, with a body to die for, she smiled serenely at everyone, lay on her sun bed, then took her bikini top off. Every man at the pool immediately got paralysis of the neck and gazed fixedly at the sky, determined not to be caught looking. It was the women who were up on their elbows, checking out this appalling social behaviour. The next morning, Sunday, we all met again, everyone smiled sweetly and, without exception, every girl on the film unit took *her* top off.

It was at that very moment of delight (to the males, anyway) that the crisis occurred. Above our heads there was a cry: "Up here. Quick, up here!" The frantic call came from Joe Dunne, stuntman extraordinaire and general double for Peter on all the Panther films. His arms flailing, he was peering over the balcony of the penthouse occupied by Blake Edwards and his wife, Julie Andrews. Lustful thoughts vanished. Previously discarded bikini tops quickly covered naked breasts, and the lifts crammed with half-dressed actors, stuntmen and technicians rose to the penthouse floor where Joe Dunne excitedly explained. There had just been a discreet knock on the door of Blake's penthouse suite by the manager of the hotel. Inclining forward, he deeply regretted disturbing the eminent director this Sunday morning, especially as he was accompanied by his delightful wife, the ever-so-famous film star Miss Julie Andrews.

He then went on to explain that he was the bearer of sad tidings. Would Mr Edwards and his lovely wife, the ever-so-famous film star Miss Julie Andrews, please vacate the penthouse suite in the next 20 minutes? Blake politely explained that, as he and Miss Andrews, plus their daughter, had been living in the suite for nearly a month, this move would not be a simple matter. And why, might he ask, was it necessary? The manager's body now inclined to an even more acute angle. "A thousand pardons, but the King has the permanent occupancy of the penthouse next to yours. He will be living in it from tomorrow. Moving into *your* suite," the bow had almost reached the acrobatic level, "to enable discussions to take place, will be the President of Chad. I am sure you will understand, we must prepare it for such an occasion!"

Blake's face, already tanned by the Moroccan sun, darkened further: "I shall immediately contact the American Ambassador and I assure you there will be diplomatic repercussions." Not for nothing had Blake been one of Hollywood's better scriptwriters for many years. Sadly, vocal fluency had no effect. As we all watched, fascinated by a scene that was far superior to any current action movie, the manager scurried to the end of the corridor, gave urgent signals and the matter took on another more bizarre dimension. In full military uniform, a young Moroccan army officer appeared. Impressive though this was, it became even more impressive when we realised he was being followed by twelve Moroccan soldiers, each carrying a rifle. Our gathered stuntmen shifted rather uneasily as the officer drew his service revolver from its holster, nodded his head to the soldiers and, in the confines of the hotel corridor, we heard the crashing sound of twelve rifle bolts being pulled back. It was all getting very, very ugly.

Then, in one of those deafening silences that always seem to happen after emotion-charged events, a figure appeared behind Blake. The ever-so-famous film star herself. As always beautifully groomed, Julie Andrews gave an imperious look to the soldiers, a dismissive glance to the manager, then stepped firmly up to the young officer. "What *do* you think you are doing?" she said. "And you can put *that* thing away as well." Her long, slim fingers quite calmly pushed the barrel of the revolver to one side. Then, with the style and elegance that only years of theatre can give you, she turned and dramatically pointed to the door of the penthouse. "My daughter is in there," she said "having a bath! We have no intention of moving until we are well and truly able to. And *you*—" a look at the officer "—will make quite certain all your cohorts will be available to help."

The officer looked at the manager and silently mouthed "Cohorts?"

The manager nodded at the soldiers. "Them," he said.

Faced by this immaculate performance, a strategic rethink was the only option open to the military and the hotel. A huddled, brief conference brought a tentative suggestion. "If the ever-so-famous Miss Andrews and her obviously equally famous husband Mr Blake Edwards would consider being moved to the adjacent penthouse across the hall here, all the visible cohorts would fetch and carry, plus as many hotel staff as necessary, and be assured you can take as long as you like." The manager swallowed hard. "Although it would be preferable *before* His Majesty gets here." A compromise had been reached. The cohorts lined up ready to be baggage carriers, the stuntmen and crew formed a phalanx outside Blake and Julie's suite ready to aid and abet, while the young officer did his best to become part of the wallpaper. The manager mopped his brow while nervously backing away to the safety of the lift shaft.

There was no option but to move, as undoubtedly the president and the King had to confer, but at least – thanks to the fortitude and bravura of the ever-so-famous Julie – there would now be unlimited assistance. It brought to mind the now oft-quoted remark of Moss Hart speaking of the lady: "She has that wonderful British strength that makes you wonder how they lost India."

Playing Pepe, a derelict Italian conman – a character that once upon a time was always played by Peter Lorre – I shuffled about Marrakech in my costume, finding social life difficult. Christopher Plummer invited me up to the balcony of a restaurant for a drink, but a vigilant policeman quickly prevented me from going up the stairs as vagrants were barred. Making matters worse, Blake invented a comedy routine which involved my fingers being constantly broken, and gradually, scene by scene, my fingers appeared tied up with wooden splints. Stuntmen, who do all those amazing action sequences, were always an important part of any Panther film and we excelled ourselves by employing Ahmed, who was a native Moroccan. He had watched the American experts and was alert and ready, should anything go wrong, to step into the breach.

Well, it did go wrong. Sliding down a rope above me, our chief stuntman got his hands badly burned. Ahmed was at the ready and, in answer to our worries as to his abilities, he assured us he was the best descender of ropes in North Africa and not to worry, as Allah had ordained all would be well. We can only presume Allah was not holding him in a favourable light, as Ahmed didn't burn his hands on the rope – he fell off it. Right on top of me. He bounced onto the marble floor, broke both his legs, and we were both rushed off to the local hospital, where I made a miraculous recovery. Peter was fascinated at my Lourdes-type revival, but I told him it was quite simple. The secret lay in the sight of the bloodstains that had never been wiped off the trolley that was wheeling me into the hospital.

Apart from that, Marrakech was splendid and I especially enjoyed working with Christopher Plummer. The film was a huge success. Composing music for the film was, once again, Henry Mancini. This gentle, courteous man had composed the first Panther film's signature tune, which became an instant hit. As the deep bass notes of the catchy tune came on the soundtrack, it got instant recognition and, in popularity, it was up there with the James Bond signature tune. We met in London while he was scoring the film and, like a schoolboy, he told me he had lifted a few bars of music. I gathered this was quite legal, as long as it wasn't more than five bars. "Seeing as you make your entrance in that hotel in Casablanca, sweaty and dishevelled, your tropical suit stained and dirty, I put a few bars of 'You must remember this' on the soundtrack." Of all the compliments I may have received in my lifetime, I think that is the one I shall remember most.

Henry then told me the wonderful story about the music he had composed for *Breakfast At Tiffany's* (another Blake Edwards film), which included the song 'Moon River', played throughout the film. Eventually, there had been a first screening for the company who had backed the film, 20th Century Fox. In the screening room, sitting in the front row in solitary splendour sat Darryl

F Zanuck, tycoon head of the company. Everyone else at the screening had to sit at the rear – no one was allowed to be in the front with him – and as the final "The End" credit came on the screen, God help anyone who dared to speak before Zanuck did.

The lights came up, the film was over. Audrey Hepburn, a vision in her little black dresses, had given a fabulous performance and they eagerly awaited Zanuck's remarks. Silence reigned, the polo mallet was swung, and then the oracle spoke: "That fucking tune has got to go!" To their eternal credit, Blake and Mancini went into action. They cajoled, they pleaded, they begged and finally they had their way. That "fucking tune", 'Moon River', made more money for the company than the film did.

13 You 'Ave The Mobilee Face

In the early '60s, I spent a lot of time in small recording studios in London, taping what started to become a great source of income for actors – the ubiquitous voice-overs. The publicity for these started with the famous PG Tips chimp commercials. Some bright advertising person had the brainwave of filming these almost human creatures and then putting voices on them. The effect was instantaneous stardom for the chimps and a lot of repeat fees for the actors, and doing a voice-over was no longer considered to be lowering oneself in the theatrical world. Leading actors and actresses vied with each other to record these very funny and very successful commercials, but it wasn't all plain sailing. The chattering of the chimps' teeth, to which we had to synchronise, was difficult to master and eventually there was only a small group of us, who became a repertory company, busily putting our voices onto the wonderful contortions of the animals. One of the commercials had the accolade of being in *The Guinness Book Of Records* as the most-televised commercial of the '70s.

One of the voices on that commercial belonged to Kenneth Connor, a diminutive actor who proved himself one of the very best. I'd worked with Kenny many times in the past (we were both in the extraordinary Goon Show on TV, *A Show Called Fred,* back in the '50s). One morning, in a De Lane Lea studio, we were booked to voice two parrots for BP petrol, the commercial to be broadcast on Nigerian radio. Sitting in the control room alongside the director was a tall, extremely well-dressed black gentleman who sat very silently while we did the usual joking around, getting the vocal cords working, and then to business. We both soon got the strange, chirpy intonation of the parrot plus the clicking, squawking noise you hear as the birds clambered over their perches. "It's BP petrol, that's what we want, BP petrol." We squawked the lines and everybody looked delighted.

The young director then got serious. "Now, do remember," he said, "this *will* be on Nigerian radio and we *do* need to make it just that teeny weeny bit more colloquial, don't we?" Under the director's tuition Kenny and I, two demented actors, highly embarrassed with the black man sitting there, were screeching "Man, dis here BP petrol man, dat's what we are wantin', BP petrol!"

There was a pause, then the Nigerian gentleman walked in from the control room. He looked at Kenny and me. "Dat's just perfect, man. Dat's just what we are wantin', man. Sho' gonna sell a lotta petrol, man."

Wartime days in Italy taught me a simple truth – Italians are, by nature, melodramatic. Divinely and wonderfully so. Not for them the clipped monosyllabic tones of the Anglo-Saxon, nor the convolutions of the American double-speak, and certainly not the measured elegance of the Asian world or the Teutonic mutterings of the Slavs.

It was in the mid '70s when I got the call from my agent. Well, strictly speaking, it was not the eminent Dennis Selinger but his female assistant. "I have just had a call from Milan from a Giorgio Romano and I do hope it wasn't you taking the piss, as he had a very sexy voice."

I assured her taking the piss was not my game and asked what Giorgio had had to say. "Well, according to him, having seen your photograph in *Spotlight* [the actors directory], you have a *mobilee* face, and they wish you to appear in a new film in Rome. I have told them that, providing they send a first-class return ticket to you, will be only too happy to oblige."

During the next few days I did keep checking in the mirror for the mobility of my face until it came time to board the flight to Rome. At the Italian airport I met the fabled Giorgio Romano who, with typical Italian *brio*, was dramatically holding a copy of *Spotlight* up in the air. Identical in size to a London telephone directory, it was open so that my picture, with its *mobilee* face, was exposed to the milling Italian populace. By rapidly glancing at the picture, then at me, Giorgio assured himself that I was the genuine article and, after steering me through customs, he flung my baggage into the back of an open Jeep. With a style that would have done credit to Stirling Moss in the Mille Miglia, he drove at full speed through the narrow back alleys of Rome. We arrived at the film location to meet the director Franco Rossi, who, satisfied with the *mobilee* face, albeit a very white one, introduced me to the gentleman I'd be acting with. Tall, extremely handsome, and oozing charm, I could well see why Shelley Winters had fallen hook liner and sinker for Vittorio Gassman. After all, she had told me, Michael Caine and any other member of the cast of *Alfie* who was willing to listen just how glorious and exciting their marriage had been. Franco, as the director, then explained the long and complicated opening scene Vittorio and I would be filming.

Very much in the continental style, the scene certainly was long. And complicated. Playing an English private detective, I had to demonstrate to Vittorio all the tricks of the investigator's trade, including hidden microphones, two-way mirrors and the whole mystique of secret surveillance. After clothes and make-up had been decided on, Franco finally turned to me and, with the devastating charm that every Italian seems to be born with, placed his arm affectionately about my shoulders. "Grame, I see you in the Peenk Panthers, and I know you weel be very good in a thees part." Well, they may have charm, but they also have cunning.

Franco gave another shoulder squeeze and the smile was even wider. "You know in Italy we dub every feelm." I nodded sagely, as it was common knowledge that Italian actors always added their voices to the film *after* it was made – not a system adhered to by English and American cinema, but that was the Italian way. "So," another squeeze from Franco, "for the purpose of theese, Vittorio weel play the scene in Italian." A purposeful nod as he quickly moved behind camera ready to call out whatever the Italian word was for action.

I moved just as quickly and caught him up. "You do realise," I said, "that I do not speak a word of Italian. How will I know when he gets to the end of his line?"

The majestic head of Vittorio turned dramatically and he gazed at Franco. "'Eesa right, Franco. 'Ow will 'e know?"

I stood between the two Italians, wearing the smug expression of the Englishman having put one up on Johnny Foreigner. Nonplussed, they gazed at me. Then came another head-turn from Vittorio. A true leading actor, he never underplayed. "I 'ave it!" he declared, bringing his face close to mine. "You are an *actore grande*. I see with my own eyes you 'ave the expert technique. Now!" Having the full attention of both Franco and myself, his performance subtly enlarged. "On the table 'ere we 'ave a cup. At the end of my first line I will move it, so." The cup was shifted an inch. "At the end of my second line I will scratch my ear, so!" Graphically, he described how, at every end of every speech or line, he would give me a visual cue. Finally, Franco called whatever they do call for action and Vittorio and I went into the long scene, which, for originality of playing, must take some beating.

Underplaying the devious English detective, I watched Vittorio like a hawk as he gabbled some meaningless Italian. He then moved the cup on the table and I came in with my first line, which happened to be "I'm glad you asked me that!" More Italian while I waited for the ear scratch. And so it went on. The film, under the English title of *Virginity*, has been shown here on television and I have watched, with awe, our long scenes together – Vittorio, moving and gesturing with style, me watching every movement like a cobra ready to strike. Strangely enough, it was very effective.

The arrival of my two new children had meant a larger house and we had all settled there happily, but as the three children started to grow the cycles lay in the hallway, the dolls lolled on the staircase (carefully placed so you were bound to trip on them while carrying a tray to watch television) and there was the problem of my photography. A darkroom was desperately needed, so off to the estate agent's we marched and the details of dozens of totally unsuitable homes were sent to us. Finally, one arrived – as they always do – that quite fitted the bill, and through the hell of moving to a new house we went. Following in the tradition of my mother, there was a large sports ground to look at, but sadly not at the front. However, having it at the rear meant the children could have a lovely roll on the grass occasionally.

It was the age of the au pair and no home with children was complete without one. We had the usual procession of them and some became great friends. (One girl took Christopher, aged twelve, back to Sweden for the Festival of Lights, sending him home by plane, and he was treated like a king by the airline.)

I soon found I was getting the reflected glory of the enormous publicity engendered when I was best man at Peter's wedding to Britt. A young girl from Italy with the unlikely name of Emma was one of the better au pairs and she very happily looked after the children, flicked her feather duster around the house and ate her food with gusto. Well built, in the Italian manner, she seemed content, until one day, giving me a fixed stare and in her heavy Italian accent, she asked me, "Ees right you were the best man for Peeter Sellers and Breet Ekland?" I told her yes. She digested this, then said, "'Ow long Breet Ekland in England before she meet Peeter Sellers?" The news that it was only a few days brought a slight gleam to her eye. "And now she ees a feelm star?" I gave a nod and left it at that.

Two nights later, I told her that my agent, Dennis Selinger, was coming to dinner. "What ees agent?" she said. "Ees like a pradoocer?"

Once more taking the easy route, I gave a nod. "Just like a producer," I said, thereby neatly sealing Dennis' fate.

All through dinner that night, wearing clothes several sizes smaller than she usually wore, plus a perfume that hit you at ten feet, Emma was a sensation. Constantly leaning provocatively across the table so Dennis could get a better view of her ample cleavage, she gave him the full treatment. Leaving the house, Dennis looked at me accusingly: "I never knew you had an au pair who looked like that!"

I gave a slight shake of the head. "Until tonight, neither did I."

Fortunately for Dennis, she became enamoured of a small bearded youth and, giving up all thoughts of film stardom, vanished into the wilds of Tufnell Park, never to be heard of again.

The Return Of The Pink Panther, made in Marrakech, set box-office records worldwide, and gave Peter's career a revival. Clouseau-speak became fashionable again, with a million bad impressions of the extraordinary voice Peter had invented circulating at parties. It became certain another Panther film would be made. And it was. The pleasure of working for Blake was that, when it came to going on location, there was nobody who had more style. He knew that, not only did the wonderful character of Clouseau entrance the public but also the exotic scenery surrounding him. Now it was Bavaria and *The Pink Panther Strikes Again*.

Blake intended me to play a comic hotel porter who, by some misfortune, was Hitler's double. I got pompous and said I thought the idea was very unfunny, especially as we were filming in the lobby of the Bayerischhof Hotel, which Hitler used many times. It was embarrassing to talk about the war. However, Blake, a perfect gentleman, said that if it didn't work he wouldn't use it. Well, we needn't have worried. As I turned to face Peter, with my perfect Hitler make-up and using a high-pitched German voice, he began to laugh. And he wouldn't stop. Germans in the lobby were standing watching, which made Peter's hysteria worse. Blake surrendered. "Forget it," he said. "We'll think of something else."

Within days cars drove us south through the glorious scenery of Bavaria, until we came to the fairy-tale castle of King Ludwig II at Hohenschwangau. Perched halfway up a mountainside, it was so exquisite that one could half excuse Ludwig for bankrupting his country by building it. There, in a small room, I appeared as another hotelier – thankfully not Hitler, just a genial old, doddery innkeeper with a small dog. Peter looked at it and said the immortal line, "Does your dog bite?" and, as I shook my head, he patted the dog and it bit him. He said, "I thought you said your dog did not bite?" then I said, "That is not my dog." The joke went worldwide. It's really an old pantomime routine, but the public loved it and repeated it *ad nauseam*.

I thought we had reached some peak of laughter with the scene in Munich, but there was worse to come. Before shooting, Blake asked if anybody had ideas. Without a pause, I said, "A pipe. A big Meerschaum pipe, and I can blow smoke all over Clouseau, who will gradually disappear." Blake loved it, and the pipe was produced. They stuffed the bowl full of what they assured me was herbal tobacco, I puffed away and gradually the room filled with smoke. I started to laugh and so did Peter. The crew, apparently loving what we were doing, started laughing as well. I got a terrible headache, and it got a bit out of control, but Blake sobered us up as he knew I was finishing on the film the next day and had to fly back to England for another picture. We pulled ourselves together, opened the doors briefly to let the smoke out, then finished the scene.

Then back to my favourite Pinewood once more, and back to another castle, but this time one set a little earlier in history. Now it was *The Prince And The Pauper*, set in the times of Henry VIII (played by Charlton Heston). With his shoulders, plus the magnificent costume he wore, you had a problem getting past Charlton in the corridor. My history of dancing came to my aid, as my character, Tom the Court Jester, was a famous dancer. So, with the film world's obsession with getting everything right, I was sent off to an expert in medieval dancing, where for several days, to the music of the lascivious lute, I leapt to and fro.

Needless to say, not one leap did I eventually perform in front of the camera. Instead, we all sat rather dourly in the grand hall while Henry/Charlton tried to decide whether or not Rex Harrison (as the Duke of Norfolk) should have his head chopped off. Just as he was about to proclaim Norfolk as a traitor, Blake walked on the set. As an old friend of our director Richard Fleischer, he came to pay the standard courtesy call but, mid-handshake, he caught sight of me dressed in my ludicrous cap and bells. "For Christ's sake," he said, "is there nothing you won't do for a laugh?" Then he gave Fleischer a look. "How come you're using a well-known drug addict like him?"

The effect was instantaneous. Dick Fleischer gave a nervous smile, Charlton Heston started to adjust the garter round his leg and Rex Harrison gazed into the middle distance. Blake saw the look of horror on my face and gave a grin. "You mean, you didn't know what happened on the day we did the dog scene? Someone filled your pipe with pot. All through that scene you were as high as a kite." Suddenly, it was all clear – the headache, the crew's hysteria as the room filled with smoke, Peter out of control. No wonder they were all laughing.

Fleischer was a "checking his notes" director. Every morning, while we actors were getting slowly attuned to our costumes, making sure the swords came out of scabbards easily, that the spurs on our heels weren't going to trip us up or, in my case, that none of the bells on my costume hadn't fallen off, Fleischer was peering at a piece of paper in his hand. We stood in awkward groups while the first assistant director ran to each of us in turn passing on directions and then, finally, when all the messages had been delivered, action was called and we all did our bits. Two days went by, then Rex Harrison, standing next to me said, "Has he actually spoken to you yet?" I told him no. "Thank God," said Harrison. "He hasn't spoken to me, either. I thought it was something I'd said."

Then came the day I was dreading: Heston had his great dying scene. With what relish film actors grasp at the final exit from life! – Edward G Robinson crying, "Is this the end of Rico?" as he squirmed artistically on the ground in *Little Caesar*, Olivier spinning like a mechanical doll in *Richard III*, Marlon Brando crashing to the earth in the vineyard in *The Godfather*. And now, as the script so tersely put it, Tom was to sit at the head of the bed and cry uncontrollably as his master, Henry VIII, dies. I had read David Niven's bestselling *The Moon Is A Balloon* and remembered his story of how director William Wyler dramatically explained to the entire cast and crew of *Wuthering Heights* that they had an actor present who couldn't act, when Niven had nervously said he couldn't summon up tears as Cathy lay dying. Tentatively, I spoke to our monosyllabic director. Could he tell me what level of intensity my crying should reach? "Loud," Fleischer said. "And don't stop."

Years later, Niven was delighted when I told him that his story, plus the terse directions, prompted such fear in me that I burst into tears as soon as the scene started. I cried all the time Heston went through his dramatic lines, "Monks, monks, monks," and even after Fleischer said "Cut" I went on sobbing. The mother of Alexander Salkind (the film's producer), a Mexican lady, walked over to me and gave me a small hug. "Don't be so sad," she said. "Eet's only a feelm."

A sad call in July of 1973 – Jimmy Beck, a stalwart of one of the greatest (some people say *the* greatest) British situation comedy shows, suddenly died. *Dad's Army* was a saga of the days of wartime Britain when a Home Guard was formed of older men volunteering to guard the homes and streets against what seemed like certain invasion by Germany. At the beginning, they had pitchforks, pieces of wood with nails in, even broom handles with knives stuck in the top – anything to fight with. Pathetically, they drilled in village halls, hoping to (as they boasted) have a crack at the Hun. It was laughable, but it was wonderful. The series – starring Arthur Lowe, John Le Mesurier and Clive Dunn, amongst others – was the most successful comedy show of the '70s, and even today TV repeats of it get enormous viewing figures. It transferred to radio, and it was during this series that I was asked to take over. It meant a reunion for me and Clive Dunn, who had made my first summer season, at Cromer, such a success.

For an actor, writing an autobiography is quite simple. He or she thinks back to that part, or that film, or that television as reference points – tiny peaks that had to be climbed. Arguments about a costume, the idiot actor who would upstage and the nightmare show in Great Yarmouth. And the critics! What Dilys Powell wrote in 1964, the terrible press that certain shows got from the television critics of the daily papers. Then there are the cuttings. Yellowing with age, curling at the edges, they are instant reminders, along with youthful pictures, of how we used to be.

My diaries go back to 1951 and have been kept ever since, but it hasn't anything to do with being a budding Pepys, simply work. In the wonderful steam-radio days, when there were four or five shows a week, you had no option. "Archie 3.30pm Paris, Lyons 8pm Aeolian Hall" simply meant that *Educating Archie* was recording at half past three at the Paris Cinema, Lower Regent Street, and *Life With Lyons* was recording at Aeolian Hall, Bond Street. Where famous names were concerned, the diaries could become the name-dropper's bible.

A terse entry for 1975 simply read, "John Huston, Claridge's, 6.30." To someone like myself, brought up on films such as *The Maltese Falcon*, *The Treasure Of The Sierra Madre* and *The African Queen*, the name stood for everything that was best in Hollywood movies, and even reading that name today reminds me of the sense of excitement I had at the thought of meeting him.

Behind it all was my agent, Dennis. He had become one of the premier agents in the country and had two clients, Michael Caine and Sean Connery, whom Columbia were trying to sign for a picture directed by Huston, *The Man Who Would Be King*. Huston had first tried to set up this story (by Rudyard Kipling) as a film for Clark Gable and Humphrey Bogart 20 years earlier but without success. Now, with the help of Dennis, it looked as if it might go into production. "There is a part," Dennis explained, "of a Gurkha soldier called Billy Fish. Very good, and very important. I've suggested you to Huston. Go and meet him."

The corridors at Claridge's are long and dark. Timidly, I knocked on the door, which swung open at once. The tall bearded figure invited me in and gave me a long, hard look. "Why on earth has Dennis sent you? You're totally wrong." It was a brave try by Dennis, and Huston was quite right, but it was worth the trip just to meet him.

14 I Hope It Isn't Too Long
Before We See You Again

The joy of being a character man in films is that, with a false nose, a cunningly applied moustache, a different hat and costume, *voilà*, you are another person – there's no chance for the audience to get tired or bored with your appearance. A Hollywood character actor of stature, Walter Brennan, holder of a record three Oscars for Best Actor, had a neat trick. Cast in yet another major supporting role, he would merely inquire of the director, "Do you want the teeth in or not?" For those who might feel the Walter Brennan approach was rather cynical, it never stopped him from always giving a marvellous performance. Most actors have shorthand. Peter Sellers had to get the walk right, Alec Guinness insisted on wearing the clothes first and I've always been rather partial to hats, always asking if I can keep them when the film is over.

In 1969, I was asked to appear in *The Picasso Summer* as a village postman in the south of France, where I found myself in the wardrobe mistress' hands. They are such experts and you can be sure that the uniform they put you in will be perfection; every button, every inch of apparel, checked and rechecked. Luckily, French postmen have great hats. Even a local cycle was supplied, and a few spins along the local concourse had me fit and ready for my performance.

The history of the film was chequered, to say the least, as it had originally been started in 1968 but sadly ground to a halt. (I'm told the finance came originally from Bill Cosby, but all had not been well.) A story of a young couple hoping to meet up with the great Picasso was filmed in the glamorous south of France and starred Albert Finney and Yvette Mimeaux. A director shot away for a few weeks, but then it was found that only a very short amount of film was usable, so at once the picture was stopped, shelved and numerous cans of film lay in desolate storage. Like pebbles in a shoe, like grit in the eyeball, those cans lay like an irritant, especially to the financiers, who gazed at the unfinished account books of the film. Surely something could be resuscitated, they thought.

A year later, the company was reassembled again, once more in the south of France, with a rewritten script, a new director and a few extra characters. I was one of those extra characters and soon found myself in Nice, occupying a suite at the Negresco, one of the great hotels of Europe. Like all actors on such a location, one immediately elevates oneself to one's surroundings and, with chameleon-like suppleness, takes on the mantle of an incredibly wealthy personage, to whom elegance is the norm. The sumptuous lobby, with its elegant parade of ludicrously extravagant shops, became the morning meeting place of myself, Albert and Yvette as we graciously permitted the staff to indulge us with coffee and croissants while viewing the passing parade of the other beautifully dressed guests.

Just occasionally, the film company instructed us that we would soon be required in front of the camera but, in the meantime, to please make certain that we check up on the social life. Being redoubtable Englishmen, Albert and I decided to explore and bravely faced "Le Promenade Anglais" – straight across the lobby, through the revolving doors and there, stretched all the way round the glorious bay, it was. Strolling along the front with Albert was to encounter various stages of "the vapours" among the female population. He had just had worldwide exposure in the cinema in *Tom Jones* and the scene where he sat opposite Joyce Redman, lustily eating his way through a meal, had become a byword for seduction. The local ladies regarded Albert, then clutched each other in apparent seizures while murmuring Gallic expletives. I seriously suggested to him that he should be entered for the Mexico Olympics as chief stud for England, but naturally he would have to practise with oxygen cylinders around his neck, as Mexico City was at 9,000 feet.

The film company, worried that the actors might be getting bored, announced the yacht trips, and the next Sunday we were confronted by a vessel that Onassis would have been happy to own and up the gangway we trooped, glancing inside the large cabin, which had supplies of food capable of lasting us for several crossings of the Mediterranean. Convinced by now that the financing of the picture was in the hands of Howard Hughes, I had sent for my wife, Audrey, my son Christopher and our au pair, Anna Esta Navarro Navarro. The next trip, we lay on the sun deck, adopting the mien of the indolent millionaire yachtsmen and watched as St Tropez got closer. There was no sign of Brigitte Bardot. To make up for this loss, the motorboat slung at the stern was lowered and Albert and I went water-skiing. That is, Albert went water-skiing while I sadly let go of the wooden towing bar, which immediately hit me across the thighs, giving a rainbow hue to my legs.

The fates did seem to have it in for me. While the rest of the unit sensibly lay on their towels on the pebbly breach outside the hotel, I leapt into the surf, gesturing to Audrey to let Christopher join me. Bravely, waist-deep in the water, he managed to reach me at the exact moment that the wave from *The Poseidon Adventure* hit me and, as we both disappeared under this enormous torrent of water, the French coastguards gave an irritable tut-tut and ran up the red flag.

We finally did do some filming, but not what was intended. The final sequence in the script had a meeting between Albert, Yvette and Picasso, and wondrous drawings on the sands by the master were to be the highlight of the film. Unfortunately, no one had thought to mention this to the gentleman in question and, when asked to perform alongside the other actors, Picasso politely declined. Perhaps he hadn't worked out how he was going to walk or what he was going to wear.

A request from a women's magazine to shoot some pictures of Laura Milligan, Spike's daughter, on her 21st birthday was, I felt, quite right and proper, as I was responsible for her being here in the first place.

It was usually Ward Bond. This tough Hollywood actor played supporting roles, invariably as either a plain-clothes policeman or in uniform – *The Maltese Falcon* was one of the high spots of his early career. In the action-packed movies of the '30s the hero and heroine would race through the California sunlight, the roof down on their convertible, speeding to tell the National Guard about the crack they had just noticed in the Grand Coulee Dam or trying to get the Governor to pardon the heroine's innocent young brother, who was about to occupy the electric chair. However, there was one golden rule: no matter how many road signs existed, *they always got lost*! Agonised close-up of heroine looking at hero: "You and your short-cut!" Equally agonised close-up of hero: "Now what do we do?" And that was Ward Bond's great moment – the camera swung away from the tortured couple and there, at the roadside, was the American speed cop at the ready. This glamorous figure, goggles masking the imperturbable face, sat on what looked like two tons of gleaming steel and chrome. The handlebars, firmly grasped by his gloved hands, were at least three feet long and decorated with every gadget under the sun.

This shot was held long enough to establish his authority and style. He smoothly coasted over to the couple, uttering the first of his two immortal lines: "You folks got a little trouble?" The heroine always got the explanation. Fluttering a pair of Hollywood's best artificial eyelashes, she would breathlessly explain all, and our policeman would nod sagely. Then the famous action – up came the knee, the foot kicked the accelerator pedal down, the bike engine sprang into life and he would then speak the second of his immortal lines: "Follow me!" With a twist of the throttle, and siren screaming, they would be off, driving through every red light they encountered!

But none of these things were in my mind that quiet Sunday morning, many years ago, when the telephone tore me away from the newsprint. "Not a bleeding cab in north London," said Spike Milligan, "and the pains have started!"

As I knew that Spike's wife was expecting a baby, this message was not as bizarre as it sounded. "Be there in ten minutes," I said and leapt into my Standard Eight drop-head coupé, a tiny car quite capable of reaching a top speed of 63 miles per hour – providing it was going downhill. Owing to a design oversight, the Standard's front seat had not been built with a nine-months-pregnant woman in mind, but June Milligan did her best. Spike, the mere male, had been wedged into what was laughingly called the occasional seat, at the rear. The roof dipped a bit so he had to lie down on his side, but at least we were on our way. I set off at a brisk ten miles per hour and June looked at me. "It won't fall out, you know. You *can* go a bit faster." She gave a minor spasm. "In fact, I would strongly advise you to." I gradually built up to a reckless 20 miles an hour and we soon arrived at the nursing home.

The matron did some terrible overacting at the doorway as she opened the car door and glared at June. "You're two weeks early! Got no room here!" She then glared at me – "Take her to Barnet General!" – then gave an imperious look and made a grand exit left.

"Oh Christ," said Spike, and buried his head in his hands. Fortunately, he didn't have to bend too far, as he was still lying on his side. Through mysterious streets we drove, hunting for the elusive Barnet General while June was getting noticeably paler. I realised the only tools in the car were the jack and a pair of pliers. I didn't really think they would be much use, so I carefully increased speed to a steady 30 as I tried to remember all I could about the umbilical cord. To knot or not to knot, that was the question. Or was it a straightforward cut? At the old Blue Star Garage, just north of Swiss Cottage, I forked left and started down the dual carriageway towards Mill Hill.

Then I saw him. An English motorbike policeman. No dark glasses, no throbbing monster machine, just a rather sedate motorbike, upon which he primly sat, well wrapped up in a smart, dark-blue raincoat. The interesting touch was the peaked cap with small flaps down over the ears. A cord from each flap fastened beneath the chin fetchingly finished this off.

As crime seemed at an all-time low in Hampstead Garden suburb that quiet Sunday morning, my dramatic plea, as I pulled the car alongside him, made him start. "Barnet General!" I declaimed.

Completely unruffled, he proved himself a graduate of Hendon College by speaking in a classic upper-class drawl. It was a very passable impression of George Sanders. "What," he inquired, "is all the rush?"

He was on the driver's side, so I leant back in my seat so he could look past me at June and I pointed at her. "That," I said, "is the rush!"

He looked June's swollen figure as, right on cue, she gave a painful groan. I then realised he had sat and watched those Hollywood movies as well, and this was the moment he had been waiting for all his life. His leg kicked down on the starter, the engine roared. "Righty ho!" he said. "Just you jolly well follow me!" I needn't have worried about his prim appearance, as that lad had a few tricks Evel Knievel would have been proud of, and I want to tell you that being driven through half a dozen red lights at high speed, the siren on the bike going full-blast, was an experience not easily forgotten. June's lips were moving, I think in silent prayer, while in the rear-view mirror I could see Spike (still horizontal) occasionally bouncing up to the roof. Even the old Standard Eight rose to the occasion, and we very nearly touched the magic 60 miles an hour on a bit of dual carriageway north of Hendon.

It was all systems go at the Barnet General and June was whisked away, which was quite fortunate as she gave birth to Laura 20 minutes after our arrival. Milligan struggled out of the back seat, giving a fair impression of Quasimodo, but managed to straighten up enough to thank the policeman, who looked rather pleased with himself. There was a certain swagger and a touch of the Errol Flynn in his farewell salute before he roared off on his bike.

The pictures I finally took of Laura for her 21st (her name came from the haunting melody, composed for the film of the same name, that Spike played on his trumpet as the finale of his stage act) were rather marred by the make-up lady they inflicted on me. Instead of going for unspoilt prettiness and an

English-rose complexion, this lady decided that, as freckles were in that year, Laura would have them instead. Laura appeared, apparently with advanced-stage measles, I went quite mad with rage and demanded the awful mess be wiped from her face and then finally got the pictures I was after.

Another call, this time from Spike himself. "WH Smith are paying a lot of money for a photograph of me in a studious pose," he said. "They want me to look intelligent. With your photographic expertise, I'm sure you could take just the picture they require."

The young art director, on behalf of his clients, fussed and twittered. "*Knowledge*, that is the key to it all. If Mr Milligan can appear to have...*knowledge*...that will be splendid." At once, a mortarboard was produced and we were all set. It went quite well but lacked that august, intelligent note, as I felt we hadn't quite got the scholarly look the picture needed.

We were on the last shot of the film when inspiration struck. "Pull the neck of the sweater up to your nose," I said. He did, and there it was – Milligan at his most erudite.

Peter Sellers kept coming to the house, spending time with Audrey and me, as nostalgia had such a hold on him. He desperately needed to look at old photographs, spend time in the darkroom – anything between films to fill in what had become an essentially empty life. He would drive us past all the old houses he had lived in, stopping at each one, reliving the past. Outside the block of flats opposite Highgate Woods, where I had lived in before the war, the car stopped again. I said, "But this is where *I* used to live before the war." It was not until then that Peter and I realised we had lived next door to each other for two years when we were schoolboys.

Then we heard a noise and we saw Peter, his head on the steering wheel, his shoulders heaving. "Oh Christ, Gra," he said. "Whatever happened to Leading Aircraftsman Sellers?"

Fortunately, as we thought at the time, he got a new wife, Lynne Frederick, and as luck would have it there was a new film as well. The Panther series had now become an awesome money-making machine (each new film in the series took more money at the box office), so in 1968 it was off to yet another glamorous location – Hong Kong. *Revenge Of The Pink Panther* was soon cast, as Blake was loyal to his own personal repertory company, and once more Herbert Lom, Burt Kwouk and myself were assembled, this time with the addition of Dyan Cannon.

The character I was to play was a *mittel*-European conman, crawler and supposed expert at disguises with the improbable name of Dr Balls. As I read the script, the thought of Peter and I playing a scene using that name and trying not to laugh loomed in my mind. However, you do not start a film telling the director he's got to change the name of your character, so I went to the studio to be fitted with a wig by the make-up man, Harry Frampton.

Blake Edwards was having lunch. He gave a smile and said, "What are you doing here?" I told him I had come for a wig-fitting as I was shooting the first scene as Dr Balls the next Tuesday. He smiled again and said, "You may be here as Dr Balls, but we shall be in Hong Kong filming the firework sequence." Casually, he asked if I fancied a trip to Hong Kong and, seeing the smile that automatically came on my face, he had me booked up to go with them.

Three weeks in a fantasy, the shops with showcases bursting with every type of clock, calculator and camera are there to confuse you, as how can you possibly choose from the hundreds and thousands of glittering gadgets? Peter and I tried but eventually gave up. You didn't want to look a trip of a lifetime in the mouth, but truthfully the magic of Hong Kong soon palled and the claustrophobia of the colony soon got to you. The filming was very efficient and I benefited from my friendship with Burt Kwouk, yet again playing the ever-faithful Cato, as (speaking fluent Mandarin) he took it as a personal insult if I had to pay more than necessary when we went shopping together.

Back in London, we started on the rest of the film. All my predictions about playing Dr Balls came true as Peter, needless to say, started laughing as we tried to get through the scenes. Declaiming the poem

In Winter, Summer, Snow or Hail,
Whether Long or Short, Dark or Pale,
Remember that when duty calls,
You've got Balls.

simply meant that Peter had to leave the set because he was laughing so much.

Two phone calls about photography came almost at the same time; the first from the Marchioness of Tavistock, at Woburn: "My mother tells me you have taken the best photograph of me she's ever seen, and I've never had the chance to look at it." The photograph she was talking about had been shot the previous year. I'd gone to Woburn, put the camera on a tripod, the marchioness had walked in the room, sat in the chair I'd prepared and I'd pressed the shutter. It had taken just over two minutes. It was a lovely shot, with available light plus small reflector. They used the picture in the Kodak exhibition, where I presume her mother had seen it, so I arranged for her to have a print.

The second call was just as aristocratic: "The Marchioness of Tavistock tells me you've taken the *best* picture of her she's *ever* had!" Considering the lady on the telephone was 84 at the time, the voice was clear and strident. "This is Barbara Cartland and I should be *delighted* if you would take some pictures of me. Publicity for a new perfume being launched in America. My son will, of course, see to the business side." That conversation led to one of the most delightful shoots I've ever had.

Her son did indeed see to the business side, and very handsomely, too. Within days I arranged to see the lady in person and taking Dean Smith, my make-up artist, plus Jenny Ford, assistant and general factotum, we arrived at the Hertfordshire home of Dame Barbara, and from the off it was sheer bliss. The house was straight out of one of her books. We never actually saw dashing young squires sheathed in tight trousers and shiny top boots lashing out with their whips at all and sundry, but we were delighted to be served lunch by a liveried footman. The white-gloved minion glided from guest to guest and, as if this gamesmanship was not enough, I noted how my two assistants were sat facing the large sunlit window while I, presumably on a higher social scale, got my back to it.

Despite being put ever so slightly in their place, Jenny and Dean sat enchanted as the Grande Dame, full of vim and vigour, poured out stories that encapsulated a pre-war society. Stories of glamorous '20s society poured forth. "*Twenty-seven times* I was proposed to." Casually indicating a magnificent portrait of Lord Louis Mountbatten, she patted the head of the large black Labrador who stayed faithfully with her at all times. "A present from dear Dickie. He *knew* how I loved dogs." She never told us if dear Dickie had also given her the yapping and permanently bad-tempered pekingese who dared anybody to stroke or fuss over it.

After lunch, a dramatic gesture: "Now, let's talk clothes. I think we'll start with the hats." A room door was opened and there were the *hats*. Rows and rows of them. Large, small, flowered, plain, cartwheel, cloche, all neatly arranged in serried rows. Dame Barbara viewed them with a knowing eye. "The choice," she gave an elegant gesture, "will be yours. However, you *may* wish to see the fur coats first. Another door was opened. "As well as the *dresses.*" There were *two rooms* of them. "As you may know, I do favour pink, but *you*," the famous eyelashes fluttered in my direction, "will be behind the camera, so…"

Reverent awe could best describe the look on the faces of Dean and Jenny. When it comes to assessing clothes, the little grey cells of women work overtime. Their computers click into tabulating every fabric, every stitch and every nuance of design. Alone, as the mere male, I effaced myself when it came to the clothing selection, with one exception. In the fur-coat room I pointed to the white mink. "That," I said, "is a must. Plus the hat."

The shoot was a joy. Jenny swung the lights into position, Dean gave final touches to the make-up, avoiding even the slightest displacement of the famous eyelashes, and we were away. Dame Barbara posed like a seasoned trouper and no qualifications reared their ugly head except one. If you *could*," the charm was almost overpowering, "arrange a light right there," she pointed dramatically to as spot almost at her feet, "it will ensure that all those naughty, horrible wrinkles will be obliterated." As that light, placed right there, would almost certainly have make her look like Bela Lugosi, I agreed but made quite certain the lamp in question was not coupled to the flash circuit. It gave a nice satisfying glow but had no effect on the pictures.

We did have many changes of clothes, but my instinct about the white mink proved right, and there, with the small Blackamoor statue obediently standing behind her, she looks (to say the least) queen of all she surveys. As a lady who wrote some 600 or 700 novels, bringing delight to millions of female readers worldwide, I feel she had a right to look satisfied. Her legacy of gadzooks Lady Barbara, with bodices bursting left and right, is a memory of a delightful, wonderfully eccentric lady.

Certainly in England, if I wrote that I had taken the only known photograph of Fiona Richmond with her clothes on, it would raise a laugh. The lady's name, mentioned in masculine company, would produce guffaws, chortles, sharp intakes of breath, nudges in the ribs and assorted schoolboy jokes on the level of "I'd like to get my arm around her waist and show her what for!", and all because an astute publisher by the name of Paul Raymond took it upon himself to publish the so-called wicked thoughts and deeds of the said Fiona in his magazine *Men Only*. She toured the country, giving us detailed descriptions of the naughty natives that she met on her journeys. The whole thing was a preposterous fake, of course, but extremely well written and, most of all, just (in the minds of the male readers) possible. Wild couplings in various provincial settings were par for the course. She only had to step off a train onto a countryside railway station and at once a sex-mad railway porter assaulted her in the waiting room. Never afraid to enjoy these moments, she then regaled her readers with intimate details of the said assaults, with accompanying nude pictures. The legend of Fiona was on the way, and in no time at all a film was mooted.

Rather cleverly, the makers of the movie did not fall into the trap of trying to make a home-made version of *Emmanuelle*. The provincial cities of England just don't have the allure of exotic Thailand, as chugging along the Manchester Ship Canal on a coal barge could never have the glamour of slim narrowboats gliding beneath sun-dappled foliage in Bangkok. Instead, they fell back on the time-honoured formula of Scotland Yard pursuing a heroic figure who, needless to say, was completely guiltless. Fiona, as the heroine, understood that he was completely guiltless and aided and abetted him. The twist was to place the action in the early '50s.

Our hero's name was Laid and, as the senior Scotland Yard detective in charge of the pursuit, I was given a huge close-up as I declaimed, "Let's get Laid!" Needless to say, the screenwriters could not miss this opportunity and made my line the title of the film. This title should have given us some warning, but Fiona was delightful, and any naughty bits in the film were put in later – an old dodge, but there's nothing you can do about it.

There were some moments that only occur in the movie world, as going for reality we filmed one day in the Marylebone morgue. Large, terrifying zinc trays used for the corpses, each with its drain hole, were a prominent feature of the main room, plus piles of indescribable chromium-plated surgical instruments. The head morgue attendant was straight out of a horror movie. Tall and thin, his face had prominent cheekbones, and his voice was Boris Karloff at his most sepulchral. He had a catlike walk and glided amongst the zinc tables, giving an occasional wolfish smile. Obviously a movie fan, he was delighted to have us, if only to brighten up his life. At the end of the day he offered a rather flaccid, cold hand, giving mine a mournful shake. "It has been a pleasure having you here, Mr Stark," he said, his eyes looking about with some pride at the various slabs and trays. "And I do hope it isn't too long before we see you here again!"

The Kodak exhibition of my photography early in 1978 was an accolade I never expected but, once offered, gave me a thrill. As the greatest name in photography, Kodak do mount this sort of thing terribly well, and it started on a low key. Colin Wharton, head of their exhibition department, asked to come to the studio to see my pictures. The prints, the negatives, the transparencies, the whole accumulation of my years of taking pictures was suddenly on display and, scattered about, the sheer amount of it looked quite impressive. The collection was transported to Ruislip, where I was invited several weeks later. The mounted photographs were displayed for my benefit and the effect was shattering. To give the exhibition department a two-and-a-quarter-inch negative and then see that same negative enlarged to six feet square was overpowering. Photograph after photograph had been given the same treatment and a few weeks later, at their headquarters in High Holborn, London, they went on display. A normal viewing audience of 5,000 for the month became 12,000-plus in the autumn of 1978. The exhibition toured England and did my self-esteem no harm at all.

15 Sergeant Bilko Proposes Marriage

Sadly, I didn't have a camera with me when I worked on the half-hour film *Le Pétomane* in 1978, which contained a performance so splendid that one runs out of superlatives trying to describe it. In the '70s and '80s, Leonard Rossiter rapidly became one of the leading comic actors on British television, with a series of situation comedies, when suddenly he was asked to make this film of one of the most bizarre theatrical artists in the history of the theatre. *Le Pétomane* was the true story of a French performer who, almost unbelievably, perfected the art of (and I can put it no more tactfully than this) audible flatulence. There were scales, there were trills, there was a range of sounds which reduced audiences in France during Victorian days to hysterics. It would be difficult to imagine anything more impossible than to put this story and character on the screen, but Leonard managed it.

Someone wanted some photographs of the giant Pink Panther that the film company had made for a children's party. Life-sized, he was a wonderful creation, and I decided to photograph him with a beautiful girl who had become a regular on the Panther films. Valerie Leon had the most glorious figure and legs that I had ever seen, so it was into a long, black, slinky dress, with a thigh-high slit in the skirt, and she would sit next to our Panther on a settee and try to seduce him. With a long cigarette holder in his hand, he would play the man about town, trying to retain his virtue. Valerie was delighted to pose, and all that remained was to bring the Panther to my studio from Shepperton. I sat him in the front passenger seat of my car, strapped his safety belt across his chest, and set off for north London. Not once in that entire journey did anyone react in any way. It could only happen in England.

I had a message to meet Richard Quine, American ex-writer and actor-turned-director. He was very charming, quietly spoken, and extremely nervous about his next job, which was directing Peter Sellers in his latest film, *The Prisoner*

Of Zenda. This big-budget movie would be filmed in Vienna and was based on the famous original story. Peter would be playing both mirror twins – one a lowly English cab driver, the other the wastrel king of a minor Balkan country. On paper it looked wonderful, but in practice it was hell, as it seems there were problems before it began. Peter was trying to get out of the film and Walter Mirisch, the producer, was making sure he stayed in it. The picture never really had a chance and Quine, to use B-picture parlance, was the fall guy. Whatever attempts he made to see things went smoothly were doomed, as he was stuck in the middle of no-man's land, with Mirisch and Peter in opposite trenches. He handed me the script, my role was explained to me and we next met in the Royal Gardens of Vienna.

Dressed in Ruritanian clothes, 200 extras strolled across the grass while a brass band pumped out Victorian melodies and I met up once more with Elke Sommer, whom I had led into her first meeting with Inspector Clouseau in *A Shot In The Dark*. The film was looking beautiful, with the huge glass conservatories of the gardens as a background, but the comedy was embarrassing. Obviously, Mirisch and Quine hoped it would be in the Panther mould, as the box-office returns of Peter's last film, *Revenge Of The Pink Panther*, just released in America, were coming in and they were astronomical. The budget of *Zenda* was immediately increased in the belief that the more you spent, the better the film became. A sad mistake, as it ended up with the dubious distinction of getting onto the list of all-time disaster movies. Apart from enjoying eating a lot of cream cakes in Demels, I was quite glad to leave Vienna.

A pair of thin legs, a boyish body, a cheeky smile and a delicious Cockney accent conjured up London's '60s. A real legend in her lifetime, Lesley Hornby, rechristened Twiggy by the equally unlikely named Justin de Villeneuve, first came into my orbit when we were both cast in *There Goes The Bride*, the film version of Ray Cooney's great stage success.

The location was Vero Beach, in Miami, halfway up the Florida peninsula, and was straight out of the travel brochure. It wasn't too rich a town – only two yachts per resident. Thrilled and delighted to have a genuine "Briddish" film, the residents were even more thrilled when they realised Twiggy would be with us. "Oh my Gawd! She sooo beautiful!! And will you look at that figure!" The natural pride of the British surfaced when we realised we had something truly original and delightful with us, and believe me, she was. I was hoping to get a good picture of Twiggy – after all, she was one of the most-photographed girls in the world – when fate took a hand.

In Miami, we used an American stills man for film, but suddenly he had some business to take care of. The producer asked a favour: "As the stills man is away for a couple of hours, would you consider helping us out?" My film was loaded and camera to the eye before he had finished speaking. Like a heat-seeker latched onto a jet plane, the camera lens swung immediately to Twiggy's face and, aware that the lens was pointed in her direction, her head lowered fractionally, her eyes opened wider and her tiny tongue moistened her lips while the shoulder nearest the camera raised slightly as a delicate smile flickered across her mouth. All of this took place in slightly under a tenth of a second. I squeezed the release button, the shutter was fired and there it was. All you had to do was point the camera.

Her role in the picture was as a '20s flapper, able to appear (or disappear) at will, and in one sequence – God knows why – she was to be found some 30 feet up in a palm tree. Film crews always have the answer and a platform was built by the tree, the top just out of shot. Professional to the end, Twiggy inched her way along the branch as, platform or not, she was still more than 30 feet in the air. Realising this was a shot in a million, I stuck on a long lens (200mm), put the camera on a tripod and waved like a lunatic at Twiggy. She saw the camera and, fighting God knows what attacks of vertigo, gracefully waved back, a lovely smile on her face. Off went the shutter and there was my "Twig On A Branch".

After the final screening of *There Goes The Bride*, it was discovered that the film was five minutes under time. Ray Cooney, who had written the original script, came up with the solution. Liking what I had done so far in the film, he altered both the start and finish of the picture, making my character (a waiter) suffer a nervous breakdown. I then had to become a psychiatrist's patient, and the powers that be selected Phil Silvers to play the part of the psychiatrist.

After being in almost every film musical of the '50s, Phil Silvers became a television giant as Sergeant Bilko. The domed head above the thick horn-rimmed glasses, and the glib stream of guile and flattery that poured in a never-ending torrent from him, was irresistible. The Bilko series moved into immortality and, as far as I can tell, will be shown forever more.

Our filming was in Hollywood (my first visit) and, like every other English actor, I stayed at the Chateau Marmont Hotel, the fake towers looking down on the small pool, the antiquated plumbing gurgling in the night. But it was home from home, as you knew there'd be someone from the old country there, and sure enough Ron Moody and Donald Pleasence were in residence. On the first night, we sat on the glamorous penthouse terrace on a warm Californian night, drinks in hand, gazing out at the million twinkling lights of Los Angeles, talking non-stop about England and whether it was better to eat your chips off a plate or out of a newspaper.

A hot, hot day in Hollywood took us to the large house and grounds where the shrink – as they say in showbiz – had his home. On the set stood Phil Silvers. "Baby," he said, and a large hand cupped round the back of my neck, pulling my head close into his chest. The Bilko character couldn't leave him. "Love your work! Love your work!" Then suddenly the voice lowered as he glanced at the script he held. "Haven't had a chance to look at this. You see, my daughter's had this heart attack, and they got her in hospital and, gee, you don't think about this sort of stuff while that's going on." Of course, he *had* had a look, but he didn't know a word. It was a long and tricky scene, and at rehearsal we tried to struggle through it.

Our director went white and gave me a hard and meaningful glance. He had that "Oh Christ, what are we going to do now?" look. There was a short break and the usual gallons of coffee were offered all round while Silvers meaningfully looked through the script. The director took me aside. "Not a word," he said. "Not a word does he know. Not a word, and we fly back to England tomorrow." Hysteria was strangling his voice.

"I have a suggestion," I said.

His eyes pleaded. "Anything!"

I carefully lowered my voice a couple of levels. "Just supposing you told him that I *too* don't know a word, owing to my being on the plane for so many hours, and would he mind terribly if we stuck the words up behind the camera so I can read them? They do all their television that way. The audience will never know. Especially with him."

And, of course, you couldn't. The scene played perfectly and it was all done on the first take. Afterwards, Phil glanced at all the words written up, then gave me a look. "Yeah, I guess it would have been difficult to learn all that on the plane. By the way, will you marry me?"

In the year 1510, a certain Alfonso de Albuquerque, the well-known Portuguese conquistador, set sail from Lisbon, navigating a rather tricky course down the west coast of Africa, around the Cape of Good Hope, through the Mozambique Channel, across the Arabian Sea, finally making landfall on the coast of India some 400 miles south of Bombay. As he had happened to discover one of the great natural harbours of the world, his somewhat articulate first mate, in his delightful Portuguese accent, spoke that famous line, "Cor, thees Alfonso, he ain't half a bit of a goer!"

Leaping ashore and sticking his arquebus in the sand, Alfonso came back with the equally famous line, "That's a great name for thees a place!"

Well, perhaps it didn't happen quite like that, but Alfonso did exist, and as far as I'm concerned he can go right to the top of my favourite explorer list. Had he not happened to land there and claim Goa for his country, I could never have made Gregory Peck such a proud and happy man.

Dennis arranged a meeting and I was cast in a new film. Gregory, along with Roger Moore, David Niven, Trevor Howard and a supporting cast of almost every well-known character actor in British movies, was filming there in this epic, boys' own, whizz-bang film. It was called *The Sea Wolves*, and the director was Andrew McLagen. (Anyone who remembers the giant, ambling actor Victor McLagen will remember his performance in *The Informer*, directed by John Ford. He was awarded the Best Actor Oscar, then spent the rest of his life as a member of the John Ford Repertory Company, appearing in most of his classic films. His son Andrew became a director, was just as physically large, at six foot seven, and spent a lot of time complaining about the heights of doorways.)

The Sea Wolves was a quite extraordinary true story of derring-do in World War II, when, in the dying days of the Raj in India, German spies were sending messages from neutral Goa to German submarines lurking off the coast. With monotonous regularity, the subs kept sending our ships to a watery grave. The film re-enacted the almost unbelievable voyage, on a small tramp steamer, of a motley crew of rather past-it ex-servicemen, nicknamed the Calcutta Light Horse. These volunteers sailed the steamer all the way from Calcutta to Goa (approximately 2,000 miles) to attack and destroy the spies' broadcasting station. In the film, I stood proudly steering the little ship, and alongside me was David Niven. Playing ex-Colonel Lewis, leader of the adventurous group, was Gregory Peck. Venerated in Hollywood as the actors' leading ambassador, he really did ooze charm, as he was very intelligent, well read and a paragon of virtue. One felt rather inferior, until that magic day when filming was over and we both sat on deck, side by side, sailing back to harbour. The legendary sunset of Goa was about to start. The enormous orange disc started its leisurely slide down into the Arabian Sea while Gregory and I, feet up on the rail, watched the magnificent cabaret that nature was laying on for us. "Spice Islands," he said. "No wonder the Portuguese fought to get here first. The wealth, the money." His hands gestured. "It was the meat, you know. It went off so fast they had to have the spices to kill the taste." I nodded sagely, not wishing to interrupt the flow, but rather wishing there could be some polite way to avoid a history lesson.

Then it was my turn to speak. "How does it feel," I said, "to be part of the English language?"

Gregory's head turned, all thoughts of an exotic exposition of the spice trade banished and, in the best Hollywood tradition of the taciturn cowboy, he merely asked, "Huh?"

This was my moment. The sun may have been dipping rapidly but I felt the glow of the informant about to impart secret knowledge. "Part of the English language," I repeated. "That's what you are, part of the English language."

Gregory had no further interest in the solar extravaganza, as his whole attention was now on me. "I don't quite, er…?" he said.

"Rhyming slang," I replied. "You are part of it."

Still baffled, but all his senses tuned to the fact that some remarkable information re himself was about to be revealed, he listened intently. He had tried to give me a rapid course on the history of the Spice Islands, and now it was my turn to reveal all about the pearly kings and queens of London and the magical world of rhyming slang.

Beginning with the easy ones, like "ball of chalk" for "walk" and "pig's ear" for "beer", I soon had his education well in hand. Once he understood you used only the first word on its own ("ball" for "walk", "pig's" for "beer"), he latched on fast. Then, to his delight, I spoke of the adoption of his name during wartime London to represent the thing you fasten a collar around. The "Gregory Peck" was the neck. No doubt about it, every serving soldier, every serving sailor and every serving airman (of which I was one) used that expression, as did all the true-blue Cockneys that got a right pasting in the Blitz. "And it's still used," I said, "to this very day!"

The light was almost gone when our little ship reached the jetty and standing waiting was Gregory's delightful French wife, Véronique. She raised a hand in greeting but was swamped by him hauling me up to her on the jetty.

"Tell her!" he said, his voice low and dramatic. "Tell her what you just told me!" Then, without waiting for a reply, he spoke again. "I'm part of the English language. Hear that? *Part of the English language!"*

The very next day, free from filming, we lounged by the pool. The delightful voice of Gregory's wife was in my ear. "Oh, you naughty man! What deed you tell 'im 'e was?" I explained quite briefly and, considering she was French, obviously quite lucidly, as she stepped back, gazed at the sky, threw her arms open wide and said, very loudly, "Merde!" Then she gave me a smile. "No wondair. 'E as been phoning 'Ollywood all evening telling all 'is friends 'e is part of the Eenglish language." Then the basic French lady asserted itself and she wagged a finger. "You know, 'eet is vairy expensive, but I tell you something: 'e would rather 'ave that than an Oscar!"

A press meeting was held for all the journalists desperate to record (both verbally and on film) the four distinguished film stars cast together for the first time. Photographers battled with their long lenses to get the exclusive picture, but I – with the cooperation of Roger Moore – scooped the pool. A group of conventional canvas-backed chairs was produced, each with the star's name carefully embossed on the back. Camera at the ready, I caught Roger's eye. "Sit in the wrong chair," I said. Immediately, he saw the joke and without a pause he sat in David Niven's chair. Grinning like schoolboys, the other three followed suit, each choosing a different chair and, as the shutter fired, I knew I had a lovely shot. One of the London papers got the picture and spread it across several columns.

Euan Lloyd, the producer, smiled affably and clutched me in a bear hug "Thanks to you," he said, "we have a North American deal. That photograph alone did the trick."

There is a group of people of whom I am inordinately fond. They encompass a very varied crowd ranging from the make-up department to the electricians, from the cameramen to the scene painters. I am referring to the film crew. Through the years, I've worked with many of them in every type of location. Hong Kong, Mauritius, Hollywood, Munich, Paris, on the sunny deserts of Jordan, on the rain-soaked streets of Swansea. To walk on a set and realise most of the crew are old friends is a delight. Every one is a friend, with (I am sorry to say) one terrible exception – a legendary figure in our profession by the name of Bert Batt.

Bert has such a stature in the film world that there are directors who would not consider making a film without him, as a great first assistant can make a picture. *The Sea Wolves* was sensible enough to employ Bert, as it was without a doubt a difficult film to get made. Four very major stars, a supporting cast of very well-known character actors and a lot of action with boats. Boats are, without a doubt, the nightmare of movies as they are large, unwieldy, not prepared to stop moving when the director shouts cut and, to put it mildly, a bugger. We had two boats on *The Sea Wolves* – one carrying the camera, the other the famous tramp steamer. I was asked if I could steer this and naturally, without any hesitation, I said yes. Actors always say yes to any such query. Of course you can ride a horse, of course you can swim underwater (several lengths), and parachute jumping is second nature to you. As long as you get the job, you can worry about the truth later. Anyway, standing at the tiller, doing helmsman acting, must be fairly simple, I thought – that was, until I saw the boat.

Bert Batt took me around the floating junk heap. It was a craft that made the *African Queen* look smart. "Don't worry," he said optimistically. "The captain will be in the wheelhouse with you at all times." The wheelhouse was a rather dirty-looking broom cupboard stuck on the deck and the captain was an Indian gentleman wearing a grubby, green T-shirt and a bedraggled pair of droopy shorts. He wore no headgear. For the purposes of the film, I was to steer this craft (I cannot really bear to label it as a "boat" any longer) up and down the coast while the camera, plus crew, were to be in the other boat, sailing alongside. The wheel, which I saw myself turning with ease, kept falling off. The captain had a pair of pliers permanently at hand and kept putting it back on again, tightening the relevant nuts.

I couldn't see any other problems except that the only other occupant of the wheelhouse, and therefore my passenger, was David Niven. I had just finished reading his all-time bestseller *The Moon Is A Balloon*, which talked of his glorious exploits in pre-war Hollywood, plus his glorious exploits as wartime colonel. His charm was legendary and he had the wonderful ability to make you think *he* was the lucky one to have *you* in his company. Bert duly introduced us, placed me by the wheel, made the captain hide down out of sight (so that I was apparently in complete control) and, with Niven by my side, we were instructed to go full steam ahead. The captain passed on this instruction to what was laughingly referred to as the engine room by banging on the wheelhouse floor. The camera boat signalled that they were filming, we kept chugging along beside them, then – more by luck than judgment – I became the hero of the hour.

Misunderstanding a frantic call from the camera boat, our captain suddenly popped up like a jack in the box, grasped the wheel and gave it a hard turn to port. We swung sharply left and, within a second, it was obvious that our bow was about to cut the camera boat neatly in half. Whether he had dyslexia or was profoundly deaf we never knew, but all I could see were the headlines: "Famous Film Star, Plus Supporting Player, Drowned Off Coast Of India". The shoulder charge I gave the captain was completely a reflex action, as survival makes one do the strangest things. All I know is the poor sod went straight back down to where he'd been before while I spun the wheel back the other way. Fortunately, we had enough speed to make the bow swing hard back to starboard, but it really was a close thing. Just a couple of feet in it.

Niven then gave me the ultimate accolade that one Englishman can give another. "Jolly good show!" he said.

There was a pause in the filming and we started to talk. "Just read *The Moon Is A Balloon*," I said. Niven smiled politely. "But," I continued, knowing he adored telling stories about Hollywood, "what's the chance of you telling me all the stories you couldn't print in the book?"

Well, it may be that he was just grateful for the shoulder charge, but a delightful smile came across his face. "Dear chum," he said (an expression that let you know you were now fully accepted), "ask what you will." I really didn't know where to begin. Had Errol Flynn really made all those conquests? And, when Niven was under contract to Goldwyn, were those famous girls around? So much gossip, so much scandal, so much rumour. A name came to my lips. The gorgeous girl from my teenage years, who stunned the world by appearing in those white shorts and turban, luring John Garfield to his doom in *The Postman Always Rings Twice* – the original sweater girl. "Lana Turner," I said.

Niven gave slight reminiscent smile. "Sweet little thing," he said. "I once had her halfway up a tree."

There are moments in my life that are clear, crystal, and set forever in (as Hercule Poirot has it) the little grey cells. That is one of them. There was the image of the glorious face and figure of Lana Turner, with vague foliage swaying in the background, while Niven precariously held onto her and a branch at the same time. And it was at that precise moment that Bert Batt entered the wheelhouse. "Sorry to interrupt, Mr Niven, but we need you up at the bow for a couple of close-ups." The authority of the first assistant is absolute, so David meekly followed him and we never got back to Lana Turner. A couple of years later, I worked with Niven again on *Trail Of The Pink Panther* in Cannes, but by then the news of his last, tragic illness had been made public and already he was finding it difficult to talk. Although he summoned up enough strength to greet me with "Hello old chum," it was no time to raise the question of Miss Turner and the tree. Re the eminent Bert Batt – well, my frustration lay not at the loss of prurient detail but at the loss of hearing one of the great storytellers of the century being cut off at the beginning of what promised to be the anecdote to end all anecdotes. Halfway up a tree!

Later, it did emerge that David was rather partial to taking other people's stories and making them his own. Blake Edwards, with some indignation, referred to the famous anecdote from *The Moon Is A Balloon* where David put his testicles in a glass of spirits to save them from frostbite. "I told David I'd been skiing and that had happened to me." Blake was quite adamant. "I can assure you, the balls in the brandy were mine!"

16 There's Only Myrna Loy, Deanna Durbin And Me Left

It was nice to be back in England again, if only to return to the superior picture quality on television. Something to do with the lines, I believe.

One day, the TV set in the corner had a surprisingly badly flickering picture. Then I realised it was showing a filmed interview from abroad of an old man talking and finding it hard to breathe. White-haired and frail, he spoke irritably of people thinking that he was getting too ill to work, and then I realised I was watching Peter Sellers. I truthfully hadn't realised it was him. He had been in Paris filming *The Fiendish Plot Of Fu Manchu* all the time I had been in India, and he seemed to have aged beyond belief. We had last spoken on the telephone while he was in Switzerland and he had spent the whole call telling me what I would be playing in the new Panther film – he and Blake had parted company and Peter would be scripting the picture with a new writer. The film interview had been shot at the Cannes Film Festival, where he hoped to get an award for his remarkable performance as Chance, the gardener in *Being There*. He had told me he was coming to London shortly for a reunion dinner with Spike Milligan and Harry Secombe, but on the day before the dinner he collapsed and died at the Dorchester Hotel in Park Lane.

His funeral in a small chapel in north London might have been the work of a Hollywood scriptwriter. Just before the funeral service, a storm broke out which the special effects department at Universal Studios in the great black-and-white horror days would have been proud of. Thunder crashed, lightning forked and torrential rain poured down. The service, conducted by the Reverend John Hester (a great friend of Peter's and I for many years), ended with Peter's personal request – a playing of the Glenn Miller recording of 'In The Mood', the great swing-band hit of wartime Britain. For me, it brought back memories of Peter as that leading aircraftsman for whom, years ago, he had mourned.

Like everything in Peter's life, his death attracted enormous publicity, but not necessarily for the right reasons. Bitterness clouded everything, as Peter's will left all his money to his widow, the young Lynne Frederick, leaving token amounts to his three children. The large fortune left to Lynne, who then spent a great deal of time publicly mourning (both in person and in print) made friends of Peter's uneasy. Spike Milligan wrote her a brief note telling her that Peter, only a few days before his death, had told Spike he intended to change his will so that his children would get a fairer share. Lynne replied with an even briefer note saying that she had to carry out Peter's final wishes. Spike had this placed in a glass-fronted frame in his toilet and on it was printed, "In case of dysentery, please break glass." There was a memorial service, at which David Niven gave the address and Dave Lodge and I were ushers. Lots of people came, and lots of people stayed away.

Lynne constantly spoke and wrote of her undying love for her late husband, and then, six months to the day after his death, she married again. Every so often, she was quoted as saying that Peter had spoilt her for any other man, but then she married for a third time, had a child and died, huge and obese (mainly from drink and a certain number of drugs). I don't know what happened to the money. It was a sad and sordid ending to someone I had been friends with for so many years and with whom I had such laughs.

The most flattering thing that can happen to an actor, regarding a film, is to have a script delivered at your door with no consultation, no interview and no audition. Speed-reading as you go, you're straight through the script until the character you're going to play enters the film, then you slow down and read it twice, mentally making notes of all the good lines. Finally you check if there is any eating in it. Do you have to do any stunts or ride a horse, and is there any sex involved? Then it's onto your agent, who reveals the pittance the company is offering but reminds you it will fit in with that television he thinks you will be just right for. The script for *Victor/Victoria* arrived with the note, "For the part of the landlord." I did all the above and no, there wasn't any eating, no stunts and a horse was never mentioned, but there was some sex involved. The script was sent by Blake Edwards and read splendidly, but there was a problem. Set in Paris in the '20s, and starring Julie Andrews as a singer forced to appear as a male, my role as the landlord meant that I should attack the lady with sexual intent. As I had known Julie most of my life, it did jar. In her early days, she stopped every show she appeared in and soon featured at all the top music halls of the country. On her 18th birthday, she had been playing at the Finsbury Park Empire. I had picked her up in my little car and, by frightening her to death, got her to her home at Walton-on-Thames just before midnight so she could still celebrate the birthday. Thinking it over, I didn't fancy the sexual intent.

The luck I have had in my life through chance encounters has always amazed me. Two days after receiving the script, I walked through the dining room at Pinewood and came face to face with Tony Adams, who has always produced Blake's films. A cheery smile, and what did I think of the script? I told him they had me in the wrong part and the waiter in the restaurant was more my style. Sure enough, the next day I was playing the waiter. Filming at Pinewood once more, the sets were fabulous, period cars glided through the Paris of the '20s, and in a restaurant I obsequiously bowed to both Julie and Robert Preston, in true Gallic manner. Desperate for food, they ate everything possible and smuggled a cockroach into the salad to get away without paying. Then, the cockroach escaping, they started a fight. I wondered if Julie's contract had anything about free food, as she had to eat non-stop for days. Finally, I waved Blake goodbye.

"You're not finished yet," he said.

I stayed for weeks, Blake giving me more and more to do, and I have memories of James Garner, after the fifth week, giving me an old-fashioned look. "You bastard," he said. "You've got a better part than I have." The film was a big success in America.

In the grounds of what is undoubtedly the most luxurious house on the French Riviera, a film crew, plus actors, assembled to make *Trail Of The Pink Panther* and *Curse Of The Pink Panther*, two films, made back to back, and using the Panther name – but missing from the cast list of both was Peter Sellers as Inspector Clouseau. They had a lot of outtakes of him, but that bumbling, accident-prone, quick-to-take-offence, inept, idiot policeman was sadly missed. The checked hat, the Humphrey Bogart private-eye raincoat, the eyes ever searching for (and invariably finding) affronts to his dignity – all perpetually moving towards what we knew would be a minefield of water buckets to step in, soap bars to slip on, swinging doors to personally attack him and, most famously, small dogs to bite him.

However, there were compensations, as most of the cast of the first Panther film were there – David Niven, Capucine, Robert Wagner – but time was taking its toll. On the very first morning, Blake Edwards took me to one side and gave me the dreadful news of Niven's illness. I hadn't seen him since our time together in Goa and, as if in perfect health, he gave me the "Hello, old chum", followed by the excuse for the ever-so-slight problem with the speech. "Got this bloody disease, you see. Slows down the old tongue, what? Probably talked too much in the past, that's the trouble."

And then Robert Wagner. Two weeks before our meeting, the accident with the small boat off the island of Catalina had occurred. However terror-stricken she was of dark water, Natalie Wood – the beautiful actress he had remarried – had decided to go ashore in the middle of the night, and as she stumbled and fell, her clothing, heavy and sodden with sea water, had pulled her down into that same dark water. Nevertheless, the still-boyish-looking actor went professionally about his work.

Lunch on any film shot in France is always a delightful occasion. The stodge of England is avoided, the gargantuan portion sizes of the USA are frowned upon and delicacy is the order of the day. The French caterers did us proud. Seated on long benches, either side of the table, it was a splendid turn-out and, forgetting all personal problems, the actors were regaling each other with the latest stories and gossip. Luckily, actors have the ability to make light of problems and, faced with any audience, captivate all and sundry with their latest anecdote – what went on on the set at Pinewood during the latest costume extravaganza, as well as the sordid details of the recent sex scandal on that film in Spain.

Niven, not a muscle giving away what was happening to him, smiled benignly at all his chums and Herbert Lom chatted away in at least six languages while Capucine, elegant and very beautiful, talked clothes with Joanna Lumley. Suddenly, she went bright purple, gave a retching cough and clawed helplessly at the air. At once, Robert Wagner, seated next to her, leapt to his feet and from behind wrapped his arms tight around her waist. Tense with effort, he gave her ribcage a huge bear hug, forcing her body down onto the table and air up her windpipe. Capucine gave a gasping cough and there, on the table, was the piece of steak that had been clogging her throat. It was all so swift and neat. Wagner dismissed the praises of his action. "Let me tell you," he said. "Only a few weeks ago I was having a dinner on a yacht, same thing exactly. Girl next to me. Just a piece of meat. I did the same thing. So, naturally, I remembered." It was ironic – saving a lady's life on a yacht shortly before losing your own wife, also on a yacht.

Night shooting on any film always creates its own excitement, especially as we were filming both Panthers in Cannes. The huge film lights, aptly named

In Winter, Summer, Snow and Hail, whether Long or Short, Dark or Pale, remember that, when duty calls, you've got Balls! *The Revenge Of The Pink Panther*. Shepperton Studios, 1978

Robert Loggia lurking in Hong Kong. *The Revenge Of The Pink Panther*, 1978

Burt Kwouk shopping in Hong Kong, 1978

An off-the-set shot of Blake Edwards. Hong Kong, 1978

Each and every one in the wrong chair! *The Sea Wolves*. Goa, 1979

Dame Barbara Cartland at home. Hertfordshire, 1979

Twig on a branch: Twiggy on location at Vero Beach, *There Goes The Bride*. Miami, 1979

"How soon can we go on honeymoon?" Phil Silvers after his proposal. Hollywood, 1979

Ron Moody and Donald Pleasence on the roof terrace at Château Marmont, Hollywood, 1979

Robert Wagner on the set of *Trail Of The Pink Panther*. Nice, 1982

"And then Garbo said to me…" The one, the only Vincent Price. Elstree Studios, 1983. *Blood Bath At The House Of Death*.

Doing my best to smuggle some photographs. Jakarta Airport, 1985

Bruce Willis and Kim Basinger. *Blind Date*. Hollywood, 1986

Bruce Willis on the set of *Blind Date* before wishing me luck with the Doberman. Hollywood, 1986

"Never mind what Blake Edwards said. Just bite the bone!" *Blind Date*. Hollywood, 1986

"I want a nice tight shot of the dog's teeth!" Blake Edwards directing *Blind Date*, 1986

After the dog. *Blind Date*. Hollywood, 1986

Robson and Jerome, London, 1996

The last toilet roll in Russia! Gareth Hunt, Yalta, 1997

Jack Palance about to reconquer southern Russia. *The Adventures Of Marco Polo*. Yalta, 1997

Nigella Lawson. London, 1997

The loverly Lumley! Joanna swings. London, 1997

Rolf and Alwen Harris at home with their totem pole, 1997

brutes, were focused on the front of one of the huge Baroque hotels that line the seafront as one of our stuntmen, five storeys up, clambered across the elaborate facade. No safety harness or nets spread beneath him, he climbed out of one of the windows and, like a spider, found his way across. David Niven stood by my side, covered his eyes with a hand and said, "I can't look. Tell me when he's done it." A smattering of applause as the stuntman reached the window, and Niven took his hand away.

Nancy Davis was causing a lot of interest amongst the paparazzi who continually circled us but, as she was President Reagan's daughter, that was hardly surprising. A nice and charming girl, she had a small part in one of the Panther films and, as we gave each other a nod of recognition, a secret service man shoulder-charged me. I went into the gutter on my bottom as he shoved Nancy backwards against a wall. "Second shop doorway on your left, but we got you well covered." Another secret service man joined him, their hands ominously inside their leather jackets. They glared about, daring any terrorist to make a move as a gendarme hustled a perfectly innocent onlooker away.

Nancy helped me to my feet. "Gee, I'm so sorry. This happens all the time."

A week later, an Englishman at the hotel stared hard. Not at me, of course, but at the lady lying by my side. You couldn't really blame him, as the lady lying by my side happened to be the fantasy girl of most English men. The fact that she was wearing a bathing costume, and was elegantly stretched out as only an ex-model girl knows how, was an additional attraction. The girl was Joanna Lumley and she and I were still waiting in Nice, still waiting to film our scene together in *Trail Of The Pink Panther*. The Englishman could contain his envy no longer. "It's all right for some," he said.

I did my best to console him as I patiently explained that part of a film actor's job was to – how could I put this delicately? – hold himself, or herself, in readiness at all times. "Any day now," I explained, "we—" I vaguely waved in Joanna's direction "—will be placed in front of a camera. One hundred technicians will be crouched behind it and Blake Edwards will call out, "Action!" That is when we—" once more I gestured "—will have to deliver lines and action, immediately. No mistakes. No errors. That is why we are kept in readiness." The Englishman retired, not really satisfied with the explanation, but it was the best I could do.

Sure enough, that very evening the assistant director gave us the news: morning flight to Paris, then filming the next day. It was a long scene Joanna and I had to play and, like the very professional actress she is, we rehearsed the lines on the plane, we rehearsed them in the make-up room and we also rehearsed them in the back of the car while we waited on the banks of the Seine for Blake. The setting by the river was, of course, the eternal Paris we all knew – the wide embankments, the elegant glass-topped passenger boats gliding by. So different to the greedy property gentlemen in London, all trying to outdo each other with uglier and uglier buildings.

The scene involved Joanna, as a reporter, tracking down Hercule, Inspector Clouseau's first assistant (played by myself), who has now retired and lives on a barge on the river. And there the barge was – very large and ominous, it had been carefully towed all the way up the Seine and was now moored, festooned with plants, by the bank. The large crew of technicians had gathered, the huge Panavision camera was wheeled into view and large arc lights plus diffusers were placed in position near the barge while four enormous trailers (one for make-up, one for wardrobe, one for Joanna, one for me) came down the slipway. Several hundred eager Parisians, excited by the appearance of the camera equipment, hung over the street railings above us. Finally, in majestic convoy, three large black limousines moved down the slipway to join us, and Blake Edwards and his minions climbed out.

The ritual of the director's morning appearance on the film set has many clear, and exact, rules – so exact that the movements, and placing, of the crew become like a precisely choreographed ballet. To begin with, the first assistant director, as the director's right-hand man, takes temporary control and absolute silence must be observed until decisions are taken. It may look haphazard, but the discipline of a film crew, particularly an English one, is something to behold. The word "silence", uttered by the first (as he is known), makes everyone on the unit speechless. Even movement is frowned upon and woe betide anyone who breaks the rule. Two people then move either side of the director, the first and the lighting cameraman. Satisfied that a total blanket of silence has descended, the first leans close and quietly speaks to the director: "When you're ready, governor."

In the meantime, the lighting cameraman has his own ritual. From a hammered silver metal, velvet-lined box, he reverently lifts the viewfinder. This piece of optics is the ultimate decision-maker for every director and, by using the built-in masks and zooms, he can decide just what lens and frame will give him the shot he wants. It may be quite small and light, but it nevertheless has a chain attached. Rule number one: always put the chain around your neck, as not many film budgets will stand one of these expensive optics being shattered. Having secured the finder round his neck, now comes the director's opening and most important ritual – the director's stance. Like a dancer, he parts his legs, balances his body, then lifts the finder to his eye. Crouched, and with body slightly tilted forward, he goes into what appears to be a boxer's shuffle. The finder, held with one hand, is panned from side to side while the other hand twists the zoom ring, adjusting the focal length.

Breathlessly, and without a single movement, the assembled crew watch until the shuffle ends, the finder is lowered and final directions re the camera position are given. But today was different. Blake had adapted the stance and, with legs apart, body crouched, he swayed from side to side, the finder panning left and right and then, dramatically, he stopped dead. Fascinated, we watched as he slowly started to bend backwards, the viewfinder pointing higher and higher into the sky and, as the backward bend continued, he became like a human Tower of Pisa, defying gravity. Finally, the viewer was removed from the eye, he looked accusingly around and said, "How long has that been there?" He was pointing at the Eiffel Tower.

The first, with true British understatement, spoke quietly. "I believe it's been there quite some time."

Words spoken softly are always more effective. Blake spoke just as quietly. "In the script it clearly states Hercule has retired and lives on a barge in a quiet backwater. How do I shoot without showing that?" He pointed an accusing finger at the giant Meccano set Alexandre Eiffel had planted in the centre of Paris. "We'll shoot this sequence in London next week." The three black limousines glided back up the slipways and Blake was gone.

Joanna and I climbed into our car and there was a silence as the tension subsided, and Joanna – the beautiful model, the elegant actress – spoke a line that endeared her to me more than ever. "Oh gosh," she said, and then burst into floods of tears. Finally, dabbing at the remains of her mascara, she gave a smile. "Mind you, we did get a dishy week in the south of France, didn't we?"

The miracle of movies. As promised, that barge (God knows how) was towed down river, across the channel and up the Thames to Teddington Lock. Joanna and I shot our scene and, of course, Blake was right – the Eiffel Tower, seen pointing skyward in a quiet backwater of the Loire, would have been a bit much.

Back in England, I impressed my three children by appearing on television in a pop video with the current teen idol, Adam Ant. Like any father, I was baffled by the passion my daughter had for this boy wearing a pirate outfit with stripes on his face, assuming he was all part of the degeneracy overtaking our country. But working with him I found he was charming, quietly spoken and highly literate. Then I became a bigger hero by being cast in *Superman III*. The children walked round me slowly, seeing me in a new and favourable light. "Are you going to fly with him?" was the first question.

"I don't think so," I said. "Just a very funny sequence before and during the credit titles."

They walked some more. "Well, if he *asks* you, will you fly with him?"

I tried to explain that I thought it highly unlikely that he would ask me, and that the only flying I would be doing was to Calgary, in Canada, where the film was being shot. They weren't very happy about this reply, but it just shows where children's priorities lie. To this day, I have a window cleaner, with three sons, who apparently always refer to me as "Superman three" because of my vague connection. Anyway, I did fly to Calgary – via Air Canada, not sailing unhindered through the skies – and I instantly fell in love with the place. Put down on the vast plains of Canada, within viewing distance of the giant Canadian Rockies, it has a sparkling newness of buildings and streets that makes you realise why it was chosen as Metropolis.

It was a reunion for me with Richard Lester, who had directed (it seemed a lifetime ago) all the Goon Shows on TV. He carried on the flair when he directed the very successful *Three Musketeers: The Queen's Diamonds*, and now he was behind the camera on *Superman III*. I had very little to do with Christopher Reeve, but he seemed very much liked by the crew, which is as good a test of an actor as I know. The terrible accident that crippled him was in the future but, watching him striding about the set in his Superman clothes, so full of vigour and dash, it seems such a bitter twist of fate that such a tragedy should happen.

I had always assumed that I had the monopoly in my family when it came to flying away to exotic locations, but my youngest son, Timothy, went to his school plays and kept getting laughs. He rapidly became a very adept performer and, as it never did me any harm, I never discouraged him. Fortunately, my wife Audrey has always been an actress and, with our mutual knowledge, pressure was never put on him. He found his own way and it soon proved a very successful way. In April 1983, a first-class flight for him and his mother to South Africa was laid on for his appearance in an adventure television series there. I bravely looked after the other two children, but sadly they soon both acquired a lifelong hatred of frozen dinners and tinned rice pudding, although they had to admit that my poached eggs on toast were a work of art.

If July 1983 stands out in my memory, it is for one quiet, wonderful, rainy afternoon in a caravan parked in a field in Hertfordshire. The caravan was small and rather basic, as the film company that was paying for its hire was also small and rather basic. The small-budget film was a starring vehicle for comic Kenny Everett. A huge success on television, Kenny was now making a comedy horror film and, just so the public would have no doubts about what they were going to see, its title was *Bloodbath At The House Of Death*. The caravan had been placed in quite a pleasant bit of woodland on the outskirts of north London and served as some sort of dressing room cum place to shelter from the rain, but there was no complaint from me, as the two other occupants, both fellow actors, made up for the small and basic by their company. First, someone I had known and worked with since the early '50s, David Lodge, and the other actor I had only known since that morning.

Actors – and it's obvious when you think about it – are more stagestruck than your average person. Let them meet a legendary member of their profession and they are inclined to be overawed. A violinist meeting Menuhin, a cellist Casals, a nightclub singer bumping into Sinatra. In the confines of that caravan – and we are talking somewhere about eight feet by twelve – it did come as a shock to be continually looking at and listening to Vincent Price. How many cinemas I had sat in and watched this elegant actor showing most of the Hollywood crowd how to do it. Act, I mean. Suave, demonic, witty, with a twinkle in the eye, and all done with such wonderful panache. Was ever a cloak twirled more stylishly, a rapier wielded more delicately, words spoken more elegantly?

And here he was in person. Cast for years in horror movies, it was understandable that he would be in this comic send-up as a "guest artist". (I always think that's better billing than "special appearance of".) The guest-artist label meant we had him for at least three days, but those three days were memorable. As if to celebrate his arrival, the sky decided to give us a rainstorm of biblical proportions, and David and I gave the rain our special blessing, as we had the chance to be regaled by one of the great storytellers of Hollywood. And what stories they were! There was no one he hadn't met, acted with, ate with, been to parties with. I don't quite remember when the name-dropping started, but when it did they fell in ever-increasing numbers and, as the deluge outside continued to bounce on the caravan roof, Vincent worked in Howard Hughes, who had signed him to a seven-year contract but never let him meet him. Patriotism made me get in Princess Margaret and the night I kept calling her darling, to which he swiftly countered with Jackie Kennedy asking him what paintings should go on the White House walls.

I couldn't compete when it came to Garbo swimming nude in his pool, but I kept up the British end by telling him how Sir Thomas Beecham helped me with a comedy routine. While the wheels of the caravan continued to sink lower into the quagmire of Hertfordshire, the stories and the deluge kept going. Yes, Cecil B De Mille *was* a bully and a pig, and Myrna Loy *was* a darling! Firmly Democratic Party, Vincent gave the Reagans and the Bushes a delightful going-over, and then we got to John Wayne, the arch-conservative who had advanced (on film), bazooka in hand, destroying the might of the Third Reich almost single-handed. His successful attempt to stay right out of the war, spending sunny years in Hollywood, was recounted with zest.

Totally uncensored, we shared Anglo-American gossip and filth, and time (to coin a cliché) whizzed by at a speed that would have done credit to Concorde. Finally, the drumming on the roof ceased, the assistant director trudged through the mud to tell us the sun was about to come out, the producers put away their suicide pills and we got on with the filming. Two days later came the sad farewell to Vincent, and six days later came the envelope from California enclosing a colour postcard. The handwritten message was from Vincent and it was very funny, very complimentary and, most of all, very nostalgic for that splendid afternoon in the caravan. Apparently, Vincent's main delight was the chance to restock his larder of stories with some of mine. As a true gent, he assured me I got full credit at the dinner parties, or wherever. The name-dropping in his letter was more outrageous than ever.

The correspondence began then and, I'm happy to say, continued. In the summer of 1986, I went to Hollywood to film *Blind Date* for Blake Edwards, and naturally I called him up. He made a few pleasantries then explained that he was leaving for Canada the next day to work with Bette (Davis), Lillian (Gish) and not forgetting Ann (Sothern) on the film *The Whales Of August* – the name-dropping was done with such relish! Our correspondence continued, then suddenly the handwriting deteriorated and, almost formless and childlike, it wandered across the pages, a half-crushed spider fallen into a bottle of ink. Typically Vincent, he joked about having such a wandering hand.

Then, almost like a miracle, a different person could have written the next letter. Strong, clear, the writing flowed effortlessly and all was revealed. Parkinson's had been diagnosed but some treatment was being administered and was having an extraordinary effect. Viagra, it seems, had nothing on this, and Vincent's only worry was who was going to hold the horses! He was also concerned that so many of the "greats", as he called them, had passed on and that the number of names to drop was getting smaller. "There's only Myrna Loy, Deanna Durbin and me left!" he wrote.

Late in 1991, there were two full-page obituaries – one in the *Daily Telegraph*, the other in the *Independent*, both writing of Coral Browne, the delightful actress who was Vincent's wife. The rarity of a full-page obituary gave one an idea of how much she was admired in England, so the cuttings went off to Vincent. He was very thrilled that I'd sent them and his letter in itself was a short and very loving obituary of Coral. He wrote of her illness: "She had a long hard go of it but now is at peace at last."

Finally, Vincent's turn came and he duly made his exit into the celestial wings, no doubt giving his cloak a devil-may-care twirl as he went.

17 Return Of The Prink Pranther

John Whiting, the head of Promandis, one of the major photographic dealers in London, looked at me and said, "Remember, you must never let a Chinese gentleman lose face. You will be the Chans' guest in Singapore, and that means you never, ever try to pay for anything. You do understand, don't you?" I gave him a nod, and one of the four unbelievably beautiful Chinese ladies – our hostesses on the plane, all dressed in one of the most alluring garments known to mankind, the cheongsam – passed me another drink.

It was 30 September 1985 and, in the height of luxury, stretching our legs knowing we could never reach the seat far in front of us, we were flying first class to Singapore. The ripples of the Kodak exhibition had spread far and wide and I was being flown to the East as an ambassador for both Promandis and Polaroid, combined with the delightfully named Ruby Photo Company. Two Chinese entrepreneurs, the twin brothers Fred and Charlie Chan, owned this company and they both bowed in unison at Singapore Airport as if joined by a string. Their organisation was faultless and cars were at the ready, doors swung open at precisely the right moment. The Pavilion Hotel was a marvel – a little more bowing at reception, I filled in the register, and by the time I'd reached my room, 25 storeys up, a pile of hotel stationery with my name stencilled in gold across the top lay on the desk by the bed.

A set of lectures on glamour photography, plus a collection of my prints, plus the photographing of a local female model was the itinerary, and each lecture was packed out. It was just before the first one that I got cold feet. Would they know all the people I had pictures of and, come to think of it, would they know me? I walked on, 100 Chinese photographers looked at me and one of them, in the front row, said, "Ah, Prink Pranther!" They knew Elizabeth Taylor; they knew Yul Brynner; they were mad about Ursula Andress; and, as Singapore is full of movie fans, they were mad about all the pictures. The lady model, a local beauty queen, was a huge success and we finished by giving away lots of Polaroid film so they could take pictures themselves. Fred and Charlie bowed so much afterwards I thought their heads were coming off. Even John Whiting inclined his head several inches and said, "First class."

It was not until a few days later, when we flew to Jakarta, that trouble appeared. A huge wooden packing case, one foot by four feet by six feet, had been tailor-made to hold all the big prints I had with me and caused a sensation when it was wheeled off the plane. A customs man walked round it several times, looked at me and then vanished into a small office. After a moment, he emerged, crooked his finger and I followed him through the door, where sitting behind a desk there was a formidable set of white and gold teeth. These belonged to the head customs officer. He didn't do any bowing.

"What you got in case?" he said.

"Elizabeth Taylor, Ursula Andress, Mia Farrow," I replied. I felt that, if I got in as many glamorous names as possible, it might help, but it didn't. More of the teeth came into view and they weren't smiling, so I realised I had better explain they were just photographs and not the real thing.

A few of the teeth disappeared as he pointed at me. "Prink Panther?" I modestly smiled and he said, "500 dollars." John Whiting took care of the bribe – which, of course, it was – as we needed the pictures and Gold Teeth was quite aware of this. What he wasn't aware of was that, while all this was going on, Fred and Charlie were quietly smuggling masses of photo equipment into Jakarta. The large box acted as a splendid decoy.

The trip to Malaysia, including Singapore, Jakarta and Kuala Lumpur, was a wonderful trip, as I finished up spending a week at the Rasa Syang Hotel (a paradise in Penang) eating exotic food, my choice from the menu as guided by the Chans. A year later, their heads still bobbing in unison, they came to London, and this time I was able to play host. The obvious place for me was to dine them at Langan's (partly owned by Michael Caine), and, displaying the menu, I grandly asked the twins if they wished any guidance re the food. They smiled politely and, in unison, said, "Bif stek." And beef steak they had.

July 1986 and Dennis was on the phone: "You're on a plane to Los Angeles Tuesday, as Blake Edwards wants you in *Blind Date*. They've arranged all the work permits."

Tuesday it was, and first class (of course), so nonchalantly turning left on entering the plane, and pressing lots of buttons, I was horizontal as soon as possible. It seems Blake felt his film needed a butler, and when Hollywood thinks butlers, it thinks Englishmen.

There's a lot to be said for specialising in servile parts, but at Los Angeles Airport, set once more to win the heart of Tinseltown, all was nearly lost. I had not counted on the coincidence of Robert Morley and I arriving in Hollywood at precisely the same moment. Apparently, Robert was making a series of TV commercials for British Airways and, while a camera filmed his every movement, he was busily surveying the airport scene. Then his eye spotted me. With a delicious mock frown, he glanced at the female American customs officer who, in her smart uniform, was holding my passport and checking if the picture in it and I were in any way similar. "Surely," said Robert in his very best English-judge-on-the-bench voice, "surely you are not letting *him* into the country!"

The passport snapped shut and the customs officer, face unmoved, expressionless, and with apparently no visible sense of humour, looked at me. "Why should you not be allowed in the country?" The large book, always at the ready at every desk, was flipped open while her eyes checked the list of malcontents prepared to overthrow the American government. Robert gave me a smile, a farewell wave and, with his camera crew, moved on.

I gave the lady what I hoped would be an ingratiating smile as she searched for my name. "I do assure you," I began, knowing that any problem in America is always helped if you at once speak in an overdone English accent, making your words as pedantic as possible, "I do assure you that that is a joke. Mr Robert Morley and I are old acquaintances, and I am here to work for Mr Blake Edwards on his new film."

The book was slammed shut immediately. "Gee, you're an actor, workin' for Blake?" I realised I was in a company town where movie-makers rule. "You got a great director there," she said. "Have a nice day." The rubber stamp hit the page and I was waved through as an honoured guest of America.

I moved to the outer glass doors and, as they slid apart, I saw one of the leading men from *Dallas*, or it could have been *Baywatch*. Anyway, he stood over six feet, was very blond and handsome and wore a smart grey chauffeur's uniform. He gave a slight bow and said, "I am your driver while you are in Los Angeles. My name is Vince, and just you let me know where you want to go." He then indicated a silver stretch limousine, which seemed to occupy most of the sidewalk and, as I sank into the enormous rear seat, he settled behind the wheel giving me a smile through the rear-view mirror. "Of course, you know I only do this as a sideline," he said. "I'm really an actor!"

Concerned in the past about violence dogging my footsteps (the bombing of Liverpool, Vesuvius erupting, the V-1s as I returned to London), I was naturally not at all surprised when an earthquake hit Los Angeles the night I arrived. Friends Brian and Lisa Johnson had let me stay with them at their beach house on Pacific Coast Highway (built by an early movie hero of mine, Richard Dix) and, as the building swayed and rocked, I assumed that the piles that jutted from the shore, holding the building erect, were merely moving with the sea. But no, it was a full recorded-on-the-Richter-scale earthquake. Brian and Lisa gave a shrug of the shoulders and said, "There's a new seafood restaurant down the road we should check out."

A swish, and I mean swish, waiter paused at the table, leant closer and spoke: "I just snuck by to tell you that you were *divine* in *Victor/Victoria* and I would recommend the seafood salad." Get a good film out on release and you can own Los Angeles for at least a week.

"Winnebago" is the one word that every agent in Hollywood knows how to spell. The moment the fee for his actor is settled, then the size of the Winnebago (the giant trailer/dressing room in which his client will spend his time) is settled, and woe betide that agent if his client has a smaller one than his co-star. It is rumoured that certain artists have been seen pacing out the length of their rivals' accommodation.

The first morning on the film, I arrived to see a giant herd of these monsters parked round one of the largest swimming pools in Hollywood. Technicians scuttled to and fro as limousine after limousine arrived, disgorging actors. Vince, sun glinting on his perfect dentistry, ushered me from my car as Kim Basinger climbed out of her car and spoke in a delicious southern accent. "Ahm your greatest fan," she said. This was my first exposure to the over-praise that is the norm in the film capital. We then went into the make-up trailer. Bruce Willis also smiled but never spoke of being my fan.

While Bruce and Kim were having their make-up applied, my make-up lady, a native of Brooklyn, viewed me with deep concern, giving a worried shake of the head. She then announced loudly, "Will you look at that goddamn complexion? You goddamn Briddish are all the same, it's all that goddamn rain you get over there. Git out of that chair! You don't need any goddamn make-up." Realising I had made a good start for the old country, I went to meet Blake, who stood gazing at the huge pool, and the 200 extras gathered around it. He then turned his attention to a large black Doberman that lay by a kennel, a stout chain fastened to its neck. The heat was making it pant and its half-opened mouth revealed a set of long, white, glistening fangs. Thoughts of the hound of the Baskervilles, loping relentlessly through the fog of Dartmoor, came to mind.

Kim Basinger joined us as Blake, narrowing his eyes, gave me a look. "Tell me, Graham. What does the word *mooning* mean to you?"

I gave a slight smile and said, "Well, in England it means looking lovesick at a girl."

Blake smiled back. "It doesn't mean that in America."

Kim looked at the dog, looked at me and then said, "Oh, Blake, you're not going to...?"

The dog handler was called and gave me an encouraging smile. "You got absolutely nothing to worry about. You *can* run fast, can't you?" Then all was revealed. For plot reasons, I had to moon the dog, which simply meant exposing my bare bottom to the slavering hound, and as the animal went for the inviting pink target I had to race through a wire gate, shutting it behind me. All films in Hollywood are taken seriously, a big-budget one even more so. The hinges of the wire gate were checked and well oiled, rubber patches were stuck on the soles of my shoes in case I slipped and there was serious debate about my trousers falling the necessary amount in the required time.

"We can only do this shot once," said Blake.

"I am not sorry to hear that," I replied.

Like Roman citizens at the Colosseum, the crowd of extras gathered, the film crew took up their stations and Bruce Willis patted me on the back and wished me luck while the rest of the cast, including Kim, stood with Blake behind the camera. The dog handler, his moment arrived to show he knew what he was doing, held tight to the chain attached to the Doberman. "Make sure the dog knows he goes for Graham," said Blake.

The handler looked injured, took a small piece of meat from his pocket and offered it to the Doberman, who gave a pleased snarl and sank his teeth into it. "He knows, all right." Then he wagged his finger at me. "Whatever happens, you keep goin', OK?"

Blake nodded to the first assistant, who nodded back, and then Blake called, "Action." From the side of the pool, I slowly walked into shot, looked at the dog, a moment of confrontation, then I undid my belt buckle and slid my trousers down my thighs until, judging enough flesh to be on display, I swiftly turned and showed my bottom to the dog. The handler let go of the chain and, setting a new southern Californian sprint record, I was through the gate, the bolt was fastened and on his hind legs the Doberman, slavering wildly, gnashed his teeth with frustration above the wire meshing.

1986 became a year of international travel. I didn't get a stretch limo in Spain, but the large bus that took myself and the rest of the cast to Little Hollywood, in Almería, was quite reasonable and, apart from the Spanish drivers' habit of seeing who could do the most daredevil things with a 50-seater coach on a mountain road, we did get to the location in one piece. A TV series, *Neat And Tidy*, set us down in this curiosity of a small cowboy town, built in the foothills of the Sierra Nevada, to replicate the setting of every Western film ever made – the wooden water tower, the sheriff's office complete with jail, the saloon with honky-tonk piano, a stage for the gals of the town to dance on and a stagecoach all ready to be held up and robbed. Six very hot and dusty weeks and, almost unbelievably, another natural disaster. But first the camels.

As part of a complicated script, I once more took my life in my hands and broke the golden rule – do not work with animals! One would have thought I had learnt my lesson with the Doberman, but no. In a weak moment I agreed to ride a camel and, as anyone who has been near one of these creatures in a zoo knows full well, they spit, mainly because they are convinced they are far superior to mankind and treat us as less fortunate creatures. They are also very bad tempered. Seated on the camel I was taught the rudimentary signals to make it advance, but it was a waste of time, as it stayed quite stationary, just chewing and ruminating. Then it ruminated and chewed. It occasionally farted. What it would not do was move forward. But we did have an ingenious camel owner who signalled that all would be well, as another camel was being led onto the sand dunes ahead of us. "Prepare yourself for immediate movement," he said. The cameras turned over and my camel, with its ungainly swinging movement, was halfway up the slope towards the other camel before you could say Omar Khayyam.

"Sex is wonderful," shouted the camel owner. "You are on a gentleman camel, while up there," he said, pointing to the sand dune, "is a lady camel. I think you had better get off when they meet."

During a final film sequence on the shore there was a roar, and then a flash flood of immensity never seen before came down from the hills and hit the set, taking most of it out to sea. As I watched the remnants of the building floating out into the Mediterranean, I realised that within a week I would be flying to Mauritius to start another picture. I wondered whether I should advise the future film company to take out extra insurance.

But there was no need to worry. Flying above this magical island I was reminded of my first sight of that tiny atoll in the Maldives so many years ago. There were more people on Mauritius but, like those 30 airmen, they were just as pleased to see us. If their separation from the rest of the world has made them such a delightful race, then the sooner there are lots of islands, the better. English–French creole is the mixture and going there to film *Jane And The Lost City* was enchanting from the word go. Terry Marcel (who had made *There Goes The Bride* with Twiggy in Miami) was once more the director, and the story was based on one of the most famous cartoon characters of World War II.

Churchill was reputed to have said that Jane of the *Daily Mirror*, as she was known, was worth a whole division of troops. This young lady, in cartoon form, spent every day being divested of her clothing (accidentally, of course) so that the British serving man could feast his eyes on her partially clothed body. While this was going on, the troops were also being given weekly doses of bromide in their tea to stop lascivious thoughts entering their heads. Whether this paradox ever entered the minds of the powers that be we shall never know, but Jane was a huge success for the *Daily Mirror* and we were in Mauritius to make a story of her wartime exploits in tropical climes. It was nice working with Terry again, as well as meeting Jasper Carrott, who had a big comic reputation on English television. He also played a very important part in my future welfare on the island.

I may have spent time watching out for a rumbling volcano or a possible monsoon or two, but physically all was well, apart from the unexpected snag of a lack of marmalade. To someone not reared on the English breakfast, this is a minor matter, but to someone used to the crunch of toast in the morning, toast smeared with best butter and marmalade, it is of major importance and only a frantic phone call from myself to Audrey could settle the matter. Jasper's wife, Hazel, later flew out to join us carrying two jars of the best marmalade that money could buy.

When the film was completed, there was a royal première for the film in London and a young Prince Edward amiably mixed with the guest, as his father's charity (the Duke of Edinburgh Awards) was getting the night's proceeds. During the after-film dinner, an auction of a diamond brooch was held and I was stuck with the job. Very little was being bid until I suggested to all and sundry that it wouldn't be right to send Edward back to the palace that night without a bid, as Father would be bound to open the study door and say, "How much bloody money did you get?" This got a nice laugh, as well as a bid for £5,000.

Henrietta, the Marchioness of Tavistock, called about me taking some more pictures of her and her husband, but this time for a very personal reason. The Marquis, Robin, had suffered a severe stroke, but then had made a remarkable recovery, and Henrietta, with Angela Levin, had written the story in *A Chance To Live* to prove that a stroke of this magnitude was not necessarily fatal. Could I please take some pictures of Robin and her together for the book and, as a special favour, could they also have a photograph of the Marquis with his butler, Roger Homes, whose quick reaction on finding Robin unconscious on the floor had undoubtedly saved the Marquis' life? Naturally, I agreed and they came to my studio, I arranged the lights and the photographs were published in the book. Roger was a charming man and I tried to get a very informal picture of Robin and him together on a couch, but tradition prevailed. As his butler, Roger refused to sit in the Marquis' presence.

After so many years, the Pink Panther refused to die. Cast again as Dr Balls, I assembled in July 1992 with the other actors, this time to fly to Jordan for *The Son Of The Pink Panther*. A reunion with Herbert Lom (once more having nervous twitches at the very name of Clouseau) and Burt Kwouk (ready to pounce, day and night), and meeting Roberto Benigni (appearing as the son of the great Clouseau) for the first time. Claudia Cardinale, the star of the very first Panther, was playing his mother. It was a delightful, affectionate film to make, but Roberto, although a very fine physical comedian (he later won a Best Actor Academy Award), could not replace Peter Sellers in the public's affection. Fortunately, the pillars in the pink city of Petra did not collapse while we were there, so I began to think the jinx was going. I had the bonus of the Jordanians having an English-educated king, being brought up to enjoy English breakfasts, and to my delight marmalade was on the table every morning. The waiters, extremely courteous and good-mannered, soon sensed my passion and I was known as Mr Marmalade throughout my stay.

Nothing terrible took place in Slovenia either, when I was making *Moonacre*, a series for TV, but without any historical connection with

England the marmalade problem arose yet again. This time, a favourite actress, Miriam Margolyes, was the courier from England, bearing two jars of Chivers Olde English Thick Cut triumphantly through customs, declaring that an Englishman was in dire need.

If any author is the patron saint of character actors, it has to be Charles Dickens. The gallery of roles he created is almost endless, and what roles they are! Fagin, the Artful Dodger, Pickwick, Micawber, Copperfield, it goes on and on, but there is one name that is relatively unknown but should be enshrined, as with him Dickens began a trend in fiction that has become endless. The name is Nadgett, and I played him in the BBC TV production of *Martin Chuzzlewit*. His immortality lies in the fact that he was the very first private detective in fiction, leading the way to Sherlock Holmes and the thousands of other private eyes that followed. The section of *Chuzzlewit* that introduces Nadgett to the reader is a masterly piece of writing, explaining Nadgett's methods, his ability to disguise himself, to fade into the background, to stand all night in shaded doorways making notes in his pocket book, and is a classic example of an author falling in love with a character and his methods. Whether Conan Doyle or the other masters of detective fiction ever studied Dickens, I don't know, but the character is a true original.

BBC television has always had a love affair with the classic serial and in the summer of 1994 fell on the Dickens book with glee. With *Martin Chuzzlewit* they began by casting Paul Scofield, the actors' actor, and from then on matched him with the best cast they could provide. Shooting in King's Lynn, an unspoilt town in north Norfolk, you could swear that time had magically stood still for 150 years, as every detail of Dickensian life was recreated. Even a fully rigged sailing ship of the period was manoeuvred into the docks of Gloucester, and on its deck Julia Sawalha flirted with her murderous lover. The period clothes of the ladies, with unbelievably complicated underwear (obviously hell to wear, and very difficult to get in and out of), did make them look wonderful. Nasty stubs of guttering candles flickered in the hovels of the poor while splendid chandeliers glowed in the homes of the rich. Dastardly deeds were done, documents were forged and amorous gentlemen in tight-fitting trousers seduced the fair sex whenever they got the chance – and it was a huge success.

★

Ideas for photographs come when least expected. Gazing at the ceiling of my photographic studio, at the top of my house, I had a vision of a swing supported by ropes fastened to the twin steel bars that ran across from wall to wall. The bars were thick enough to support almost anything and high enough to give ample clearance. All it needed was the ropes, plus an elegant lady to be on the swing. Thoughts of the painter Jean Fragonard flitted through my mind, as did thoughts of Joanna Lumley (which, to be honest, often happened anyway). The lovely Lumley has always been a favourite model and I was certain – correctly, as it turned out correctly – that she would be only too happy to levitate on my behalf.

With all the talk of money about (a new millionaire every day – *Vide Press*), it's hardly surprising that there is a shop at the foot of Barnet Hill (near where I live) that sells yachts. We are not talking about the toy ones with eight-inch masts that you nervously push out onto the round pond hoping some puff of wind will get it to the other side. No, these are your genuine, ocean-goers. Teak decks, heavily varnished mahogany woodwork, polished brass fittings and gleaming white hulls, all ready to glide through the waters at Cowes. Wishing to make a purchase, I wandered into this establishment (I can't keep calling it a shop) and spoke to the salesperson.

In this day and age, one is not permitted to call them anything else under the restrictions of the Sex Discrimination Act. The salesperson I actually spoke to was wearing a smart suit, stood about six foot one, had a moustache and smelled of a rather understated aftershave lotion, so there wasn't any confusion about his sex. He smiled obligingly and I stated my needs: "I wish to buy some rope which should be quite thin but, at the same time, virtually unbreakable."

The salesperson moved with some regret from the side of a magnificent motor yacht towards a more general section of marine accessories. "Before assisting you in this matter," he said, "it would be beneficial if I could ascertain just what strain this rope may have to bear. It could well be to hoist a mainsail? Or possibly control the swing of the boom? The mooring of a smallish craft, perhaps? It would be a great help if I might inquire just what is to be held on the end of this rope. In other words, what weight must it support?"

The courtesy of his reply warranted absolute truth. "Joanna Lumley," I said. Thinking back, I feel the abrupt answer could have been better phrased as he was not to know I was a photographer, and he was not to know Joanna was a personal friend and, even more important, he was not to know I was constructing a swing on which Joanna would be posing for a photograph. The suspension of such a delicious creature meant *total safety*. Could I answer to the male population of England should any harm come to her? As I was still in need of the rope, I had no option but to elaborate on my answer. Gradually the glassy-eyed look vanished and gradually the furtive looks at the other salespersons (hinting of a deranged customer) ceased.

The ropes on display were very varied, from something suitable for mooring the *Queen Mary* to nylon cord that could have served as a shoelace. The selection was easy and I bought enough to be suitable. Joanna, a darling as usual, her legs to die for stretching endlessly, cavorted on the swing and the shoot was a wonderful success, which made me some days later go back and confront my favourite salesperson. "I can well understand your lack of belief, but without demur you did supply me with what I needed. What is more important, as you can see, the rope stood the strain." As he gazed at the picture, I wasn't sure the same was going to apply to him.

One of the regrets of the same year was a programme for an independent producer, Mike Mansfield, that was a brave attempt to be different. A wonderful Sax Rohmer, Raffles, Fu Manchu-threatening world domination comedy, it starred Tony Slattery as Tiger Bastable, playboy, *bon viveur* and self-appointed white man's shield against the dark forces of the yellow-skinned hordes of the East. Currently unbelievably politically incorrect but, set as it was in the '20s, it was terribly funny and we all had a splendid time. Sadly, it was not shown on the TV network.

Professional debts, as far as actors are concerned, are taken very seriously. Morecambe and Wise feeling they owed me something and paying me back is a perfect example. In the '60s, a young director, eager to make a pilot sequence for a modern-day version of Dickens' *A Christmas Carol*, got Ron Moody and me to jump in and out of cars on the Embankment, as well as do a couple of scenes in a small studio. Nothing came of it, however, and it finally joined the collection of the nearly-but-not-quite shows that lie in their hundreds in cans in production offices all around the country.

Thirty years later, that director, Norman Stone, gave me a call. "I know it's been a long time," he said, "but I do think you'd better come and work with me again so I can say thank you." It couldn't have been more nostalgic, as the three-part musical comedy *Ain't Misbehavin'* was set in London in World War II. The recreation of bombed streets, the "Loose Talk Is Dangerous" posters on the walls, the women's clothes (even to the seams in their stockings), the trilby hats that all men wore and the old-fashioned cars with the impossible-to-open clips on the side of the bonnets was faultless.

The film was set in the the seedy world of small-time crooks running the black market, selling parachute silk to the ladies for underwear and getting petrol on the side. The plot was roughly based around Robson Green and Jerome Flynn, as members of a dance band, diving in and out of RAF uniforms and getting mixed up with the underworld, but it was all an excuse (as far as I was concerned) to be in something that was my youth to a T.

The main feature was the band. Warren Mitchell, a fair clarinet player in real life, played a rather tatty bandleader, but the gentlemen sitting behind him were real musicians. They played several big-band arrangements, and Noël Coward's line about the nostalgia of cheap music came to mind, except it wasn't cheap. As the film went on, I found myself telling the airmen that they didn't wear their caps like that and that, if they were caught with their uniforms in that state, they'd be on a fizzer. On the final day of shooting, I made a joking remark that today, as far as I was concerned, was black armband day, as my work on the film was ended. Twenty minutes later, care of the wardrobe mistress, I turned to find the entire crew, plus Robson and Jerome, standing in a row wearing black armbands.

18 Hi, Genghis –
You Know Attila, Of Course

Normally, if you had a goddess in your studio, she would be mounted on a plinth, having been worked on for some time with a cold chisel, and would customarily be merely draped in a few cunningly placed wisps of diaphanous material, possibly holding a trident in one hand. In this case, the goddess herself, Nigella Lawson, sat in a comfortable chair and wore elegant clothes, and certainly no attempt on her person was made with a cold chisel. The 150mm Sonnar lens mounted on my Hasselblad camera was the only weapon used to depict her shape and form. My make-up artist, Ann Morgan, delighted at having bone structure to die for in front of her, produced all those magical and mysterious pots and jars that ladies rhapsodise about and set to work with a will. No ancient Roman sculptor could have been more dedicated.

"Not a lot to do," Ann confided, "but if we just…" The two female heads went into a deep and detailed conversation with a fervour and passion that made me retire, as a mere male, abruptly from the scene. Small sponges of foundation deftly applied, plus delicate strokes of eyeliner pencil; a blusher brush wielded with finesse that would have done credit to a medieval miniaturist and rapt attention as shadows were cunningly built up; the merest hint of powder; and, hey presto, all was revealed. Two sets of eyebrows were raised in my direction.

I knew how Paris, asked for his judgment, must have felt. "Delightful," I said. The two ladies exchanged blank and puzzled looks.

"But surely," Ann said, "just a trifle more on…" She gestured vaguely to the lovely cheekbones. Nigella nodded firmly, her face moving closer to the mirror. "And wouldn't you like the lips a bit more…" She pouted invitingly. "And by doing that," Ann joined in excitedly, "we'd get a more…"

I braced myself, as one must at moments of crisis. "The make-up looks wonderful, the effect is quite stunning and, as we have a lot to do, I think we should start shooting now." Perhaps the use of the words "wonderful" and "stunning" did the trick. With surprising demureness, the ladies moved to the camera area, gracefully Nigella posed, Ann did her last-minute adjustments to the hair, wielding her tail comb with the speed and panache of D'Artagnan, and gradually we started taking the pictures.

Asking her to pose for inclusion in this book, I was ahead of all the newspapers of England, who have bestowed the title of "goddess" on Nigella. She has not only delighted the whole of the country by cooking glorious dishes on television, but she has also written several exotic books on culinary matters which have topped the bestseller lists for months. The goddess label fits her perfectly, as goddesses don't have temperaments – they have the ability to make everything seem possible and they remain quite adorable no matter what the circumstances, even when a photographer starts laying down the law.

In the early 1960s, the do-it-yourself craze hit the country. Sheets of plastic were fastened with impact glue and acres of hardboard were nailed to the wooden supports and hey presto! The home would never be the same again. While all sensible males were utilising these new materials in the home, on the television, a large, broad-shouldered Australian backstroke-swimming champion flexed his muscles as well as a sheet of that same hardboard, thereby creating a rhythm that was hard to ignore. To it, he sang, "Tie me kangaroo down, sport, tie me kangaroo down," and a major record hit was born. Rolf Harris, new to our shores, came and conquered with such an original but basically simple sound, and just to make sure this was not a one-off hit, we then had 'Sun Arise' and 'Two Little Boys', which sold their respective millions. Commissioned by a magazine, I spent a day at Rolf's Thameside home taking pictures, and began to realise just what a miniature atom bomb of energy burned in this wild colonial boy. He and his delightful wife, Alwen, posed by the huge totem pole in the garden as his enthusiasm for life burst from every part of him. Needless to say, after showing to all and sundry on television his affection for animals, he then confounded the art critics, always willing to ambush anyone straying into their exclusive territory, by demonstrating that his knowledge of art wasn't confined to talking about it. Out came the easel and brushes and, by God, once more on television the paint went on the canvas to show just how those masters worked.

If you have a social sense, you naturally, on the day of a general election, wish to nip off to the polling booth in the hopes that your cross on the voting slip will usher in a new era of justice and reform. In the 1997 election, this would have been a bit difficult for me, as at that very time, the night of 30 April and 1 May, I was flying at roughly 30,000 feet over the Ukraine. Hoping that the pilot was going to stay well clear of Chernobyl, I spent a lot of time vainly signalling the lady all-in wrestler who was our flight attendant for another packet of nuts, but, having no fluency in the Russian tongue, I naturally fell back on miming my wants. Immediately, she brought me a sick bag.

My companion on the flight, fellow actor Gareth Hunt, took over the miming and was immediately successful. There is nothing bitter in my reporting this – obviously he was more dextrous, as he'd spent so long sexily playing with coffee beans on a very successful television commercial. We were *en route* to Yalta, in the Crimea, to appear in a film *The Adventures Of Marco Polo*, and the problems in the ex-Soviet Union sadly became more apparent as time went on. The first leg of the journey was the non-stop flight from London to Kiev, capital of the Ukraine, and, apart from the lack of communication between the Man Mountain lady and myself, things were reasonable – that is, while we were still in the air. However, landing on the soil of Mother Russia was another matter entirely. At Kiev Airport, Slavic eyes narrowed as two large, uniformed officials thumbed through our passports. "Purrpois of veeseet?" The *basso profundo* question rolled off the tongue.

Gareth, sensing clarity was of the utmost importance, uttered one word only: "Feelm!"

This was not much of a success. The first official looked at his companion. "Feelm?" Gareth's ability as a mime came to the rescue again, as rather stylishly he pretended to film them both and once more sign language was triumphant.

The second official, with an even deeper voice, beamed expansively and gave his comrade a meaningful nudge. "'Ollywood!"

The comrade nodded sagely and held up our passports. "You 'ave munney?" Eager to cement the goodwill that we had established, and realising this was a currency check, Gareth and I both produced our wallets. I had £120, Gareth £80. "Is perfick!" The first official took it all. "One hundred punts eeech. Landink fee!" The passports were handed back and the Brothers Karamazov indicated the exit doors.

Dragging our cases, we stood bewildered outside the airport building and matters became even more bizarre as we saw before us a huge pre-war American-styled automobile standing waiting. Enormous chromium fins jutted from the rear and ribbed supercharger pipes curved from the side of the bonnet while a Russian driver sat behind a dashboard which had enough white plastic knobs to have done credit to a giant cinema organ. He wound his window down: "Supper!" As Gareth and I were the only two people near the car, this call was obviously directed to us. Inside the back of the car, spacious enough to accommodate a fair-sized Siberian wolf, the driver once more uttered the only English word he apparently knew – "Supper!" – put his foot hard on the accelerator and, with a roar of the engine, we set off for the dreary and depressing city centre of Kiev.

The rest of the evening was straight out of Kafka's *The Trial*. Three hotels denied all knowledge of available rooms while Gareth's mime, by now up to Marcel Marceau level, did nothing to produce any food but did produce a telephone. As we shared the same agent, we were able to call him in London direct.

Our call was brief: "We are in Russia – Kiev, to be exact – and we have no food or money!" Our agent, Dennis Selinger, magician that he was, contacted Yalta (several hundred miles south) and in half an hour help was at hand. The only food available was pizzas from some local shop, but nothing from a three-star Michelin restaurant could have tasted better. Needless to say, it was our driver who delivered them to us, and with a triumphant bellow of "Supper!" he thrust them into our hands. We also got a room in a hotel which, by the sinister stains on the walls, had obvious been recently occupied by the Ogpu, the Soviet secret police.

The next day, Gareth and I, in a subdued mood, returned to Kiev Airport, this time to board the local flight to Yalta. On the far edge of the airport was a decrepit building which was trying its best to look as if it wasn't going to fall down and, standing forlornly by it, a high-winged monoplane, constructed *circa* 1935, with two propeller engines. This decrepit plane was crewed by another lady all-in wrestler, who pointed to seats, stuck a plastic dish of red cabbage in our laps and then retired behind a flapping curtain at the rear of the plane, never to be seen again. Shutting my eyes tight and commending my soul to St Christopher, I willed the plane to fly. In answer to all my prayers, we landed some hours later in the Crimea.

Yalta, conquered by Potemkin for Catherine the Great, was Russia's answer to Monte Carlo. Past holiday resort for legions of tsars and grand dukes, it had also been selected as the meeting place for the triumvirate of Stalin, Roosevelt and Churchill in the last phases of World War II. The palace where they met – indeed, the very room in which the conference took place –

was one of the locations for our filming. The round table, which could have easily seated King Arthur plus all his knights, was still there with the three imposing chairs still in place and, in front of each, a miniature flag on a miniature flagpole denoting who had sat where (interesting gamesmanship putting Stalin's chair where it had had its back to the light). Gareth and I childishly kept swapping seats, and voices. Personally, I thought my Churchill was far better than his, as I got the bizarre pronunciation of "the Naaaazis" right, but Gareth's Stalin seemed to have the correct Russian timbre. Of course, the fact that neither of us had ever actually heard Stalin speak gave him a certain advantage.

Filming began and we gradually progressed through the dialogue. It was of the "Hi, Genghis – you know Attila, of course?" variety. Starring in the film, Jack Palance, as some Asian scourge, wore a helmet that boasted horns big enough to equip him for the run with the bulls at Pamplona, but he was a serious actor and did his best. Later, we moved to another location, which was a wondrous turreted miniature castle perched high on the cliffs above the Black Sea. This pastiche castle had been built by some besotted archduke for his lady friend at the turn of the last century but, as she was a rather emotional Slav, she left for the south of France the moment he finished it. It could have been built by Disney. There was a lot of sword-slashing and hosts of tastefully dressed maidens in dire peril of losing their virtue kept rushing about – and a good time was had by one and all.

The Russian people were a delight. Hardened as it seemed to vicissitudes, they had a level of acceptance that we from the West found difficult to understand. We went along with everything until it came to the toilet paper. Stalin may have forced through some magnificent five-year plans, but he never did get around to setting up an Andrex factory in the area, and if you didn't read Russian then it was very boring gazing at the squares of so-called toilet paper in the lavatory.

Completing my section of the film, the time came to say goodbye to all my newfound comrades, as well as my steadfast companion, Gareth. He and I had fought our way past lady all-in wrestlers, the Russian airport Mafia, and survived hungry nights in Kiev. A firm handshake, then, through gritted teeth, one Englishman spoke to another. "Dear friend," said Gareth, "it has been an honour and a privilege to make this journey with you, and do give my regards to the old country."

Noble sentiments bring forth noble gestures. "Realising your command of the language is only on a level with mine," I said, "will you please accept, as a parting gift, this small token of my esteem." Into his grateful hands I pressed the remains of the only known roll of toilet paper in Yalta. "You can thank my wife for this," I said. "She had the presence of mind to enclose it in my luggage."

Jack Palance, horns akimbo, dutifully posed for a final picture on the ramparts of the miniature castle and then, carefully performing a rather classy veronica – a well-known bull-fighting manoeuvre performed by a matador – to avoid the twin threat of impalement, I shook hands with him and said goodbye. Courteous and intelligent, he was totally at variance with his image and capable of surprising us all with those amazing press-ups he performed at the Oscar ceremony.

Vincent Price, in one of his letters to me, quoted Bette Davis as saying, "Old age is not for cissies," and she was right. It also brings an obsession for reading the obituaries. Depending on your morning paper (mine is the *Times*), you do start seeing far too many names of friends, and one is filled with regret for the jokes and laughs that you won't be having with them any more. The obituaries that hit the hardest were the ones written in many papers for my agent Dennis Selinger on 2 February 1998. When I say "agent", it paints a picture of a purely business arrangement, but as he stood for so much more, it's very hard to quantify. But I'll try.

We met when he was working for the mighty Lew and Leslie Grade theatrical agency, but truthfully Dennis was not really cut out for just the world of music hall. Gradually, he entered the world of films and asked me to join him in the late '50s, just before I got married. Assuring him his ten per cent was not part of the deal, I arranged for him to be my best man. He also became godfather to my three children and, over the years, became as much part of our family as a blood relative. His range of clients became a who's who of the cinema world. Peter Sellers, Michael Caine, Sean Connery and Roger Moore were just some of the actors he represented and his attention to each and every one of his clients never faltered. Dennis coming to our house every Christmas was a bigger event to my children than Santa Claus' visit, and the presents became embarrassing. In all the years we were together, right up to his death, I never heard a word of malice spoken by him or about him. Harry Saltzman, producer of all the Bond films, always said of Dennis, "I don't need a contract; all I have to have from him is a handshake." Annually, on 20 June, Dennis held his birthday party at Langan's for his clients and these came to be the best parties in London. Six months after Dennis' death, Michael Caine and Mickey Most held the party once more as a tribute to him. It was, of course, packed to the doors. He was the best and the most loved agent in our profession.

An era of radio history came to an end when Spike Milligan died, at the end of February 2002. He had been failing for some time and the exit was expected. I called him, as I knew he possessed an 8mm black-and-white film of our magical trip on the Thames and hoped we could print a frame from it for inclusion in this book (the camera perched on deck saw us doing comical bits behind the steering wheel). "Gone," he said. "Don't know where it is. Sorry, Gra. All gone. Yes, it's all gone." The voice got fainter and fainter and the cue was obviously to place the receiver gently back on its rest.

Still capable of glorious one-liners, at an awards dinner shortly before his death, Spike tottered up to collect his statuette to be proudly told that a eulogistic letter concerning him had been received from the Prince of Wales. The attendant actors dutifully treated the letter with awe and deference while Spike, with a comedian's perfect timing, declaimed it the work of a "little grovelling bastard". He had already told Harry Secombe that he hoped Harry would die before him. "I don't want you singing at my funeral," he said. Gentleman that he was, Harry passed away the year before.

In 1990, ten years after Peter Sellers' death, I was asked by a publisher if I would care to write about him. I knew him to be tasteful gentleman and he produced a splendid-looking volume, *Remembering Peter Sellers,* which contained my memories of a friend over some 30 years. The pleasure of being an author of a book lies in the fact that it gives you *gravitas* – it's quite impressive to have a few hardback copies on the shelf in your study, even if it suggests that not every single one has been purchased.

Then you've got the signings. In a bookshop, a purchaser of one of your books, wishing for a signature, joins (you hope) a queue that winds its way towards you. You give an encouraging smile as you take a book off the pile and wait for the instructions regarding the dedication. Normally, they murmur their own name and you write the conventional best wishes, but you can get specifics like "To Auntie Maud". You can also have the occasional horror that examines the flyleaf, then puts the book back on the pile saying that the price is too high. One day, a copy was asked for, as well as a question about whether I would care to make a talking book of it. I at once said yes.

John Kaufman asked the question, and within weeks the studio was arranged, a sound engineer (with giant earphones clamped on either side of his head) was ready to adjust the volume controls and we were recording. To keep his strength up, the engineer sustained himself with large slabs of milk chocolate, and every so often one could sense his fingers feeling out towards the silver paper wrapping, but he knew that no snap of the chocolate was permitted until each chapter had ended. He got three pieces a day, which was quite good going, and, even more important, the talking book sold very well.

From that collaboration came a discussion about my photography, my career in films and the stage, radio and television shows I'd done. "How would you feel about an autobiography?" I'm afraid he wasn't too keen on the title *The Memoirs Of A Marmalade Eater*, but I said that I would persevere and, well, here it is.

"Not an ounce of rhythm in his body" will now be in public domain and the wearing of black velvet pyjamas in Earls Court has now been exposed. I hope my ignorance of the Rolls-Royce Merlin didn't harm the war effort too much and, if there are any of those 30 airmen on that Maldive island still around, I also hope they've got over their hangovers. To the WAAF chiropodist who let me wear my shoes in the war, lots of love, and especial thanks to my fellow airmen of the Gang Show. I hope the ginger-headed corporal is still bringing comfort to the ladies and that Sir Thomas Beecham isn't giving the celestial harpists too bad a time. To all the personalities who allowed me to take and publish their photographs, I can but say a heartfelt thanks, and let's hope it's still a little time before my Marylebone morgue attendant gets to see me again.

Index